A HANDBOOK

OF

BANKRUPTCY LAW

Embodying the full text of the Act of Congress of 1898, and annotated with references to pertinent decisions under former statutes

BY H. CAMPBELL BLACK

Author of "Black's Law Dictionary," and of Treatises on "Judgments," "Tax Titles," "Constitutional Law," "Statutory Construction," "Removal of Causes," "Intoxicating Liquors," etc.

ST. PAUL, MINN.
WEST PUBLISHING CO.
1898

PREFACE.

The following pages contain a complete and verbatim copy of the National Bankruptcy Act of 1898, with annotations embodying the substance of all the decisions rendered under former acts of congress on the same subject which are pertinent and likely to prove of value or importance under the provisions of the new statute.

While the endeavor has been to make the annotations as full as practicable throughout, special prominence has been given to the elucidation of those questions which will probably first come before the courts for settlement—questions, that is, of jurisdiction, of procedure, of the persons and corporations entitled to take advantage of the law, or liable to be proceeded against under it, and in regard to the acts of bankruptcy upon which a petition in involuntary cases may be founded.

It will be proper to add that the volume now offered to the profession represents the fruits of the author's study and research extending over a period of many years.

H. C. B.

TABLE OF CONTENTS.

CHAPTER I.

DEFINITIONS.

CHAPTER II.

CREATION OF COURTS OF BANKRUPTCY AND THEIR JURISDICTION.

CHAPTER III.

BANKRUPTS.

CHAPTER IV.

COURTS AND PROCEDURE THEREIN.

CHAPTER V.

OFFICERS, THEIR DUTIES AND COMPENSATION.

CHAPTER VI.

CREDITORS.

CHAPTER VII.

ESTATES.

TABLE OF CASES CITED.

INDEX.

†

THE

LAW OF BANKRUPTCY.

CHAPTER I.

DEFINITIONS.

MEANING OF WORDS AND PHRASES.

§ 1. *a* **The words and phrases used in this act and in proceedings pursuant hereto shall, unless the same be inconsistent with the context, be construed as follows: (1) "A person against whom a petition has been filed" shall include a person who has filed a voluntary petition; (2) "adjudication" shall mean the date of the entry of a decree that the defendant, in a bankruptcy proceeding, is a bankrupt, or if such decree is appealed from, then the date when such decree is finally confirmed; (3) "appellate courts" shall include the circuit courts of appeals of the United States, the supreme courts of the territories, and the supreme court of the United States; (4) "bankrupt" shall include a person against whom an involuntary petition or an application to set a composition aside or to revoke a discharge has been filed, or who has filed a voluntary petition, or who has been adjudged a bankrupt; (5) "clerk" shall mean the clerk of a court of bank-**

ruptcy; (6) "corporations" shall mean all bodies having any of the powers and privileges of private corporations not possessed by individuals or partnerships, and shall include limited or other partnership associations organized under laws making the capital subscribed alone responsible for the debts of the association; (7) "court" shall mean the court of bankruptcy in which the proceedings are pending, and may include the referee; (8) "courts of bankruptcy" shall include the district courts of the United States and of the territories, the supreme court of the District of Columbia, and the United States court of the Indian Territory, and of Alaska; (9) "creditor" shall include anyone who owns a demand or claim provable in bankruptcy, and may include his duly authorized agent, attorney, or proxy; (10) "date of bankruptcy," or "time of bankruptcy," or "commencement of proceedings," or "bankruptcy," with reference to time, shall mean the date when the petition was filed; (11) "debt" shall include any debt, demand, or claim provable in bankruptcy; (12) "discharge" shall mean the release of a bankrupt from all of his debts which are provable in bankruptcy, except such as are excepted by this act; (13) "document" shall include any book, deed, or instrument in writing; (14) "holiday" shall include Christmas, the Fourth of July, the Twenty-Second of February, and any day appointed by the President of the United States or the congress of the United States as a holiday or as a day of public fasting or thanksgiving; (15) a person shall be deemed insolvent within the provisions of this act whenever the aggregate of his property, exclusive of any property which he may have conveyed, transferred, concealed, or removed, or permitted to be concealed or removed, with intent to defraud, hinder or delay his creditors, shall not, at a fair valuation, be sufficient in amount to pay his debts; (16) "judge" shall mean a judge of a court of bankruptcy, not including the referee; (17) "oath" shall include affirmation; (18) "officer" shall include clerk, marshal, receiver, referee, and trustee, and the imposing of a duty upon or the forbidding of an act by any officer shall include his successor and any person authorized by law to perform the duties of such officer; (19) "persons" shall include corporations, except where otherwise specified, and officers, partnerships, and women, and when used with reference to the commission of acts which are herein forbidden shall include persons who are participants in the forbidden acts, and the agents, officers, and members of the board of directors or trustees, or other similar controlling bodies of corporations; (20) "petition" shall mean a paper filed in a court of bankruptcy or with a clerk or deputy clerk by a debtor praying for the benefits of this act, or by creditors alleging the commission of an act of bankruptcy by a debtor therein named; (21) "referee" shall mean the referee who has jurisdiction of the case or to whom the case has been referred, or anyone acting in his stead; (22) "conceal" shall include secrete, falsify, and mutilate; (23) "secured creditor" shall include a creditor who has security for his debt upon the property of the bankrupt of a nature to be assignable under this act, or who owns such a debt for which some indorser, surety, or other persons secondarily liable for the bankrupt has such security upon the bankrupt's assets; (24) "states" shall include the territories, the Indian Territory, Alaska, and the District of Columbia; (25) "transfer" shall include the sale and every other and different mode of disposing of or parting with property, or the possession of property, absolutely or conditionally, as a payment, pledge, mortgage, gift, or security; (26) "trustee" shall include all of the trustees of an estate; (27) "wage-earner" shall mean an individual who works for wages, salary, or hire, at a rate of compensation not exceeding one thousand five hundred dollars per year; (28) words importing the masculine gender may be applied to and include corporations, partnerships, and women; (29) words importing the plural number may be applied to and mean only a single person or thing; (30) words importing the singular number may be applied to and mean several persons or things.

CHAPTER II.

CREATION OF COURTS OF BANKRUPTCY AND THEIR JURISDICTION.

§ 2. That the courts of bankruptcy as hereinbefore defined, viz, the district courts of the United States in the several states, the supreme court of the District of Columbia, the district courts of the several territories, and the United States courts in the Indian Territory and the district of Alaska, are hereby made courts of bankruptcy, and are hereby invested, within their respective territorial limits as now established, or as they may be hereafter changed, with such jurisdiction at law and in equity as will enable them to exercise original jurisdiction in bankruptcy proceedings, in vacation in chambers and during their respective terms, as they are now or may be hereafter held, to (1) adjudge persons bankrupt who have had their principal place of business, resided, or had their domicile within their respective territorial jurisdictions for the preceding six months, or the greater portion thereof, or who do not have their principal place of business, reside, or have their domicile within the United States, but have property within their jurisdictions, or who have been adjudged bankrupts by courts of competent jurisdiction without the United States and have property within their jurisdiction; (2) allow claims, disallow claims, reconsider allowed or disallowed claims, and allow or disallow them against bankrupt estates; (3) appoint receivers or the marshals, upon application of parties in interest, in case the courts shall find it absolutely necessary, for the preservation of estates, to take charge of the property of bankrupts after the filing of the petition and until it is dismissed or the trustee is qualified; (4) arraign, try, and punish bankrupts, officers, and other persons, and the agents, officers, members of the board of directors or trustees, or other similar controlling bodies, of corporations for violations of this act, in accordance with the laws of procedure of the United States now in force, or such as may be hereafter enacted, regulating trials for the alleged violation of laws of the United States; (5) authorize the business of bankrupts to be conducted for limited periods by receivers, the marshals, or trustees, if necessary in the best interests of the estates; (6) bring in and substitute additional persons or parties in proceedings in bankruptcy when necessary for the complete determination of a matter in controversy; (7) cause the estates of bankrupts to be collected, reduced to money and distributed, and determine controversies in relation thereto, except as herein otherwise provided; (8) close estates, whenever it appears that they have been fully administered, by approving the final accounts and discharging the trustees, and reopen them whenever it appears they were closed before being fully administered; (9) confirm or reject compositions between debtors and their creditors, and set aside compositions and reinstate the cases; (10) consider and confirm, modify or overrule, or return, with instructions for further proceedings, records and findings certified to them by referees; (11) determine all claims of bankrupts to their exemptions; (12) discharge or

refuse to discharge bankrupts and set aside discharges and reinstate the cases; (13) enforce obedience by bankrupts, officers, and other persons to all lawful orders, by fine or imprisonment or fine and imprisonment; (14) extradite bankrupts from their respective districts to other districts; (15) make such orders, issue such process, and enter such judgments in addition to those specifically provided for as may be necessary for the enforcement of the provisions of this act; (16) punish persons for contempts committed before referees; (17) pursuant to the recommendation of creditors, or when they neglect to recommend the appointment of trustees, appoint trustees, and upon complaints of creditors, remove trustees for cause upon hearings and after notices to them; (18) tax costs, whenever they are allowed by law, and render judgments therefor against the unsuccessful party, or the successful party for cause, or in part against each of the parties, and against estates, in proceedings in bankruptcy; and (19) transfer cases to other courts of bankruptcy.

Nothing in this section contained shall be construed to deprive a court of bankruptcy of any power it would possess were certain specific powers not herein enumerated.

JURISDICTION.

General Jurisdiction of Bankruptcy Courts.

The proceeding in bankruptcy is equivalent to the general creditors' bill in chancery, and is a plenary proceeding, its practice being prescribed by the statute, and to that extent varying from the chancery practice obtaining in creditors' bills. So far as not varied by statute, the practice should be the same. The collateral proceedings incident to and arising in the course of a bankruptcy proceeding, in the form of petitions and motions nisi, against persons already parties to the bankruptcy proceeding, are of the same character as like collateral proceedings incident to and arising in a creditors' bill in chancery, and are summary only where they would be so in a creditors' bill, except where allowed by statute. In re Anderson, 23 Fed. 482. The proceeding in bankruptcy is in the nature of a proceeding in rem; the acquisition of jurisdiction is based upon the taking possession, by the court, of the debtor's whole property and effects, and upon its adjudication as to his status. Hence the federal court in which the bankruptcy proceedings are commenced has jurisdiction of the debtor's whole estate, wherever situate, and it is the only court which can enjoin a mortgage creditor from foreclosing his mortgage in a state court, notwithstanding the creditor resides within another circuit. Markson v. Heany, 1 Dill. 497, Fed. Cas. No. 9,098. So, the bankruptcy court has power to issue an injunction to restrain the sheriff of a state court from proceeding to sell the property of the estate under execution issuing from the state court on a judgment obtained prior to the institution of the bankruptcy proceedings. In re Mallory, 1 Sawy. 88, Fed. Cas. No. 8,991. So, the court has jurisdiction of an action by the trustee in bankruptcy of a voluntary bankrupt to recover a balance due from a principal to the bankrupt as his factor, for such a suit is essential to the winding up of the proceedings in bankruptcy, and jurisdiction in it depends upon the subject-matter, not the parties. Kelly v. Smith, 1 Blatchf. 290, Fed. Cas. No. 7,675. But the court of bankruptcy is created such by the statute, and has no powers but those conferred upon it, either expressly or by necessary implication, for the just and full execution of the law. Clark v. Binninger, 38 How. Prac. 341; In re Morris, Crabbe, 70, Fed. Cas. No. 9,825. Nevertheless, the federal courts, exercising their statutory powers in matters of bankruptcy, are not to be regarded as limited or inferior tribunals, in such sense that their jurisdiction must affirmatively appear on the face of the record in order to the validity of their judgments; jurisdiction will be presumed, as in the case of all the higher courts. Hayes v. Ford, 15 N. B. R. 569; Chemung Canal Bank v. Judson, 8 N. Y. 254; Reed v. Vaughn, 10 Mo. 447. But when the want of jurisdiction appears on the face of the petition in bankruptcy, the consent of the parties cannot give jurisdiction, and the court of its own motion should take notice of the point. Hopkins v. Carpenter, 18 N. B. R. 339, Fed. Cas. No. 6,686. A stranger to a bankruptcy proceeding may come into it voluntarily by petition or other appropriate method, and submit to the bankruptcy court his rights touching property in the custody of the court claimed as assets by the trustee in bankruptcy. In re Anderson, 23 Fed. 482. A proceeding in involuntary bankruptcy is not one for the recovery of a creditor's debt, but to secure a distribution of the debtor's property among all his creditors; and therefore the prosecution of an action by the creditor for the recovery of his debt is not a bar to his proceeding against the debtor in bankruptcy. In re Henderson, 9 Fed. 196.

Ancillary Jurisdiction.

Any district court of the United States may, in the exercise of its ancillary jurisdiction, and in aid of the court in which proceedings are pending, grant injunctions, stay proceedings, enforce the provisions of composition resolutions, or administer other summary relief as a court in bankruptcy, as to persons or property within the district, if the relief sought is such as the court in which the proceedings are pending would grant if the person or property to be affected were within reach of the process of that court, provided that court is disabled from giving the same relief by reason of the persons or property not being subject to its process. In re Tifft, 19 N. B. R. 201, Fed. Cas. No. 14,034; McGehee v. Hentz, 19 N. B. R. 136, Fed. Cas. No. 8,794; Moore v. Jones, 23 Vt. 739, Fed. Cas.

No. 9,768; Sherman v. Bingham, 3 Cliff. 552, Fed. Cas. No. 12,762.

Power to Restrain State Courts.

Rev. St. U. S. § 720, provides that "the writ of injunction shall not be granted by any court of the United States to stay proceedings in any court of a state, except in cases where such injunction may be authorized by any law relating to proceedings in bankruptcy." The bankruptcy act provides that "a suit which is founded upon a claim from which a discharge would be a release, and which is pending against a person at the time of the filing of a petition against him, shall be stayed until after an adjudication or the dismissal of the petition." And further, the courts of bankruptcy are given power to "make such orders, issue such process, and enter such judgments as may be necessary for the enforcement of the provisions of this act." Under these provisions, when the bankruptcy law cannot be properly administered by the court having jurisdiction, in consequence of the interference of a state court and its determination to adjudicate upon the rights of parties and property in the bankruptcy court, the latter ought not to hesitate to assert its authority; for in this matter the courts of the United States and the courts of the state are not of co-ordinate authority, but the federal court is superior. In re Miller, 6 Biss. 30, Fed. Cas. No. 9,551, per Drummond, J. But after process of execution issuing from a state court has been executed by a sale of the bankrupt's property, it is too late for the bankruptcy court to interfere by injunction or otherwise, the purchaser having acquired a good title. In re Fuller, 1 Sawy. 243, Fed. Cas. No. 5,148. And a bankrupt, after litigating for five years and to a final decree an action in the state court, cannot have an injunction from the federal court against the execution of such decree, on the ground that the assignee in bankruptcy was joined as a party to such action without leave of the bankruptcy court. Price v. Price, 48 Fed. 823. The state courts have no jurisdiction, for fraud or any other cause, to interfere with or set aside a sale of the bankrupt's property by the trustee in bankruptcy. Akins v. Stradley, 51 Iowa, 414, 1 N. W. 609.

Marshaling of Assets.

Where a creditor held several judgment notes of his debtor, and also some mortgages and two insurance policies as collateral, and caused judgment to be entered on the notes and execution to be issued thereon, and shortly afterward a petition was filed against the debtor and he was adjudged a bankrupt, it was held that the court had power so to marshal the assets as to require the creditor to foreclose a mortgage before resorting to the general fund. In re Sauthoff, 7 Biss. 167, Fed. Cas. No. 12,379. The fact that the bankruptcy court has power to ascertain and liquidate all liens and other specific claims on the bankrupt's estate, and to compel all lien-holders to appear and submit their claims, does not necessarily imply that this jurisdiction must be exercised in all cases. If the trustee and the general creditors are satisfied that a given debt against the bankrupt is valid, and that the property upon which it is secured is of no more value than is sufficient to pay it, it may be abandoned to the creditor holding the lien. Second Nat. Bank of Louisville v. Nat. State Bank, 10 Bush, 367. And see The Ironsides, 4 Biss. 518, Fed. Cas. No. 7,069.

Summary and Equitable Powers of Bankruptcy Courts.

The bankruptcy court is always open and has no separate terms, and may therefore re-examine any order or decree made in the cause at any time and vacate it or set it aside on a proper showing, provided no vested rights are thereby disturbed. Boutwell v. Allderdice, 2 Hughes, 121, Fed. Cas. No. 1,708. The design with which a summary power so extended and comprehensive was conferred upon the district courts in this connection was undoubtedly to facilitate the dispatch of bankruptcy business and bring the cases to a speedy termination. This, indeed, is the obvious policy and intent of the whole statute. It has been broadly stated that the bankruptcy courts are authorized by summary proceedings to administer all the relief which a court of equity could administer under the like circumstances upon regular proceedings. In re Wallace, Deady, 433, Fed. Cas. No. 17,094; Ex parte Foster, 2 Story, 131, Fed. Cas. No. 4,960. So, the court has summary jurisdiction over all contracts made with itself respecting the bankrupt's property, such as (in this case) a forthcoming bond for goods seized by the direction of the court in the hands of a third person as assets of the estate. Rosenbaum v. Garnett, 3 Hughes, 662, Fed. Cas. No. 12,053. So, any claimant may proceed, if he so chooses, by summary petition against the trustee in bankruptcy in respect to any funds in the latter's hands; for the trustee is an officer of the court and his possession is that of the court. Ferguson v. Peckham, 6 N. B. R. 569, Fed. Cas. No. 4,741; In re Evans, 1 Low. 525, Fed. Cas. No. 4,551. The converse, however, is not the case; the trustee has no right to take similar action against third persons. Id. Again, the summary jurisdiction of the court extends to the ascertainment and liquidation of an alleged lien. Samson v. Clarke, 6 N. B. R. 108. And the trustee may proceed by summary petition to have an order for a sale declared null and void. In re Major, 14 N. B. R. 71, Fed. Cas. No. 8,981. But, on the other hand, jurisdiction to foreclose mortgages upon the bankrupt's estate is not included in the powers to be exercised summarily, (In re Casey, 10 Blatchf. 376, Fed. Cas. No. 2,495) nor for the sale of property which is not in the trustee's possession but in that of receivers appointed by a state court who are not made parties to the petition. Bradley v. Healey, 1 Holmes, 451, Fed. Cas. No. 1,781. And see, generally, In re Ulrich, 6 Ben.

483, Fed. Cas. No. 14,328; In re Kirtland, 10 Blatchf. 515, Fed. Cas. No. 7,851. The jurisdiction of the courts of bankruptcy extends as well to bills in equity on behalf of the trustee, in regard to the recovery of assets, as to actions at law. Flanders v. Abbey, 6 Biss. 16, Fed. Cas. No. 4,851.

Jurisdiction as Dependent on Residence.

Under the terms of the statute, the residence or domicile of the bankrupt within the territorial jurisdiction of the court, or his having carried on business within the district, for the prescribed period of time before the filing of a petition against him, is an essential jurisdictional fact, without the existence of which the court will have no authority to proceed; or, in other words, it is the fact which determines the court in which the proceedings are to be taken. In re Leighton, 4 Ben. 457, Fed. Cas. No. 8,221; In re Little, 3 Ben. 25, Fed. Cas. No. 8,391; In re Palmer, 1 N. B. R. 213, Fed. Cas. No. 10,680; Fogarty v. Gerrity, 1 Sawy. 233, Fed. Cas. No. 4,895. See In re Burton, 9 Ben. 324, Fed. Cas. No. 2,214. Under the act of 1867, it was held that the proceedings in involuntary bankruptcy must be instituted with reference to the debtor's actual residence, or the place where he carries on his business, and not with regard to his domicile; the two terms not being synonymous as used in the bankruptcy law. And hence, where a person, resident with his family in one place, bought a stock of goods in another, and went there for business, leaving his family in the former place, it was held that the petition was properly filed in the place where he transacted such business. In re Watson, 4 N. B. R. 613, Fed. Cas. No. 17,272. In a case where the petitioner in voluntary bankruptcy had lived with his father in New Jersey for four years, and had kept books for a firm in New York City for six months prior to filing his petition in the southern district of New York, it was held that that court had no jurisdiction. In re Magie, 2 Ben. 369, Fed. Cas. No. 8,951. But a fugitive from justice, whose domicile was within a given district at the time of his flight, and who has acquired no domicile elsewhere, may be proceeded against in such district after his flight. Cobb v. Rice, 130 Mass. 231.

Jurisdiction of Corporations.

Where the same corporation enjoys a corporate existence, by legislative authority, in two states at once, and successive petitions in bankruptcy are filed against it in the federal courts within each of those states, that court which first acquires jurisdiction by the filing of a petition will retain it to the exclusion of the other, and must be permitted to exercise its jurisdiction to the fullest extent without interference by any other court. In re Boston, H. & E. R. Co., 9 Blatchf. 101, Fed. Cas. No. 1,677. The district court has power to declare a corporation bankrupt although it has previously been dissolved by a decree of a state court. In re New Amsterdam Ins. Co., 6 Ben. 368, Fed. Cas. No. 10,140. A corporation, subject to the provisions of the bankruptcy law, which has committed an act of bankruptcy, and is in existence when the petition against it is filed, and when the proper papers are served on its proper officer, cannot oust the jurisdiction of the bankruptcy court to proceed, on the return day, to an adjudication, because a decree dissolving the corporation has been made after such service and before such return day. Platt v. Archer, 9 Blatchf. 559, Fed. Cas. No. 11,213.

Appointment of Receiver.

Among the enumerated powers of the courts of bankruptcy is the power to "appoint receivers, or the marshals, upon applications of parties in interest, to take charge of the property of bankrupts after the filing of the petition and until it is dismissed or the trustee is qualified." There was no provision in the act of 1867 expressly authorizing the appointment of receivers by the bankruptcy court; but it was held to be within the general equity powers of a court of bankruptcy, after an adjudication and before the selection of a trustee, to appoint a receiver for the temporary care and custody of the estate, when special circumstances rendered it desirable. Lansing v. Manton, 14 N. B. R. 127, Fed. Cas. No. 8,077; Sedgwick v. Place, 3 Ben. 360, Fed. Cas. No. 12,619. For example, a receiver may be appointed where the apparent titles to property are such on their face that the marshal cannot act efficiently under the usual warrant. Keenan v. Shannon, 9 N. B. R. 441, Fed. Cas. No. 7,640. But no appointment will be made unless the party alleged to hold the property adversely to the complainant is served with process (Hyslop v. Hoppock, 5 Ben. 447, Fed. Cas. No. 6,988), nor where, upon the hearing of the motion, it is not apparent that the ultimate determination of the suit in favor of the complainant is reasonably probable. Wilkinson v. Dobbie, 12 Blatchf. 298, Fed. Cas. No. 17,670.

Power to Call in Stock Subscriptions.

The court of bankruptcy has jurisdiction and authority to order delinquent stockholders of a corporation to pay up their subscriptions to the capital stock, and if they fail to do so, the trustee has the same right of action that the corporation itself would have had to compel such payment. Sanger v. Upton, 91 U. S. 56; In re Republic Ins. Co., 3 Biss. 452, Fed. Cas. No. 11,704; Payson v. Stoever, 2 Dill. 427, Fed. Cas. No. 10,863. And a provision in the subscription and in the stock certificate that the balance was to be paid on the call of the directors, "when ordered by a vote of a majority of the stockholders themselves," does not prevent the effectual exercise of this power by the court; as a court of equity it has all the power of the directors, or the stockholders, or both collectively. Upton v. Hansbrough, 3 Biss. 417, Fed. Cas. No. 16,801.

CHAPTER III.

BANKRUPTS.

ACTS OF BANKRUPTCY.

§ 3. *a* Acts of bankruptcy by a person shall consist of his having (1) conveyed, transferred, concealed, or removed, or permitted to be concealed or removed, any part of his property with intent to hinder, delay, or defraud his creditors, or any of them; or (2) transferred, while insolvent, any portion of his property to one or more of his creditors with intent to prefer such creditors over his other creditors; or (3) suffered or permitted, while insolvent, any creditor to obtain a preference through legal proceedings, and not having at least five days before a sale or final disposition of any property affected by such preference vacated or discharged such preference; or (4) made a general assignment for the benefit of his creditors; or (5) admitted in writing his inability to pay his debts and his willingness to be adjudged a bankrupt on that ground.

b A petition may be filed against a person who is insolvent and who has committed an act of bankruptcy within four months after the commission of such act. Such time shall not expire until four months after (1) the date of the recording or registering of the transfer or assignment when the act consists in having made a transfer of any of his property with intent to hinder, delay, or defraud his creditors or for the purpose of giving a preference as hereinbefore provided, or a general assignment for the benefit of his creditors, if by law such recording or registering is required or permitted, or, if it is not, from the date when the beneficiary takes notorious, exclusive, or continuous possession of the property unless the petitioning creditors have received actual notice of such transfer or assignment.

c It shall be a complete defense to any proceedings in bankruptcy instituted under the first subdivision of this section to allege and prove that the party proceeded against was not insolvent as defined in this act at the time of the filing the petition against him, and if solvency at such date is proved by the alleged bankrupt the proceedings shall be dismissed, and under said subdivision one the burden of proving solvency shall be on the alleged bankrupt.

d Whenever a person against whom a petition has been filed as hereinbefore provided under the second and third subdivisions of this section takes issue with and denies the allegation of his insolvency, it shall be his duty to appear in court on the hearing, with his books, papers, and accounts, and submit to an examination, and give testimony as to all matters tending to establish solvency or insolvency, and in case of his failure to so attend and submit to examination the burden of proving his solvency shall rest upon him.

e Whenever a petition is filed by any person for the purpose of having another adjudged a bankrupt, and an application is made to take charge of and hold the property of the alleged bankrupt, or any part of the same, prior to the adjudication and

pending a hearing on the petition, the petitioner or applicant shall file in the same court a bond with at least two good and sufficient sureties who shall reside within the jurisdiction of said court, to be approved by the court or a judge thereof, in such sum as the court shall direct, conditioned for the payment, in case such petition is dismissed, to the respondent, his or her personal representatives, all costs, expenses, and damages occasioned by such seizure, taking, and detention of the property of the alleged bankrupt.

If such petition be dismissed by the court or withdrawn by the petitioner, the respondent or respondents shall be allowed all costs, counsel fees, expenses, and damages occasioned by such seizure, taking, or detention of such property. Counsel fees, costs, expenses, and damages shall be fixed and allowed by the court, and paid by the obligors in such bond.

ACTS OF BANKRUPTCY.

Insolvency of Debtor.

It will be observed that some of the acts of bankruptcy enumerated in the statute can be committed only by a person who is insolvent. As the term was used in former laws on the subject of bankruptcy, "insolvency" was defined as the inability to pay one's debts and meet his engagements as they matured in the usual and ordinary course of his business as persons in trade usually do. But the first section of the present act (clause 15) declares that a person shall be deemed "insolvent," within the provisions of the act, when the aggregate of his property, excluding such as he may have fraudulently conveyed or transferred, or concealed or removed, shall not be sufficient in amount, at a fair valuation, to pay his debts.

The failure to pay a single debt when due, it is said, is not sufficient to establish the fact of insolvency. Driggs v. Moore, 1 Abb. (U. S.) 440, Fed. Cas. No. 4,083.

Fraudulent Conveyances.

A conveyance, sale, transfer, or assignment of property which is fraudulent at common law is an act of bankruptcy; and so is every conveyance or assignment which contravenes the objects and provisions of the bankruptcy law, although it might have been good at common law. Gassett v. Morse, 21 Vt. 627, Fed. Cas. No. 5,264. Thus, a sale of a stock in trade, in gross, without invoice, at night, and for cash, is not a sale made in the ordinary course of business, and may be an act of bankruptcy. Davis v. Armstrong, 3 N. B. R. 33, Fed. Cas. No. 3,624. But a sale of property by a person who is in fact insolvent is not necessarily, and without regard to its character, void under the bankruptcy law. If it was made in good faith and for the honest purpose of discharging a debt, and in the confident expectation that by so doing the person could continue his business, it will be upheld. But if he made it to avoid the provisions of the bankruptcy act, and to withdraw his property from its control, and the vendee either knew or had reasonable cause to believe that the vendor's intention was of this character, it will be avoided. Tiffany v. Lucas, 15 Wall. 410. The sale of a stock of goods will not be considered an act of bankruptcy where the only object of the seller was to change his business, and the purchaser acted in good faith. In re Valliquette, 4 N. B. R. 307, Fed. Cas. No. 16,823. It is not an act of bankruptcy for a railroad corporation to convey its property in trust to secure bonds to be issued and sold, and the proceeds to be applied to pay all its unsecured debts, the same being done in good faith and with a view to enable the company to continue its legitimate business, though it may be technically insolvent, or likely soon to be so. In re Union Pac. R. Co.,

10 N. B. R. 178, Fed. Cas. No. 14,376. Again, where a person who is solvent agrees to transfer certain property to another as collateral security for advances made, but the transfer is not then completed, and subsequently, after he becomes insolvent, the transfer is concluded in pursuance of the agreement, this is not an act of bankruptcy. Ex parte Potts, Crabbe, 469, Fed. Cas. No. 11,344. The giving of a mortgage by an infant is not an act of bankruptcy, because it is not an absolute transfer, but is subject to his election to affirm or disaffirm it when he comes of age. In re Derby, 6 Ben. 232, Fed. Cas. No. 3,815. The subject of fraudulent gifts or transfers of the debtor's property, the suffering or procuring judgments to be entered against him, and the creation of illegal preferences, will be more fully discussed in connection with the subject of the discharge of the bankrupt and the several grounds of opposition to such discharge.

Assignment for Benefit of Creditors.

In this country it is well settled upon the authorities that a general assignment made by an insolvent debtor under the state laws, in contemplation of bankruptcy, is an act of bankruptcy, although it embraces all his property, and purports to be made for the equal benefit of all his creditors, and creates or intends no preferences, and is free from fraud, and although he denies any intention to evade or defeat the bankruptcy act; and such assignment is void or voidable as against the trustee in bankruptcy, because its necessary effects and consequences are to withdraw the estate from the administration of the court of bankruptcy, and so to obstruct or defeat the operation of the law. Boese v. King, 108 U. S. 379, 2 Sup. Ct. 765; In re Burt, 1 Dill. 439, Fed. Cas. No. 2,210; Cragin v. Thompson, 2 Dill. 513, Fed. Cas. No. 3,320; In re Beisenthal, 14 Blatchf. 146, Fed. Cas. No. 1,236; In re Frisbee, 14 Blatchf. 185, Fed. Cas. No. 5,129; In re Croft, 8 Biss. 188, Fed. Cas. No. 3,404; In re Smith, 4 Ben. 1, Fed.

Cas. No. 12,974; Globe Ins. Co. v. Cleveland Ins. Co., 14 N. B. R. 311, Fed. Cas. No. 5,486; Barnes v. Rettew, 8 Phila. 133, Fed. Cas. No. 1,019; McLean v. Johnson, 3 McLean, 202, Fed. Cas. No. 8,883; McLean v. Meline, 3 McLean, 199, Fed. Cas. No. 8,890; In re Randall, Deady, 557, Fed. Cas. No. 11,551; Jackson v. McCulloch, 13 N. B. R. 283, Fed. Cas. No. 7,140; Barton v. Tower, 1 N. Y. Leg. Obs. 8, Fed. Cas. No. 1,085; In re Chamberlain, 3 N. B. R. 710, Fed. Cas. No. 2,574; Perry v. Langley, 1 N. B. R. 559, Fed. Cas. No. 11,006; Jones v. Sleeper, 2 N. Y. Leg. Obs. 131, Fed. Cas. No. 7,496. It is presumed that the debtor intended to delay or defeat the operation of the bankruptcy law upon him; his denial has no rebutting force; he is presumed to intend the necessary consequences of his own acts. In re Smith, 4 Ben. 1, Fed. Cas. No. 12,974. And the fact that an assignment for the benefit of creditors is defectively executed does not make it any the less an act of bankruptcy. In re Lawrence, 10 Ben. 4, Fed. Cas. No. 8,133; In re Mendelsohn, 3 Sawy. 342, Fed. Cas. No. 9,420. So an application by a debtor for the benefit of a state insolvency law is an act of bankruptcy. Van Nostrand v. Carr, 30 Md. 128. But if the assignment be made more than six months (now four) before proceedings in bankruptcy are taken against the debtor, his trustee cannot assail the assignment nor claim the property from the assignee. Mayer v. Hellman, 91 U. S. 496.

Giving a Preference.

Where an insolvent trader gives a mortgage to one of his creditors, in contemplation of bankruptcy, and for the purpose of giving such creditor a preference over the others, it is an act of bankruptcy within the meaning of the statute. Arnold v. Maynard, 2 Story, 349, Fed. Cas. No. 561; Baldwin v. Rosseau, 1 N. Y. Leg. Obs. 391, Fed. Cas. No. 803. A creditor who knows his debtor to be insolvent may sue him, and proceed to judgment, and take his property on legal process, in such a manner as would operate to give a preference to himself if carried into full execution, and may then allege these facts as an act of bankruptcy and have the debtor adjudicated a bankrupt. Coxe v. Hale, 10 Blatchf. 56, Fed. Cas. No. 3,310. And a preference in contemplation of bankruptcy is no less an act of bankruptcy because yielded to the threats and coercion of the creditor. Atkinson v. Farmers' Bank, Crabbe, 529, Fed. Cas. No. 609. "Suffering his property to be taken on legal process with intent to give a preference" is an act of bankruptcy although the debtor did not know that there was any such law as the bankruptcy law in existence, and therefore could not have directly intended to defeat or evade it. In re Craft, 2 Ben. 214, Fed. Cas. No. 3,316.

Suffering Creditor to Obtain Preference by Legal Proceedings.

It is declared to be an act of bankruptcy if the debtor, while insolvent, shall have "suffered or permitted any creditor to obtain a preference through legal proceedings," provided the debtor does not, "at least five days before the sale or final disposition of any property affected by such preference," vacate or discharge the preference. In construing a similar provision in the act of 1867, it was held that something more than passive non-resistance on the part of an insolvent debtor is necessary to invalidate a judgment and levy on his property when the debt is due and he has no defense. In such a case, there is no legal obligation on the debtor to file a petition in bankruptcy to prevent the judgment and levy, and a failure to do so is not sufficient evidence of an intent to give a preference to the judgment creditor, or to defeat the operation of the bankruptcy law. But very slight circumstances which tend to show the existence of an affirmative desire on the part of the bankrupt to give a preference or to defeat the operation of the act may, by giving color to the whole transaction, render the lien void. Wilson v. City Bank, 17 Wall. 473. In deciding the question whether the giving of a warrant of attorney to confess judgment is an act of bankruptcy, the character of the alleged bankrupt's business may be taken into consideration; and where it appears that the purpose of the warrant of attorney may have been to enable the debtor to continue his business, and that there was no intention to defeat or delay the operation of the bankruptcy law, it is not a sufficient ground for an adjudication of bankruptcy. In re Leeds, 6 Phila. 468, Fed. Cas. No. 8,205. The giving by a debtor, for a consideration of equal value, of a warrant of attorney to confess judgment is not an act of bankruptcy, though the warrant is not recorded, but kept in the creditor's custody unknown to others. Blabon v. Hunt, 26 Pittsb. Leg. J. 180, Fed. Cas. No. 1,455.

Concealing Property.

Under this clause, it has been held that the secreting or concealment of goods which constitutes an act of bankruptcy, distinct from a fraudulent conveyance of them, must be an actual, not a constructive, concealment of them by the bankrupt himself, or by his procurement, while they continue, in his intention, his own goods. Livermore v. Bagley, 3 Mass. 487. And see Fox v. Eckstein, 4 N. B. R. 373, Fed. Cas. No. 5,009. But the better opinion seems to be that procuring an attachment upon a fictitious debt, in order to forestall or prevent an attachment by a bona fide creditor, comes fairly within the language of this clause; because the words mean not only the physical removal or concealment of property, but also the concealment of the actual title and position of the property of whatever kind. In re Williams, 3 N. B. R. 286, Fed. Cas. No. 17,703; In re Hussman, 2 N. B. R. 437, Fed. Cas. No. 6,951. And see O'Neil v. Glover, 5 Gray, 144, 159; Anonymous, 1 Pac. Law Rep. 173, Fed. Cas. No. 466.

Voluntary Petition as Act of Bankruptcy.

The act of 1867 contained a clause providing that the filing of a voluntary petition in bankruptcy should constitute an act of bankruptcy. No such provision is found in the present statute; but since it is made an act of bankruptcy if the debtor shall have "admitted in writing his inability to pay his debts and his willingness to be adjudged a bankrupt on that ground," it is probable that the filing of a voluntary petition will be held to produce the same result. In relation to this clause in the earlier statute, it was said: "He does not become a bankrupt by the adjudication, but he becomes one by the filing of the petition, provided that adjudication is afterwards made. The adjudication is merely a certificate or order made by an authorized officer to the effect that the petitioner became a bankrupt by the filing of his petition." In re Patterson, 1 Ben. 517, Fed. Cas. No. 10,815. As the filing of the petition is an act of bankruptcy, a single creditor cannot resist the adjudication by plea and proof that the debtor is really able to pay his debts. In re Fowler, 1 Low. 161, Fed. Cas. No. 4,998.

Acts of Bankruptcy by Corporation.

The appointment by a state court of a receiver to take possession of the property and assets of a corporation is a "taking on legal process," within the meaning of the bankruptcy law. "The receiver of a court of chancery is its executive officer, as much so, to all intents and purposes, as a sheriff of a court of law; and the goods or property in his hands are as much in the custody of the law as if levied upon under an execution or attachment." In re Merchants' Ins. Co., 3 Biss. 162, Fed. Cas. No. 9,441.

WHO MAY BECOME BANKRUPTS.

§ 4. *a* **Any person who owes debts, except a corporation, shall be entitled to the benefits of this act as a voluntary bankrupt.**

b **Any natural person, except a wage-earner or a person engaged chiefly in farming or the tillage of the soil, any unincorporated company, and any corporation engaged principally in manufacturing, trading, printing, publishing, or mercantile pursuits, owing debts to the amount of one thousand dollars or over, may be adjudged an involuntary bankrupt upon default or an impartial trial, and shall be subject to the provisions and entitled to the benefits of this act. Private bankers, but not national banks or banks incorporated under state or territorial laws, may be adjudged involuntary bankrupts.**

WHO ARE SUBJECT TO BANKRUPTCY LAW.

Voluntary Bankruptcy.

An alien may file his own petition in bankruptcy as soon as he has acquired the necessary residence in the United States. In re Goodfellow, 1 Low. 510, Fed. Cas. No. 5,536. Where a petition in involuntary bankruptcy was filed, and the debtor, before adjudication, filed his voluntary petition and was duly adjudged a bankrupt, it was held that the pendency of the first proceeding was no bar to the institution of the second, and that the court would proceed in the latter, and the further prosecution of the former would be stayed. In re Flanagan, 5 Sawy. 312, Fed. Cas. No. 4,850. But if the debtor files two successive petitions, setting forth the same debts, proceedings under the second will not be allowed to continue while the first is still pending. In re Wielarski, 4 Ben. 468, Fed. Cas. No. 17,619. The debtor may appropriate so much of his effects as may be necessary to raise the means to maintain his application in bankruptcy. Flournoy v. Newton, 8 Ga. 306. As to whether infants, lunatics, and married women may take advantage of the bankruptcy law, or are amenable to its provisions in proceedings in invitum, see, infra, further notes to this section.

A state court will not grant an injunction to restrain a debtor from applying for the benefit of the national bankruptcy law. Fillingin v. Thornton, 49 Ga. 384.

A voluntary bankrupt may be allowed, for good reasons shown, to withdraw his petition at any time before adjudication. Ex parte Bennett, 1 Pa. Law J. 145, Fed. Cas. No. 1,309; Dudley's Case, 1 Pa. Law J. 302, Fed. Cas. No. 4,114; In re Randall, 5 Law Rep. 115, Fed. Cas. No. 11,550. But this he cannot claim as a matter of right; he cannot withdraw his petition, if any of the creditors oppose it, at his own pleasure or without showing good cause therefor. In re Harris, 3 N. Y. Leg. Obs. 152, Fed. Cas. No. 6,110. Before an adjudication has been made, it is within the sound discretion of the court whether to dismiss or retain the petition. In re Randall, 5 Law Rep. 115, Fed. Cas. No. 11,550. But after an adjudication, it seems that it cannot be dismissed without the concurrence and assent of all the creditors. In re Gile, 5 Law Rep. 224, Fed. Cas. No. 5,423.

Infants.

It has been held that an infant is entitled to the benefit of the bankruptcy act, and that the proceedings may be had in his own name; the intervention of a guardian or next friend is not necessary. In re Book, 3 McLean, 317, Fed. Cas. No. 1,637. But the better opinion appears to be that an infant cannot be adjudged a bankrupt either on his own petition or on an adverse petition. Nor can he come into court after attaining majority, and, by presenting a petition to that effect, ratify and confirm involuntary proceedings begun against him during his minority. The court never acquired jurisdiction over him, and jurisdiction cannot be conferred upon it by any such retroactive process. In re Derby, 6 Ben. 232, Fed. Cas. No. 3,815. In Massachusetts, it has been held that proceedings in insolvency (under the state law) against an infant, who is not represented by a guardian ad litem, are void. Farris v. Richardson, 6 Allen, 118. Whether such proceedings would be good if the minor were represented by a guardian was doubted but not decided in this case. But a person against whom and his partner proceedings in insolvency have been instituted under such law, cannot avoid them on the ground that his partner was an infant when the proceedings were begun, if the infant was then represented by a guardian ad litem and has ratified the proceedings after coming of age. Winchester v. Thayer, 129 Mass. 129.

Lunatics.

The disabilities of a lunatic or insane person are such that he cannot commit an act of bankruptcy, and consequently he cannot be adjudged a bankrupt for any acts or transactions of his done or committed during his insanity. In re Marvin, 1 Dill. 178, Fed. Cas. No. 9,178; In re Weitzel, 7 Biss. 289, Fed. Cas. No. 17,365. But if a person, being at the time sane, commits such acts as make him amenable to the operation of the bankruptcy law, he may be adjudged a bankrupt upon compulsory proceedings, notwithstanding his supervening insanity; for a commission of bankruptcy is as much an action as any other species of proceeding, and the fact of lunacy, under the circumstances supposed, could not be pleaded in defense of an action at law. Shelford, Lunat. 429; Anonymous, 13 Ves. 590; Ex parte Stamp, 1 De Gex, 345; In re Pratt, 2 Low. 96, Fed. Cas. No. 11,371; In re

Marvin, 1 Dill. 178, Fed. Cas. No. 9,178. Nor is the consent of the lunatic's guardian or committee essential to the petition. In re Weitzel, 7 Biss. 289, Fed. Cas. No. 17,365. The fact that a person has been declared a lunatic by the proper court of the state of his domicile, and a guardian appointed for him, will not invalidate the action of the bankruptcy court in subsequently passing an adjudication of bankruptcy upon him on his own petition; for the decree of the state court merely establishes that he was insane at the time it was made, and does not exclude the supposition that he may since have become sane. Saunders v. Mitchell, 61 Miss. 321.

Married Women.

There has been some doubt and uncertainty as to the power of courts of bankruptcy to proceed against married women; but the true rule on this subject appears to be that the federal court, when called upon to adjudge a feme covert bankrupt, must regard the laws of the state of her domicile; and if, in that state, by enabling statutes, her common-law disabilities have been taken away to such an extent as to allow her to make valid and enforceable contracts in the way of trade or business, then she is amenable to the bankruptcy law,—that in any case where a plea of coverture would not avail her in an action on the debt, she may be proceeded against in bankruptcy. These views are supported by both the English and American cases. Lavie v. Phillips, 3 Burrows, 1783; Johnson v. Gallagher, 3 De Gex, F. & J. 494; In re Matthewman, L. R. 3 Eq. 781; Picard v. Hine, L. R. 5 Ch. App. 274; McHenry v. Davies, L. R. 10 Eq. 88; In re Kinkead, 3 Biss. 405, Fed. Cas. No. 7,824; In re Lyons, 2 Sawy. 524, Fed. Cas. No. 8,649; In re Collins, 3 Biss. 415, Fed. Cas. No. 3,006; In re O'Brien, 1 N. B. R. 176, Fed. Cas. No. 10,397. And see an interesting review of the authorities on this point in 13 Am. Law Reg. (N. S.) 129. Thus, in Illinois, where a married woman has entire control of her separate estate, whether owned before marriage or since acquired, and may make contracts in respect to the same, enforceable either at law or in equity, and may engage in trade, using her own property, it was held that where she formed a business partnership with her husband, contributing her separate money to the capital of the concern and her time and skill to the management of its affairs, the firm might be adjudged bankrupt, and it was thought that the wife might be so adjudged individually. In re Kinkead, 3 Biss. 405, Fed. Cas. No. 7,824. So, where a married woman was authorized by her husband to carry on business as a partner with other members of a firm, and was separate in property from her husband, it was held that it was not necessary to make the husband a party in a proceeding in involuntary bankruptcy against the firm. Lastrapes v. Blanc, 3 Woods, 134, Fed. Cas. No. 8,100. But, on the other hand, if the statutes of the state have not removed the common-law disabilities of a married woman, so that she is still incompetent to contract, a petition in bankruptcy will not lie against her, at least where it is not shown that she has a separate estate. In re Goodman, 5 Biss. 401, Fed. Cas. No. 5,540. And in the case of In re Howland, 2 N. B. R. 357, Fed. Cas. No. 6,791, where a petition in involuntary bankruptcy was filed against a married woman, having a separate estate, founded on the nonpayment of certain promissory notes made by her, it was held that, inasmuch as it did not appear on the face of the notes that it was her intention to bind her separate estate, and there being no allegation that they were given for the benefit of the separate estate, or in the course of trade, the petition must be dismissed, but with permission to amend. A married woman, where no fraud is intended, may take advantage of bankruptcy with respect to debts contracted while she was sole. Lawver v. Gladden (Pa. Sup.) 1 Atl. 659.

Corporations.

By the express provisions of the act corporations are debarred from taking the benefit of the act by the filing of a voluntary petition in bankruptcy. But the provisions for involuntary bankruptcy apply to unincorporated companies and to corporations "engaged principally in manufacturing, trading, printing, publishing, or mercantile pursuits;" so that any company, incorporated or not, which answers to this description, may be proceeded against under the statute, if it owes debts to the amount of one thousand dollars and has committed an act of bankruptcy.

Under the bankruptcy law of 1867, where no specific exceptions were made, but the law applied to "all moneyed, business, or commercial corporations and joint-stock companies," it was universally held that railroad companies must be included under the designation of "business corporations," and that they were therefore liable to be thrown into bankruptcy. New Orleans, S. F. & L. R. Co. v. Delamore, 114 U. S. 501, 5 Sup. Ct. 1009. In this case it was said: "The jurisdiction of the bankruptcy court to adjudicate a railroad company bankrupt and to administer its property, under the bankruptcy act, has been sustained by several circuit courts of the United States. No circuit court before which the question has been brought has denied the jurisdiction. As they were the courts of last resort upon this question, and valuable rights may depend upon their judgments upon the point, we think the question should be considered as settled by the authorities cited, and are unwilling at this late day to re-examine it." And see In re Greenville & C. R. Co., 5 Chi. Leg. News, 124, Fed. Cas. No. 5,787; Alabama & C. R. Co. v. Jones, 5 N. B. R. 97, Fed. Cas. No. 126; In re California Pac. R. Co., 3 Sawy. 240, Fed. Cas. No. 2,315; Rankin v. Florida, A. & G. C. R. Co., 1 N. B. R. 647, Fed. Cas. No. 11,567; In re Southern Minn. R. Co., 10 N. B. R. 86, Fed. Cas. No. 13,188; In re Alabama & C. R. Co., 9 Blatchf. 390, Fed. Cas. No. 124; Adams v. Boston, H. & E.

R. Co., 1 Holmes, 30, Fed. Cas. No. 47; Sweatt v. Boston, H. & E. R. Co., 3 Cliff. 339, Fed. Cas. No. 13,684; Winter v. Iowa, M. & N. P. R. Co., 2 Dill. 487, Fed. Cas. No. 17,890. In the case of Alabama & C. R. Co. v. Jones, supra, it was observed that a corporation carrying on and pursuing any lawful business, defined and clothed by its charter with power to do so, is clearly a business corporation and amenable to the bankruptcy law, and that it seemed to be the clear intent of the law to bring within its scope all corporations, except those organized for religious, charitable, literary, educational, municipal, or political purposes. But under the present statute, since a railroad company neither trades, manufactures, prints or publishes, as the principal part of its business, it cannot be amenable to the bankruptcy law, unless it should be considered that its business is a "mercantile pursuit," which the courts are not at all likely to hold.

Insurance companies duly authorized under the laws of a state to transact the business of insurance, in any of its branches or departments, were held to be subject to the operation of the bankruptcy law, since they plainly came within the general descriptions given in the statute of 1867; but whether this is also the case under the terms of the present act is more doubtful. See In re Merchants' Ins. Co., 3 Biss. 162, Fed. Cas. No. 9,441; In re Independent Ins. Co., 1 Holmes, 103, Fed. Cas. No. 7,017; In re Hercules Mut. Ins. Co., 6 Ben. 35, Fed. Cas. No. 6,402.

Since the act declares that the word "persons" shall include corporations, service of process is to be made personally on a corporation by delivering a copy of the petition and order to show cause on its head or principal officers; and the "usual place of abode" must be construed to mean the principal place of business where alone it can be said to reside. In re California Pac. R. Co., 3 Sawy. 240, Fed. Cas. No. 2,315. A corporation, for all essential purposes, is as effectually dissolved by the commencement of proceedings in bankruptcy against it as if a solemn judgment were pronounced to that effect. It is such a dissolution as will afford creditors a remedy against the individual stockholders where they are made liable upon the dissolution of the corporation. State Savings Ass'n v. Kellogg, 52 Mo. 583. Compare Holland v. Heyman, 60 Ga. 174.

Trading Corporations.

Bankruptcy laws were originally confined to such persons as were "traders"; and former laws of the United States on this subject required that "traders" should keep books of account, in order to be entitled to a discharge. While this restriction is no longer in force, as respects natural persons, the present statute provides that proceedings in involuntary bankruptcy may be instituted against corporations which are "engaged principally in trading." The construction of this term should clearly be the same as that which was established under former bankruptcy laws, since it must be presumed that it was adopted by congress with an understanding and knowledge of what had previously been decided by the courts as to its meaning. Hence the decisions on the interpretation of the word "trader," made under the earlier statutes, will now be of importance and value.

Among those who have been held to be "traders," within the meaning of the bankruptcy law, may be instanced the following: A baker, who buys flour which he makes into bread, and sells the bread to daily customers (In re Cocks, 3 Ben. 260, Fed. Cas. No. 2,933), a man who boards horses (In re Odell, 9 Ben. 209, Fed. Cas. No. 10,426), a person who keeps a liquor saloon and sells there, for cash and on credit, at retail, cigars and liquors bought in quantity, partly on credit (In re Sherwood, 9 Ben. 66, Fed. Cas. No. 12,773), a stair-builder, who buys nails, lumber, and other necessary materials, and works them into stairs for persons who give him orders for such stairs and pay him a gross price therefor (In re Garrison, 5 Ben. 430, Fed. Cas. No. 5,254). Also, within the meaning of the bankruptcy law, a butcher is a tradesman. In re Bassett, 8 Fed. 266. On the other hand, a man who speculates in stocks, buying and selling them through brokers, but not keeping an office for that purpose nor acting as a commission broker for others, is not a trader. In re Marston, 5 Ben. 313, Fed. Cas. No. 9,142; In re Woodward, 8 Ben. 563, Fed. Cas. No. 18,001. One who contracts with a railroad company to grade and build its road is not a merchant or trader. In re Smith, 2 Low. 69, Fed. Cas. No. 12,981. One who is engaged in farming and trading live stock is not within the act. In re Ragsdale, 7 Biss. 154, Fed. Cas. No. 11,530. A person who from time to time buys oil paintings and places them in a public gallery and sells them at auction, but is regularly engaged in a totally different business, is not a trader. In re Chapman, 9 Ben. 311, Fed. Cas. No. 2,601. One who superintends the running of a steamer, and, as treasurer of the corporation owning her, receives and disburses the money earned by the vessel, is not a merchant or tradesman within the act. In re Merritt, 7 Fed. 853. Nor is a teamster who, even to a very considerable extent, buys and sells hay and straw for the bona fide purpose of keeping his team from standing idle. In re Kimball, 7 Fed. 461. Nor is a theatrical manager who buys costumes, machinery, etc., for use in his business, and who on a few occasions has sold some such property. In re Duff, 4 Fed. 519.

Merchants and Manufacturers.

A merchant is one who buys to sell again, and who does both, not occasionally or incidentally, but habitually and as a business. Com. v. Natural Gas Co., 32 Pittsb. Leg. J. 310. It has also been held that a banker is a merchant, according to both the commercial and the civil law. Brown v. Pike, 34 La. Ann. 578. But this point is not now of importance, since incorporated banks, whether state or national, are expressly excepted from the provisions of the present bankruptcy law. But a commercial traveler is not a merchant, since he does not sell his own goods. Ex parte Taylor, 58 Miss. 481. The proprietor of a steam saw-mill, in which are prepared boards and shingles from lumber grown on his own land, and placed on the market for sale, is a manufacturer within the meaning of the act, though perhaps not a trader. In re Chandler, 1 Low. 478, Fed. Cas. No. 2,591. But a corporation engaged in the business of printing and publishing a weekly newspaper, is not a manufacturer. In re Capital Publishing Co., 3 MacArthur, 405. Compare In re Kenyon, 6 N. B. R. 238. (Such a corporation, however, is made subject to the institution of proceedings in involuntary bankruptcy against it by the express language of the present law, which applies to corporations "engaged principally in printing and publishing.") A builder or repairer of vessels is not a manufacturer. People v. Dry-Dock Co., 63 How. Prac. 453. Nor is a cooper who makes barrels from staves (New Orleans v. Le Blanc, 34 La. Ann. 597), nor an ice-cream confectioner. New Orleans v. Mannessier, 32 La. Ann. 1075.

National and State Banks.

The present act, it will be perceived, expressly excepts national banks from the class of persons who may be adjudged bankrupts. Former statutes on the subject contained no such exempting clause. Yet the courts always held that a national bank was not liable to be proceeded against in bankruptcy. The bankruptcy act, it was said, did not repeal or supersede the provisions of the act in relation to the winding up of insolvent national banks and the appointment of receivers for them (Rev. St. U. S. §§ 5120–5140). Nor could the two acts exist together as furnishing concurrent or co-ordinate remedies. The remedies prescribed in such a case under the bankruptcy act are not so ample and complete as those under the statute specially relating to national banks; and the fact that creditors cannot of their own motion institute proceedings under the latter statute does not change the construction of the acts. Nor did congress intend to inject the provisions of the bankruptcy act into the other statute, so that creditors could apply the remedies of the one, and the controller of the currency the remedies of the other. Such a construction would inevitably produce confusion and conflicts of jurisdiction. In re Manufacturers' Nat. Bank, 5 Biss. 499, Fed. Cas. No. 9,051.

Under the act of 1867, it was held that a bank incorporated under the laws of a state was subject to the operation of the national bankruptcy law. Thornhill v. Bank of Louisiana, 3 N. B. R. 110, Fed. Cas. No. 13,990. But it will be noted that this rule is changed by the present statute, which expressly provides that its involuntary features may apply to "private bankers," but shall not apply to "banks incorporated under state or territorial laws."

Decedent's Estate.

The bankruptcy act does not authorize the institution of proceedings against the individual estate of a deceased person; nor does the court acquire jurisdiction of the individual estate of a decedent by proceedings against a firm of which he was a member. Adams v. Terrell, 4 Woods, 337, 4 Fed. 796.

Aliens.

The benefit of the bankruptcy act is not by its terms restricted to citizens of the United States. Consequently, an alien resident within this country and owing debts here may take advantage of the act by filing his voluntary petition in bankruptcy. In re Boynton, 10 Fed. 277; In re Goodfellow, 1 Low. 510, Fed. Cas. No. 5,536.

Wage Earners.

These persons, by the express terms of the act, are exempt from liability to be adjudged bankrupts. The word "wage earners" is not a technical term of the law, but has come to be much used of late years, especially by writers on political and social economy, as a substitute for the phrase "laboring classes." It may be expected that difficulties will arise in its construction, in view of the complex conditions of modern business life and the manifold nature of the relation of employer and employed. The first section of the statute provides that the term "wage earner" shall mean "an individual who works for wages, salary, or hire, at a rate of compensation not exceeding one thousand five hundred dollars per year." But obviously the terms of this definition require explanation, and especially the words "wages" and "salary." According to Webster, the former expression means "hire, reward, that which is paid or stipulated for services, but chiefly for services by manual labor, or for military and naval services. We speak of servants' wages, a laborer's wages, or soldiers' wages; but we never apply the word to the rewards given to men in office, which are called fees or salary." Another authority defines wages as "the agreed compensation for services rendered in a menial or subordinate capacity." Abbott, Law Dict.; Ryan v. Hook, 34 Hun, 185. Bouvier defines the same term as "a compensation given to a hired person for his or her services." Bouvier, Law Dict. In a recent work of high authority, "wages" is defined as "that which is paid for a service rendered; what is paid for labor; hire. In common use the word 'wages' is applied specifically to the payment made for manual labor or other labor of a menial or mechanical kind, distinguished (but somewhat vaguely) from 'salary,' and from 'fee', which denotes compensation paid to professional men, as lawyers and physicians." And a wage earner is "one who receives stated wages for labor." Century Dict. s. v. "The word 'wages,' in its popular use, signifies the remuneration of hired labor. As so used, it is more or less disparaging, being commonly placed in contrast with the words 'salaries,' 'fees,' 'honorarium,' etc., by which it is sought to denote the remuneration of services of a higher or more intellectual character." F. A. Walker, in Lalor's Polit. Cyclop.

In the case of Com. v. Butler, 99 Pa. St. 542, Chief Justice Sharswood observed: "The truth is, and this the lexicographers seem to hold, that if there is any difference in the popular sense between 'salary' and 'wages,' it is only in the application of them to more or less honorable services. A farmer pays his farm hand, in common speech, wages, whether by the day, the week, the harvest, or the year. If for any reason he has occasion to employ an overseer, his compensation, no matter how measured, is called a 'salary.' An ironmaster pays his workmen wages; his manager receives a salary. A merchant pays wages to his servant who sweeps the floor, makes the fire, and runs his errands; but he compensates his salesman or clerk by a salary." See, also, South & North Alabama R. Co. v. Falkner, 49 Ala. 118; People v. Remington, 45 Hun, 338. In another case it is said: "'Fees' are compensation for particular acts or services, as the fees of clerks, sheriffs, lawyers, physicians, etc. 'Wages' are the compensation paid or to be paid for services by the day, week, etc., as of laborers, commissioners, etc. 'Salaries' are the per annum compensation to men in official and some other situations." Cowdin v. Huff, 10 Ind. 85. But according to another opinion, "this compensation to a laborer may be a specified sum for a given time of service, or a fixed sum for specified work; that is, payment may be made by the job. The word 'wages' does not imply that the compensation is to be determined solely upon the basis of time spent in service; it may be determined by the work done. It means compensation estimated in either way." Ford v. St. Louis, K. & N. W. R. Co., 54 Iowa, 728, 7 N. W. 126.

A fixed annual compensation paid to the secretary of a business corporation is a salary; it is not wages. Gordon v. Jennings, 9 Q. B. Div. 45. Where the receiver of a railroad corporation is directed by the order of the court to pay "wages of employés" out of the income of the road, this term does not include the services of counsel employed for special purposes. Louisville, E. & St. L. R. Co. v. Wilson, 138 U. S. 505, 11 Sup. Ct. 405. So, in People v. Remington, 45 Hun, 329, it is held that the term "wages" does not include the salary of the president, manager, or superintendent of a business corporation; nor sums payable to attorneys at law for professional services rendered to the corporation upon occasional retainers; nor the compensation of a person who is employed by the company to sell its goods in a foreign country, at a fixed annual salary, with the addition of a commission and his traveling expenses. Again, the term "wages" is not applicable to the compensation of the public officers of a municipal corporation, who receive annual salaries, which are not due till the end of the year, and who are entitled to be paid so long as they hold their offices without regard to the services rendered. People v. Meyers, 25 Abb. New Cas. 368. A person who takes a contract to execute a certain cutting on a railway, at a certain sum per cubic yard, and employs several men under him to assist in doing the work, is not a "workman" or "laborer," although he does a portion of the work himself; and his compensation is not "wages." Riley v. Warden, 2 Exch. 59. So again, where manufacturers receive raw material from another, and work it up for him into a finished or partly finished product, by the use of their machinery and the labor of their employés, under a contract specifying a fixed rate of payment, the money due them therefor is not "wages." Lang v. Simmons, 64 Wis. 525, 25 N. W. 650; Campfield v. Lang, 25 Fed. 128. But on the other hand, in Texas, under a constitutional and statutory provision that "current wages for personal service" shall not be subject to garnishment, it has been held that the exemption might be claimed by one who was employed by a live-stock company as manager, at a monthly salary of $200, though he was also a stockholder of the company. Bell v. Indian Live-Stock Co., 11 S. W. 344.

If it were not for the definition contained in the act itself, we should be justified in concluding, from these authorities, that "wage earner" must be taken as synonymous with "laborer," as the latter term is ordinarily employed in statutes and in legal speech, or as denoting one who subsists by his physical labor, as distinguished from one who subsists by professional skill. Weymouth v. Sanborn, 43 N. H. 173; Pennsylvania & D. R. Co. v. Leuffer, 84 Pa. St. 168. But since the bankruptcy act makes the term "wage earner" include not only a person who works for "wages," but also one who works for "salary" or "hire," it will probably be held to include almost all classes of employés, whatever be the nature of their labor, who are compensated at a fixed rate, not exceeding $1500 per annum, but excluding independent contractors and all those persons whose remuneration is given for specific services rendered upon an occasional employment, and not under a permanent engagement, and who are employed in such occupations as require something more than mere physical labor or mere clerical ability.

PARTNERS.

§ 5. *a* A partnership, during the continuation of the partnership business, or after its dissolution and before the final settlement thereof, may be adjudged a bankrupt.

b The creditors of the partnership shall appoint the trustee; in other respects so far as possible the estate shall be administered as herein provided for other estates.

c The court of bankruptcy which has jurisdiction of one of the partners may have jurisdiction of all the partners and of the administration of the partnership and individual property.

d The trustee shall keep separate accounts of the partnership property and of the property belonging to the individual partners.

e The expenses shall be paid from the partnership property and the individual property in such proportions as the court shall determine.

f The net proceeds of the partnership property shall be appropriated to the payment of the partnership debts, and the net proceeds of the individual estate of each partner to the payment of his individual debts. Should any surplus remain of the property of any partner after paying his individual debts, such surplus shall be added to the partnership assets and be applied to the payment of the partnership debts. Should any surplus of the partnership property remain after paying the partnership debts, such surplus shall be added to the assets of the individual partners in the proportion of their respective interests in the partnership.

g **The court may permit the proof of the claim of the partnership estate against the individual estates, and vice versa, and may marshal the assets of the partnership estate and individual estates so as to prevent preferences and secure the equitable distribution of the property of the several estates.**

h **In the event of one or more but not all of the members of a partnership being adjudged bankrupt, the partnership property shall not be administered in bankruptcy, unless by consent of the partner or partners not adjudged bankrupt; but such partner or partners not adjudged bankrupt shall settle the partnership business as expeditiously as its nature will permit, and account for the interest of the partner or partners adjudged bankrupt.**

Jurisdiction in Partnership Cases.

One or more partners may file their petition in bankruptcy without making the others parties, but notice of the pendency of the proceedings must be given to the other partners. In re Moore, 5 Biss. 79, Fed. Cas. No. 9,750; In re Gorham, 9 Biss. 23, Fed. Cas. No. 5,624. So where two partners of a firm of three have petitioned to have the firm adjudicated bankrupt, the district court has jurisdiction over the partnership property, notwithstanding the third partner is proceeding in a state court for a settlement of the partnership concerns, and has procured himself to be appointed receiver, and is in possession of the joint assets. In re Hathorn, 2 Woods, 73, Fed. Cas. No. 6,214. But where one of two partners files a voluntary petition in bankruptcy, alleging that the other will not join him, and praying to have him declared a bankrupt, this, as to the other partner, is a case of involuntary bankruptcy. Medsker v. Bonebrake, 108 U. S. 66, 2 Sup. Ct. 351.

Involuntary Bankruptcy.

A petition in bankruptcy against a firm, naming only two of the three partners, cannot be amended so as to make the third a party after all the testimony is taken and the cause is before the court upon hearing, and the firm cannot be adjudged bankrupt upon a petition so defective. In re Pitt, 8 Ben. 389, Fed. Cas. No. 11,188. And an adjudication in bankruptcy against a firm must be made in one proceeding and on one petition; the adjudication of one member of a firm in one proceeding; and of the remaining members of it in a separate proceeding, with such effect as to bring the firm into bankruptcy, is a thing not contemplated by the statute. In re Plumb, 9 Ben. 279, Fed. Cas. No. 11,231. But proceedings in one district against a firm constitute no bar to similar proceedings in another district against another firm some of whose members were also members of the former firm. In re Jewett, 7 Biss. 473, Fed. Cas. No. 7,307. But in a case where a firm composed of three persons did business, and they all resided within one district, and two of these partners constituted another firm, doing business under another name in a different district, and the former firm was adjudged bankrupt and a trustee appointed, who took possession of all the property of all three partners, and subsequently a similar petition was filed in the other district against the firm composed of the two partners; it was held that the said trustee had acquired all the interest of the partners in the second firm, which firm was ipso facto dissolved by the bankruptcy; that the creditors of the second firm would be entitled to be first paid out of the assets of that firm, and such right would be recognized in the bankruptcy proceedings already instituted; and that the court to which the latter petition was presented would not proceed to an adjudication thereon while proceedings were pending in the other district. In re Leland, 5 Ben. 168, Fed. Cas. No. 8,228.

Dissolution of Partnership.

A dissolution of the firm by the act of all or any of the partners does not put an end to the power of the bankruptcy court, so long as any unfinished business, debts, credits, or assets remain. In Re Noonan, 3 Biss. 491, Fed. Cas. No. 10,292; In re Crockett, 2 Ben. 514, Fed. Cas. No. 3,402; In Re Stowers, 1 Low. 528, Fed. Cas. No. 13,516.

Secret Partner.

It is not essential to the validity of an adjudication in bankruptcy against a partnership that a secret or dormant partner should have been made a party defendant; where only the ostensible partners are served and proceeded against, this will at least bind the partnership property. Metcalf v. Officer, 5 Dill. 565, Fed. Cas. No. 9,496.

Presumptive Partner.

One who permits himself to be held out as a partner, though he has actually retired from the firm, may be made bankrupt as a member of the firm at the suit of creditors. In re Krueger, 2 Low. 66, Fed. Cas. No. 7,941.

Dissolution by Death of Partner.

A partnership dissolved by the death of one of the members cannot be treated as still subsisting so as to be subject to the provisions of the bankrupt law. The status of a deceased person cannot be passed upon by a bankruptcy court, nor has he any property the title to which can vest in a trustee appointed in a proceeding by or against the surviving partner. In Re Temple, 4 Sawy. 92, Fed. Cas. No. 13,825. Nevertheless a surviving partner may be adjudged bankrupt on an act of bankruptcy committed by him in respect to the joint property and in the course of the administration of the assets of the dissolved partnership. In Re Stevens, 1 Sawy. 397, Fed. Cas. No. 13,393. And where a surviving partner files his petition in bankruptcy, both individually and as surviving partner of a firm, the court has authority to adjudge him bankrupt in both characters. Briswalter v. Long, 7 Sawy. 74, 14 Fed. 153.

Acts of Bankruptcy by Partners.

A sale by one partner to his co-partner, when the firm is insolvent and on the eve of bankruptcy, is presumptively fraudulent as to firm creditors, the effect of such transfer being to change the order of payment and prefer private creditors to firm creditors, and the court should set it aside and distribute the property as firm property. In Re Cook, 3 Biss. 122, Fed. Cas. No. 3,150. But it is not an act of bankruptcy on the part of one member of a firm to influence or procure the departure of another from the state, though the circumstances are such that the absconding partner makes himself amenable to the law. In re Terry, 5 Biss. 110, Fed. Cas. No. 13,836.

Effect of Adjudication of one Partner.

An adjudication of bankruptcy against one member of a partnership dissolves the firm, and makes the solvent partner and the trustee of the bankrupt tenants in common of the partnership effects. Halsey v. Norton, 45 Miss. 703; Blackwell v. Claywell, 75 N. C. 213; McNutt v. King, 59 Ala. 597.

Distribution of the Estate.

Partnership property must first go to satisfy partnership debts in preference to separate debts due by a partner. In re Wiley, 4 Biss. 214, Fed. Cas. No. 17,656. But the rule is now well settled, in accordance with the English doctrine, that where there are both partnership and individual debts, but no partnership assets and no solvent partner, the debts of the firm and of the members can both be proved and the general estate is to be distributed pari passu among all the creditors joint and several. In re Knight, 2 Biss. 518, Fed. Cas. No. 7,880; In re Litchfield, 5 Fed. 47; In re Blumer, 12 Fed. 489; In re Lloyd, 22 Fed. 88. The firm creditors have a right to share pari passu with individual creditors in the individual estate where the firm assets are not more than sufficient to pay the costs and expenses properly chargeable to the firm estate. In re Litchfield, 5 Fed. 47. The test of available assets for such purpose is whether, at the time of the filing of the petition in bankruptcy, there was an available fund to pay firm creditors; and a neglect by the firm creditors to avail themselves of such fund then existing, whereby it has been dissipated or lost to them, does not enlarge their equity against the individual estate, although in fact they have been paid nothing on their debts. Id. But when all the partners are in bankruptcy, it was the general rule that the separate estate of one partner should not claim against the joint estate of the partnership in competition with the joint creditors, nor the joint estate against the separate estate in competition with the separate creditors. In re Lloyd, 22 Fed. 90. But the present statute expressly provides that the court "may permit" this to be done. Where a firm composed of three persons gave, in settlement of part of a debt due to one creditor, the note of the firm with the indorsement of one of the partners, and for other parts of it, severally, three notes, each made by one of the partners and indorsed by the others, and the firm was adjudged bankrupt, and the creditor proved his debt against the makers alone of the four notes, it was held that he was entitled to dividends according to such proofs, out of the several estates, joint or separate, against which the proofs were made. Mead v. National Bank of Fayetteville, 6 Blatchf. 180, Fed. Cas. No. 9,366. And see In re Bradley, 2 Biss. 515, Fed. Cas. No. 1,772. Where three of the four members of a firm, and the firm itself, settled with creditors under a composition in a bankruptcy proceeding to which the fourth member, A., was not a party, and afterwards, in another proceeding, A. was adjudged a bankrupt, it was held that the firm creditors were not entitled to share with A.'s individual creditors in the distribution of the fund realized from A.'s individual estate, except the holders of certain notes made by the firm on which A. was liable as an indorser. In re Adams, 29 Fed. 843. A debt founded on a judgment against the two members of a firm jointly, in a suit on a partnership note, does not entitle the creditors to dividends out of the separate estate of each member of the firm, on an equal footing with the separate creditors of each member. In Re Berrian, 6 Ben. 297, Fed. Cas. No. 1,351. And where two partners signed an agreement, as individuals, to transfer certain property as security for a partnership liability, but failed to make the transfer, and subsequently became bankrupt, it was held that such liability was not provable against the separate estate of one of the partners. Gauss v. Schrader, 10 Biss. 289, 48 Fed. 816. And again, a claim founded on a bond signed by the individual members of a firm, but not given for a firm debt, is not entitled, as against partnership creditors, to be paid out of the assets of the firm; it is a joint but not a partnership debt. In re Roddin, 6 Biss. 377, Fed. Cas. No. 11,989. An agreement between two traders to unite their stocks in trade as the capital of a partnership to be formed between them, and to convert the separate business debts of either into joint debts of the firm will not entitle a separate creditor who has not acceded in any way to the arrangement before bankruptcy, to prove his claim as a joint creditor of the firm against the partnership estate. In re Isaacs, 3 Sawy. 35, Fed. Cas. No. 7,093. A joint creditor, in case of the separate bankruptcy of one member of the firm, has a right to prove his joint debt, and vote for the trustee, in the separate bankruptcy. In re Webb, 4 Sawy. 326, Fed. Cas. No. 17,317. It is also held that the exemption provided for by the statute is not to be allowed to the individual partners out of the firm assets. In re Croft, 8 Biss. 188, Fed. Cas. No. 3,404; In re Hughes, 8 Biss. 107, Fed. Cas. No. 6,842.

Discharge of Partners.

The discharge of a member of a firm, upon his individual petition in bankruptcy, and without any proceedings by or against the firm, does not discharge such member from the firm or partnership debts. Hudgins v. Lane, 2 Hughes, 361, Fed. Cas. No. 6,827; In re Little, 1 N. B. R. 341, Fed. Cas. No. 8,390; In re Noonan, 10 N. B. R. 330, Fed. Cas. No. 10,292. And a discharge in bankruptcy of two general partners cannot be set up in favor of a special partner, in an action against the three as general partners on the ground that the special partner has made himself liable as a general partner. Abendroth v. Van Dolsen, 131 U. S. 66, 9 Sup. Ct. 619. Where a firm is proceeded against as such, unless the court acquires jurisdiction of all the partners it cannot grant a discharge to any. In re Beals, 9 Ben. 223, Fed. Cas. No. 1,165. A proceeding in bankruptcy by a partner against his copartner is not an involuntary proceeding as respects the copartner, and therefore the latter cannot obtain his discharge without the assent of creditors or the amount of assets required in voluntary proceedings by the act of July 27, 1868. In re Wilson, 2 Low. 453, Fed. Cas. No. 17,784. But, as to such a proceeding being voluntary, compare Medsker v. Bonebrake, 108 U. S. 66, 2 Sup. Ct. 351. When objections are filed to the discharge of partners who are bankrupts, the trial may be joint, but the verdicts and decrees must be several. In re George, 1 Low. 409, Fed. Cas. No. 5,325.

EXEMPTIONS OF BANKRUPTS.

§ 6. *a* This act shall not affect the allowance to bankrupts of the exemptions which are prescribed by the state laws in force at the time of the filing of the petition in the state wherein they have had their domicile for the six months or the greater portion thereof immediately preceding the filing of the petition.

Exemptions.

It is provided by section 47 of the present act that the trustee shall set apart the bankrupt's exemptions and report the items and estimated value thereof to the court. But the right of the bankrupt to the property exempted by the law of the state is a fixed and determinate right, not dependent upon the discretion of the trustee, and where it is claimed and illegally refused before the trustee sells the property, it may be asserted against the proceeds of the same while in the hands of the court for distribution. In re Jones, 2 Dill. 343, Fed. Cas. No. 7,445. It is further provided, by section 7 of the present act, that it shall be the duty of the bankrupt to make a claim for such exemptions as he may be entitled to. And section second confers upon the bankruptcy court jurisdiction to "determine all claims of bankrupts to their exemptions."

Title to Exempt Property.

Property exempt by the law of the state does not pass to the trustee in bankruptcy at all; he acquires no title to it, and the title of the owner is not impaired or affected by the proceedings in bankruptcy. In re Hunt, 5 N. B. R. 493, Fed. Cas. No. 6,883; In re Hester, 5 N. B. R. 285, Fed. Cas. No. 6,437; Bush v. Lester, 15 N. B. R. 36; Wilkinson v. Wait, 44 Vt. 508; Felker v. Crane, 70 Ga. 484. Hence it remains the absolute property of the bankrupt and subject to any specific liens on it created by his voluntary act or by legal proceedings. Robinson v. Wilson, 15 Kan. 595. But a trustee in bankruptcy, like a sheriff levying execution, is entitled to at least temporary control of the exempted property until it can be set apart from the rest. Sheldon v. Rounds, 40 Mich. 425. As the title to such property does not pass to the trustee, the owner may bring and maintain suits in respect to the same without regard to the pendency of his bankruptcy proceedings. Henly v. Lanier, 75 N. C. 172. He may maintain an action for the recovery of it in specie, or for damages for wrongs done in respect to it, independently of the trustee. Winn v. Morse, 59 N. H. 210. The right of action for trespass to exempt property is not in the trustee but in the bankrupt himself. Seiling v. Gunderman, 35 Tex. 545. The trustee is not entitled to any of the exempted property, and it is no concern of his who may have the right to it; upon the death of the bankrupt, the title to such property vests in the executor or administrator. In re Hester, 5 N. B. R. 285, Fed. Cas. No. 6,437. When exempted property is designated and set apart to the bankrupt, under the orders of the bankruptcy court, as such property does not pass to the trustee, and does not further concern the court nor the estate, the court has no jurisdiction to defend such property from adverse liens that may or may not be extinguished by the bankruptcy. Jeffries v. Bartlett, 20 Fed. 496. A sale made after the filing of the petition in bankruptcy, of property exempt both by the bankrupt act and the state law, under a levy made prior to the commencement of the proceedings in bankruptcy, will be set aside. In re Griffin, 2 N. B. R. 254, Fed. Cas. No. 5,813. Land which has been set aside as exempt, and for a homestead, in bankruptcy proceedings, to which no exception has been made by any of the creditors, is the absolute property of the bankrupt and his alienees and those claiming under them, as against a party claiming the property under an execution sale upon a judgment recovered by certain fiduciary creditors of the bankrupt subsequent to the allotment of the homestead. Simpson v. Houston, 97 N. C. 344, 2 S. E. 651. Where land has been set apart to a bankrupt as an exemption by the bankruptcy court, this has the same effect in holding off prior liens of creditors, or liens existing at the time of the adjudication, as if the exemption had been regularly set apart by a proceeding in the state court having jurisdiction, in the method prescribed by the state laws. Barrett v. Durham, 80 Ga. 336, 5 S. E. 102; Collier v. Simpson, 74 Ga. 697.

Who may claim Exemption.

A wife cannot have a homestead on the land of her bankrupt husband, as against the trustee, or against those claiming title to the same under a sale made by the trustee. Lumpkin v. Eason, 44 Ga. 339. The individual members of a bankrupt partnership are not entitled to exemptions out of the partnership property. Their interest, as individuals, in the joint property, is an interest in the surplus only. In re Corbett, 5 Sawy. 206, Fed. Cas. No. 3,220; In re Hafer, 1 N. B. R. 147, Fed. Cas. No. 5,896; In re Price, 6 N. B. R. 400, Fed. Cas. No. 11,410; In re Handlin, 12 N. B. R. 49, Fed. Cas. No. 6,018; In re Tonne, 13 N. B. R. 170, Fed. Cas. No. 14,095; In re Sauthoff, 16 N. B. R. 181, Fed. Cas. No. 12,380; Wright v. Pratt, 31 Wis. 99; Pond v. Kimball, 101 Mass. 105; Guptil v. McFee, 9 Kan. 35; Kingsley v. Kingsley, 39 Cal. 665. See, per contra, In re Young, 3 N. B. R. 111, Fed. Cas. No. 18,148; In re Richardson, 11 N. B. R. 114, Fed. Cas. No. 11,776; Stewart v. Brown, 37 N. Y. 350.

Liens on Exempt Property.

Property cannot be exempted to the prejudice of a creditor who holds a valid vendor's lien thereon. The lien must prevail. Congress did not intend that the bankrupt act should override cases of that nature. In re Perdue, 2 N. B. R. 183, Fed. Cas. No. 10,975; In re Whitehead, 2 N. B. R. 599, Fed. Cas. No. 17,562; In re Brown, 3 N. B. R. 250, Fed. Cas. No. 1,980. Since a discharge in bankruptcy does not divest the lien which a creditor may have on the property of the bankrupt, set apart to him as an exemption and unadministered by the bankruptcy court, therefore his discharge will not prevent the re-issue of an execution on a judgment antedating the discharge, which judgment was a lien on property that had been set apart in the bankruptcy proceedings as a homestead. Fowler v. Wood, 26 S. C. 169, 1 S. E. 597. The debtor may lawfully mortgage or convey his exempt property, and such a preference is not in violation of the act nor a fraud upon it. Schlitz v. Schatz, 2 Biss. 248, Fed. Cas. No. 12,459. Since the title to the bankrupt's homestead does not pass to the trustee, the latter cannot maintain a bill to set aside a prior mortgage on the homestead, otherwise valid, as giving a preference contrary to the act, nor to restrain the foreclosure of such mortgage in the state courts. Rix v. Capitol Bank, 2 Dill. 367, Fed. Cas. No. 11,869. A general creditor of an insolvent cannot subject a homestead to liability for his debts, notwithstanding the insolvent had applied property in his hands to the payment of a debt which was a lien on the homestead. In re Henkel, 2 Sawy. 305, Fed. Cas. No. 6,362.

Forfeiture or Waiver of Exemption.

The bankrupt cannot claim any exemption in property conveyed by him prior to the commencement of the proceedings in bankruptcy in fraud of his creditors, and afterwards recovered to the estate. The sale is good as against him, and in attempting to place his property beyond the reach of his creditors, he has placed his exemption beyond his own reach. In re Graham, 2 Biss. 449, Fed. Cas. No. 5,660; Keating v. Keefer, 5 N. B. R. 133, Fed. Cas. No. 7,635. But compare Bartholomew v. West, 2 Dill. 290, Fed. Cas. No. 1,071; McFarland v. Goodman, 6 Biss. 111, Fed. Cas. No. 8,789. A bankrupt who is a fugitive from justice, and who has failed to account to the assignee for $5,000 and other property in his hands, has no right, after ten years acquiescence, to claim an exemption out of cash in the hands of the assignee, the proceeds of property sold by him. In re Moyer, 15 Fed. 598. A purchase of a homestead by an insolvent trader upon the eve of bankruptcy, with knowledge of his insolvent condition and for the purpose of placing the property beyond the reach of process, is a legal fraud, and the court will declare it void as to creditors. In re Boothroyd, 14 N. B. R. 230, Fed. Cas. No. 1,652. Where a bankrupt built a block for business purposes upon ground where his dwelling stood, and moved his family into it, he cannot, upon becoming insolvent, claim it as exempt under the state laws. In re Lammer, 14 N. B. R. 460, Fed. Cas. No. 8,031. But a bankrupt is not deprived of his right to a homestead exemption by the fact that he had previously waived his homestead rights in favor of a particular creditor; for such waiver only applies to persons claiming under the instrument in which the waiver was made, and does not inure to the benefit of the trustee in bankruptcy or the other creditors. In re Poleman, 5 Biss. 526, Fed. Cas. No. 11,247.

By what Law Governed.

In setting out the exemption to the bankrupt, it is the lex domicilii which governs; and property which is exempt by the laws of the state where the debtor resides and where the petition in bankruptcy is filed will be protected wherever it may be actually situated; and if it is situated in another state, the court will not inquire into the laws of that state to see if it would be exempt there, for that question is entirely immaterial. In re Stevens, 2 Biss. 373, Fed. Cas. No. 13,392. In construing the state exemption laws, for the purposes of the bankrupt act, the federal courts will follow the decisions of the highest courts of the state. In re Wyllie, 2 Hughes, 449, Fed. Cas. No. 18,112. See, also, Holland v. Withers, 76 Ga. 667.

DUTIES OF BANKRUPTS.

§ 7. *a* The bankrupt shall (1) attend the first meeting of his creditors, if directed by the court or a judge thereof to do so, and the hearing upon his application for a discharge, if filed; (2) comply with all lawful orders of the court; (3) examine the correctness of all proofs of claims filed against his estate; (4) execute and deliver such papers as shall be ordered by the court; (5) execute to his trustee transfers of all his property in foreign countries; (6) immediately inform his trustee of any attempt, by his creditors or other persons, to evade the provisions of this act, coming to his knowledge; (7) in case of any person having to his knowledge proved a false claim against his estate, disclose that fact immediately to his trustee; (8) prepare, make oath to, and file in court within ten days, unless further time is granted, after the adjudication, if an involuntary bankrupt, and with the petition if a voluntary bankrupt, a schedule of his property, showing the amount and kind of property, the location thereof, its money value in detail, and a list of his creditors, showing their residences, if known, if unknown, that fact to be stated, the amounts due each of them, the consideration thereof, the security held by them, if any, and a claim for such exemptions as he may be entitled to, all in triplicate, one copy of each for the clerk, one for the referee, and one for the trustee; and (9) when present at the first meeting of his creditors, and at such other times as the court shall order, submit to an examination concerning the conducting of his business,

the cause of his bankruptcy, his dealings with his creditors and other persons, the amount, kind, and whereabouts of his property, and, in addition, all matters which may affect the administration and settlement of his estate; but no testimony given by him shall be offered in evidence against him in any criminal proceeding.

Provided, *however*, **that he shall not be required to attend a meeting of his creditors, or at or for an examination at a place more than one hundred and fifty miles distant from his home or principal place of business, or to examine claims except when presented to him, unless ordered by the court, or a judge thereof, for cause shown, and the bankrupt shall be paid his actual expenses from the estate when examined or required to attend at any place other than the city, town, or village of his residence.**

Requisites of Schedule.

Partnership property, as well as individual assets, should be included in the schedules of a bankrupt. But an interest in an action of tort need not be included. In re Brick, 4 Fed. 804. The omitting to name a creditor in the schedule is not fraudulent, if done with such creditor's assent. In re Needham, 2 N. B. R. 387, Fed. Cas. No. 10,081. Where a petition in voluntary bankruptcy stated the present residences of certain creditors to be unknown, but gave their former residences, it was held that the statement as to the present residences was sufficient, and the statement as to former residences was surplusage, but the bankrupt should show, either in the schedules or by separate affidavit, what efforts he had made to ascertain the residences of such creditors. In re Pulver, 1 Ben. 381, Fed. Cas. No. 11,466. Debts barred by the statute of limitations should be placed in the schedule (In re Perry, 1 N. B. R. 220, Fed. Cas. No. 10,998) though it seems that this will not have the effect to revive a debt so barred. In re Ray, 1 N. B. R. 203, Fed. Cas. No. 11,589. There is nothing in the bankrupt act which requires that a voluntary petition should be signed or verified by the debtor in person, in order to give the court jurisdiction of the proceeding. Wald v. Wehl, 18 Blatchf. 495, 6 Fed. 163. It is held that material additions to the schedule are not allowable, after the first meeting of creditors, except upon such conditions as will prevent injustice. In re Ratcliffe, 1 N. B. R. 400, Fed. Cas. No. 11,578. But an application by a bankrupt for leave to amend his schedule of creditors for the purpose of inserting the name of a creditor inadvertently omitted, is grantable of course, and is properly an ex parte proceeding, requiring no notice to creditors. To such an amendment creditors have no right to object. In re Hill, 5 Fed. 448. Where there is no reason to withhold a discharge on the ground of fraud against the bankrupt laws, the court will order formal amendments made to the schedules which were omitted by the bankrupt through ignorance and mistake, and the case continued, in order that such proper returns may be made; and, upon compliance with the orders of the court, an application for discharge may be made at some future time. In re Townsend, 2 Fed. 559.

Practice in Regard to Meetings.

The debtor is not required to be present at a meeting of the creditors called to consider a resolution to vary a composition which has been accepted; and the absence of the debtor (unless it be shown that information was required of him, or that a creditor would be injuriously affected) is no ground for refusing to confirm the proceedings of such meeting. In re Dumahaut, 15 Blatchf. 20, Fed. Cas. No. 4,124. If it is clearly shown that the object of the meeting failed, by reason of the mistakes or mis-instructions of attorneys for the creditors, the court may direct a second meeting to be held. In re McDowell, 6 Biss. 193, Fed. Cas. No. 8,776.

Examination of Bankrupt.

Where a bankrupt is summoned to an examination at the instance of a creditor who has proved his claim, counsel for other creditors have no right to interpose any objections to his examination. In re Winship, 7 Ben. 194, Fed. Cas. No. 17,878. The bankrupt is to be examined and cross-examined like any other witness. In re Levy, 1 Ben. 496, Fed. Cas. No. 8,296. "A bankrupt under examination has the right to be cross-examined, or further examined, in his own behalf, after the creditor or assignee is done with him, so far as may be necessary to explain or qualify any matters brought out on the direct examination, which may seem to bear unfavorably upon his conduct or dealings, or which are obscure." In re Noyes, 2 Low. 352, Fed. Cas. No. 10,370. But he has no right to consult with his attorney before answering a question, unless the examining magistrate shall see good cause for allowing it; but the attorney may attend and object to improper questions. In re Tanner, 1 Low. 215, Fed. Cas. No. 13,745. He cannot refuse to answer a question as to his having lost money at gaming, on the ground that it will criminate or degrade him. In re Richards, 4 Ben. 303, Fed. Cas. No. 11,769. When the referee directs the bankrupt to produce certain books and papers, which order the bankrupt disobeys, he is guilty of a contempt and may be imprisoned. In re Allen, 13 Blatchf. 271, Fed. Cas. No. 208. A bankrupt who has fully submitted to an examination, has a right to be protected against unreasonable demands for further examination; and where the examination already had is apparently full, unless it be made to appear that such examination was collusive, or deficient in some material and specified particulars, an application for further examination may properly be refused. In re Frisbie, 13 N. B. R. 349, Fed. Cas. No. 5,131. The summary jurisdiction of the bankruptcy court over the person of the bankrupt ceases upon his discharge; after that he cannot be required by summary order to submit to an examination in reference to property alleged to have been concealed; a plenary suit is necessary for the recovery of such property. In re Dole, 11 Blatchf. 499, Fed. Cas. No. 3,964. See In re Solis, 4 Ben. 143, Fed. Cas. No. 13,165. If it appears to the court that the bankrupt has neglected or refused to surrender any property which ought to come into the custody of the trustee, or fails or refuses to give a satisfactory account of his property or his dealings previous to bankruptcy, the court may order him to surrender such property, or properly account for it, and on his failure to do so, he may be committed for contempt. In re Salkey, 6 Biss. 269, Fed. Cas. No. 12,253.

DEATH OR INSANITY OF BANKRUPTS.

§ 8. *a* **The death or insanity of a bankrupt shall not abate the proceedings, but the same shall be conducted and concluded in the same manner, so far as possible, as though he had not died or become insane:** *Provided*, **that in case of death the widow and children shall be entitled to all rights of dower and allowance fixed by the laws of the state of the bankrupt's residence.**

PROTECTION AND DETENTION OF BANKRUPTS.

§ 9. *a* A bankrupt shall be exempt from arrest upon civil process except in the following cases: (1) When issued from a court of bankruptcy for contempt or disobedience of its lawful orders; (2) when issued from a state court having jurisdiction, and served within such state, upon a debt or claim from which his discharge in bankruptcy would not be a release, and in such case he shall be exempt from such arrest when in attendance upon a court of bankruptcy or engaged in the performance of a duty imposed by this act.

b The judge may, at any time after the filing of a petition by or against a person, and before the expiration of one month after the qualification of the trustee, upon satisfactory proof by the affidavits of at least two persons that such bankrupt is about to leave the district in which he resides or has his principal place of business to avoid examination, and that his departure will defeat the proceedings in bankruptcy, issue a warrant to the marshal, directing him to bring such bankrupt forthwith before the court for examination. If upon hearing the evidence of the parties it shall appear to the court or a judge thereof that the allegations are true and that it is necessary, he shall order such marshal to keep such bankrupt in custody not exceeding ten days, but not imprison him, until he shall be examined and released or give bail conditioned for his appearance for examination, from time to time, not exceeding in all ten days, as required by the court, and for his obedience to all lawful orders made in reference thereto.

Privilege from Arrest.

This section does not relieve from arrest one who is already in custody at the time his petition in bankruptcy is filed. In re Walker, 1 Low. 222, Fed. Cas. No. 17,060; Hazleton v. Valentine, 1 Low. 270, Fed. Cas. No. 6,287. Where the bankrupt is under arrest under process from a state court, he should make application to that court to obtain his release, before coming into the bankruptcy court, as this practice is less likely to produce conflict of jurisdiction. In re O'Mara, 4 Biss. 506, Fed. Cas. No. 10,509. Where a debtor has been arrested on execution from a state court, and has claimed the benefit of the state law for the relief of poor debtors, before proceedings in bankruptcy, the court will not enjoin the creditor from proceeding under his execution. Minon v. Van Nostrand, 1 Holmes, 251, Fed. Cas. No. 9,641. If the debtor is held under arrest in a civil action in a state court founded on a debt contracted by his defalcation while acting in a fiduciary capacity, that is a claim from which his discharge in bankruptcy would not release him, and therefore he is not entitled to be released on habeas corpus from the bankruptcy court. In re Seymour, 1 Ben. 348, Fed. Cas. No. 12,684; In re Whitehouse, 1 Low. 429, Fed. Cas. No. 17,564. But in a case where, before adjudication, the creditor had obtained judgment for a tort, and after the institution of bankruptcy proceedings sued out a ca. sa. and had the debtor arrested, the bankruptcy court released him from arrest, notwithstanding that the state court had already refused to do so. The jurisdiction of the district court, as it was held, is exclusive and its authority paramount, and it will protect the bankrupt in the manner contemplated by law. In re Wiggers, 2 Biss. 71, Fed. Cas. No. 17,623. As to the power of the bankruptcy court, on a writ of habeas corpus, to inquire into the question whether the debt for which the arrest is made is one from which the bankrupt's discharge would release him, see In re Valk, 3 Ben. 431, Fed. Cas. No. 16,814.

Arrest of Bankrupt.

The arrest of the debtor under the provisions of this section is not intended as a means of security or satisfaction of the moving creditor's demand. It is designed merely to secure the attendance of the bankrupt from time to time, as the court shall order, and hence it is to that purpose only that bail is required of him. In re Sheehan, 8 N. B. R. 345, Fed. Cas. No. 12,737. The warrant may issue against the person and property of the bankrupt, or either of them. In re Muller, Deady, 519, Fed. Cas. No. 9,912.

EXTRADITION OF BANKRUPTS.

§ 10. *a* **Whenever a warrant for the apprehension of a bankrupt shall have been issued, and he shall have been found within the jurisdiction of a court other than the one issuing the warrant, he may be extradited in the same manner in which persons under indictment are now extradited from one district within which a district court has jurisdiction to another.**

Extradition.

It is provided by Rev. St. U. S. § 1029, that "only one writ or warrant is necessary to remove a prisoner from one district to another. One copy thereof may be delivered to the sheriff or jailer from whose custody the prisoner is taken, and another to the sheriff or jailer to whose custody he is committed, and the original writ, with the marshal's return thereon, shall be returned to the clerk of the district to which he is removed." The preliminary examination of an alleged offender, arrested in another district, must be according to the usages of law in the state where the arrest is made. U. S. v. Brawner, 7 Fed. 86.

SUITS BY AND AGAINST BANKRUPTS.

§ 11. *a* **A suit which is founded upon a claim from which a discharge would be a release, and which is pending against a person at the time of the filing of a petition against him, shall be stayed until after an adjudication or the dismissal of the petition; if such person is adjudged a bankrupt, such action may be further stayed until twelve months after the date of such adjudication, or, if within that time such person applies for a discharge, then until the question of such discharge is determined.**

b **The court may order the trustee to enter his appearance and defend any pending suit against the bankrupt.**

c **A trustee may, with the approval of the court, be permitted to prosecute as trustee any suit commenced by the bankrupt prior to the adjudication, with like force and effect as though it had been commenced by him.**

d **Suits shall not be brought by or against a trustee of a bankrupt estate subsequent to two years after the estate has been closed.**

Stay of Proceedings in State Courts.

The power of the bankruptcy court to prohibit any proceeding in a state court by a creditor to enforce a lien upon the bankrupt's property is to be exercised summarily, and does not require a formal suit. In re Clark, 9 Blatchf. 372, Fed. Cas. No. 2,801. This power of the district court to stay proceedings extends not only to the state courts, but also to the admiralty side of the same court, and a libel against the bankrupt's vessel, filed under such circumstances, will be enjoined. In re People's Mail S. S. Co., 3 Ben. 226, Fed. Cas. No. 10,970. But the power is not vested in any other district court than that in which the bankruptcy proceedings are pending. In re Richardson, 2 Ben. 517, Fed. Cas. No. 11,774. And the mere adjudication of bankruptcy will not compel a stay of proceedings in the state court, without a restraining order from the bankruptcy court. Howes v. Holmes, 2 Mo. App. 81. Where, after verdict and before judgment, in a cause pending in a state court, the defendant files his petition in bankruptcy, the court in which the prior action is pending, on the filing of a certificate of his having been adjudged a bankrupt, on motion of the defendant, should stay further proceedings until the bankruptcy court passes upon his discharge, and on the discharge being shown, render judgment on the verdict against the defendant, with a perpetual stay of execution. Hill v. Harding, 116 Ill. 92, 4 N. E. 361. Where, in an action upon a judgment of a court of another state, it appeared that the judgment was obtained intermediate the commencement by the defendant of voluntary proceedings in bankruptcy and the granting of his discharge therein, and that the judgment was upon a debt provable in such proceedings and which existed at the time of their commencement, it was held that the discharge operated upon the judgment and was a good defense to the action. McDonald v. Davis, 105 N. Y. 508, 12 N. E. 40. And see Boynton v. Ball, 121 U. S. 457, 7 Sup. Ct. 981. But this section of the act does not prohibit the *commencement* of an action upon a provable claim against a person who has been adjudged a bankrupt under the national bankruptcy law. Davidson v. Fisher, 41 Minn. 363, 43 N. W. 79.

Foreclosure of Mortgages.

The bankruptcy court has power to restrain the holder of a mortgage on the bankrupt's property from foreclosing it, and it is generally proper to do so when the value of the property exceeds the amount secured by the mortgage, or when the validity or the amount of the mortgage is in doubt. In re Iron Mountain Co., 9 Blatchf. 320, Fed. Cas. No. 7,065; In re Sacchi, 10 Blatchf. 29, Fed. Cas. No. 12,200. But at the same time, a bill to foreclose a mortgage, to which the bankrupt and his trustee are made defendants, may well be entertained in a state court, and its prosecution will not be a contempt of the bankruptcy court, unless the latter court deems it advisable to interfere by injunction. In re Moller, 14 Blatchf. 207, Fed. Cas. No. 9,700.

What Actions not Stayed.

The act does not prevent a plaintiff in a state court from having judgment against a bankrupt debtor when he is sued jointly with others in an action ex contractu; in such case, judgment may be rendered against all, and an order made staying execution as to the bankrupt until the question of his discharge is determined. Byers v. Bank, 85 Ill. 423. And the execution of a decree for partition in a state court is not arrested because one of the parties to the suit becomes a bankrupt; his share of the property vests in his trustee. Baum v. Stern, 1 S. C. 415. The state tribunals are not deprived, by mere force of an adjudication in bankruptcy, of jurisdiction over suits against the bankrupt. The bankruptcy court has power to arrest or control the proceedings in such suits, when it becomes necessary for the purposes of justice, but when such power is not exercised, the jurisdiction of the ordinary courts remains unimpaired and their judgments are valid. In re Davis, 1 Sawy. 260, Fed. Cas. No. 3,620. See also Hewett v. Norton, 1 Woods, 68, Fed. Cas. No. 6,441. No stay is authorized which hinders the use of the orderly methods for the collection of taxes during the pendency of the bankruptcy proceedings. In re Duryee, 2 Fed. 68. After the property of a bankrupt has been sold and the proceeds received, and neither the court nor the assignee nor the creditors have any further interest in it, the court will not interfere, at the instance of the purchaser, to prevent, by injunction, parties from asserting any claims they may have, or pretend to have, against the property, in any of the courts of the several states; and this, notwithstanding no final distribution has been made in the bankruptcy. The bankruptcy court will not interfere where no advantage can result to the bankrupt's estate. Adams v. Crittenden, 17 Fed. 42. In dealing with this subject-matter, the act of 1867 provided that suits in the state courts should be stayed "upon the application of the bankrupt." And under this clause it was held that the debtor was under no obligation to obtain a stay. He might allow the suit to proceed to judgment without forfeiting his right to avail himself of his discharge, if he should subsequently obtain it. Whyte v. McGovern, 51 N. J. Law, 356, 17 Atl. 957. It was also the rule prescribed by the earlier statute that such suits should only be stayed when there was "no unreasonable delay on the part of the bankrupt in endeavoring to obtain his discharge." Rev. St. § 5106. Under this clause, it was held that a stay should not be granted when the application for discharge had been pending without action by the bankrupt for more than eight years. In re Sweet, 36 Fed. 761.

Effect of the Stay.

"The stay does not operate as a bar to the action, but only as a suspension of proceedings until the question of the bankrupt's discharge shall have been determined in the United States court sitting in bankruptcy. After the determination of that question in that court, the court in which the suit is pending may proceed to such judgment as the circumstances of the case may require. If the discharge is refused, the plaintiff, upon establishing his claim, may obtain a general judgment." Gray, J., in Hill v. Harding, 107 U. S. 633, 2 Sup. Ct. 404. A defendant in an action at law, who has been adjudged a bankrupt, may interpose his plea to that effect at any time before judgment. Block v. Fitche, 33 La. Ann. 1094. A sale under execution issuing from the state court during the pendency of bankruptcy proceedings against the judgment debtor is invalid and passes no title. Stemmons v. Burford, 39 Tex. 352; Stinson v. McMurray, 6 Humph. 339.

Violation of Order Staying Suits.

Where a bankrupt obtained an injunction order from the bankruptcy court staying all suits and proceedings against him on the part of certain creditors, their agents and attorneys to collect certain specified debts, and thereupon a suit by one of the creditors was discontinued, and afterwards a new suit was brought through the same attorneys in the state court for the recovery of the same debt, with allegations of fraud, it was held that this was a violation of the injunction order. In re Schwarz, 14 Fed. 787.

Intervention of Trustee in Pending Suits.

When there is a suit pending at the time of the adjudication, in which the bankrupt is the plaintiff on the record, the trustee may either have himself substituted as plaintiff, or he may consent that the bankrupt shall continue to prosecute the action in his own name. Thatcher v. Rockwell, 105 U. S. 467. The right of action is the same if the bankrupt be one of several joint plaintiffs. Thus, where husband and wife were jointly prosecuting a suit in respect to the wife's *chose in action*, and during its pendency the husband went into bankruptcy, his trustee should join with the wife in the further conduct of that suit. In re Boyd, 2 Hughes, 349, Fed. Cas. No. 1,745. But the trustee has his option whether to intervene or not; and if he is satisfied that nothing is to be gained for the estate by his prosecuting or defending the suit, his duty requires him to take no part in the litigation, and no court has power to compel him to become a party to the action. Serra v. Hoffman, 29 La. Ann. 17. If he elects to proceed, it must be in his own name and not in that of the bankrupt. Dessau v. Johnson, 66 How. Prac. 4. And if he declines to prosecute a right of action which is pending at the time of bankruptcy, the bankrupt may maintain a suit thereon in his own name and for his own benefit. Ramsey v. Fellows, 58 N. H. 607. An action which is in progress when the defendant is adjudged a bankrupt may, upon due notice to the trustee, be prosecuted to final judgment against the latter in his representative capacity, provided the bankruptcy court does not see fit to arrest the proceedings; but such judgment is not effectual for purposes of execution, but only as an ascertainment of the amount due the creditor and as a basis of dividends. Norton v. Switzer, 93 U. S. 355; Eyster v. Gaff, 91 U. S. 521. Where an action is pending in a state court of competent jurisdiction to enforce a specific lien on property of the debtor, the subsequent bankruptcy of the debtor does not divest the state court of its jurisdiction to proceed to a final decree in the cause and execute the same. The trustee in bankruptcy may intervene in such action, but the jurisdiction of the state court and the validity of its decree are not affected by his failure to do so. Kimberling v. Hartly, 1 Fed. 571. Tenants in common must join in an action to recover the earnings of their vessel, unless there is an excuse for the severance of the claim; but the bankruptcy of one owner is not an excuse; in such case the assignee of the owner who is in bankruptcy must be joined with the solvent owners, or if an assignee has not been appointed when the suit is commenced, an action may be supported in the names of the bankrupt and other owners until an assignee comes in. Stinson v. Fernald, 77 Me. 576, 1 Atl. 742.

Limitations of Actions by and against Trustees—What is a Suit within this Clause.

Where a judgment in a state court was rendered against one who was shortly thereafter adjudged a bankrupt, the suing out a writ of error to that judgment by the trustee was held to be a "suit" within the meaning of the clause of limitations. Jenkins v. International Bank, 106 U. S. 571, 2 Sup. Ct. 1; International Bank v. Jenkins, 107 Ill. 291. But the substitution of the trustee as plaintiff in a pending action is not to be regarded as a bringing of suit by him within the meaning of the statute; the suit begins when the summons or other process is issued. Chicago &c. R. R. v. Jenkins, 103 Ill. 588. And where an action is pending in which the bankrupt is plaintiff, and the trustee, after the statute of limitations has run against him, applies to be made a party thereto by amendment, such amendment will not have the effect to relate back to the commencement of the suit and make the trustee a party ab initio; for this would amount to an evasion of the statute. Cogdell v. Exum, 69 N. C. 464. The limitation does not apply to a bill in equity brought by trustees under a will to obtain the instructions of the court, in which a trustee in bankruptcy of one of the cestuis que trust under the will is a party defendant. Minot v. Tappan, 127 Mass. 333.

To what Actions the Statute Applies.

The clause "applies to all judicial controversies between the assignee and any person whose interest is adverse to his, in behalf of the bankrupt's estate." Scovill v. Shaw, 4 Cliff. 549, Fed. Cas. No. 12,552; Walker v. Towner, 4 Dill. 165, Fed. Cas. No. 17,089; Bailey v. Glover, 21 Wall. 342. It applies to suits by trustees to collect the debts and assets of the estate, as well as to actions relating to specific property. Payson v. Coffin, 4 Dill. 386, Fed. Cas. No. 10,858; Ross v. Wilcox, 134 Mass. 21. It applies to all cases where adverse claims are made to property which the trustee found in the possession of the bankrupt and of which he took charge in good faith as the property of the bankrupt. Esmond v. Apgar, 76 N. Y. 359. It applies to an action by the trustee of a bankrupt corporation to enforce against stockholders the payment of their unpaid shares. Payson v. Coffin, 5 Dill. 473, Fed. Cas. No. 10,-859. It also applies to actions brought in the name of the trustee though wholly for the benefit of a third party. Pike v. Lowell, 32 Me. 245. But a suit in equity, brought against a bankrupt and his trustee, to foreclose a mortgage executed by the bankrupt, is not barred by the limitation. Gildersleeve v. Gaynor, 4 Woods, 541, 15 Fed. 101. And it has no reference to suits growing out of the dealings of the trustee with the estate after it comes into his hands; "these are matters for which he may be made personally responsible, and no reason existed for changing the general period of limitation any more than in the case of any other trustee dealing with trust property." Nelson, J., in Re Conant, 5 Blatchf. 54, Fed. Cas. No. 3,086. And further, the limitation applies only to actions by and against the trustee in respect to interests existing in some claimant other than the bankrupt himself. Phelps v. McDonald, 99 U. S. 298; Clark v. Clark, 17 How. 315.

Concealed Frauds.

When the cause of action on which the trustee sues is based on a secret transfer or fraud concealed by the parties thereto, which he could not earlier have discovered by the exercise of due diligence, the limitation is not to be considered as running against him until the discovery of such fraud. Tyler v. Angevine, 15 Blatchf. 536, Fed. Cas. No. 14,306; Rosenthal v. Walker, 111 U. S. 185, 4 Sup. Ct. 382; Bailey v. Glover, 21 Wall. 342; Cook v. Sherman, 4 McCrary, 20, 20 Fed. 167.

Accruing of Trustee's Title.

The limitation does not begin to run against the trustee, in respect to rights in property previously assigned for the benefit of creditors, until he has procured a decree setting aside the assignment, and has thus clothed himself with the title of the assignee. Tappan v. Whittemore, 15 Blatchf. 440, Fed. Cas. No. 13,750. But the fact that a trustee in bankruptcy did not discover his right to certain property of the bankrupt until after the expiration of two years from the time an action accrued to him therefor, does not remove the bar of the statute. Norton v. De La Villebeuve, 1 Woods, 163, Fed. Cas. No. 10,350. But the limitation does not apply to suits by trustees or their grantees for the recovery of real estate until after two years from the taking of adverse possession. Banks v. Ogden, 2 Wall. 57.

COMPOSITIONS, WHEN CONFIRMED.

§ 12. *a* **A bankrupt may offer terms of composition to his creditors after, but not before, he has been examined in open court or at a meeting of his creditors and filed in court the schedule of his property and list of his creditors, required to be filed by bankrupts.**

b **An application for the confirmation of a composition may be filed in the court of bankruptcy after, but not before, it has been accepted in writing by a majority in number of all creditors whose claims have been allowed, which number must represent a majority in amount of such claims, and the consideration to be paid by the bankrupt to his creditors, and the money necessary to pay all debts which have priority and the cost of the proceedings, have been deposited in such place as shall be designated by and subject to the order of the judge.**

c **A date and place, with reference to the convenience of the parties in interest, shall be fixed for**

the hearing upon each application for the confirmation of a composition, and such objections as may be made to its confirmation.

d **The judge shall confirm a composition if satisfied that (1) it is for the best interests of the creditors; (2) the bankrupt has not been guilty of any of the acts or failed to perform any of the duties which would be a bar to his discharge; and (3) the offer and its acceptance are in good faith and have not been made or procured except as herein provided, or by any means, promises, or acts herein forbidden.**

e **Upon the confirmation of a composition, the consideration shall be distributed as the judge shall direct, and the case dismissed. Whenever a composition is not confirmed, the estate shall be administered in bankruptcy as herein provided.**

Constitutionality.

That clause of the bankrupt law which relates to compositions with creditors is valid and constitutional, inasmuch as the power given to Congress by section 8 of article 1 of the Constitution must be held to be general, unlimited, and unrestricted, over the whole subject of bankruptcy. In re Reiman, 7 Ben. 455, Fed. Cas. No. 11,673; Id., 12 Blatchf. 562, Fed. Cas. No. 11,675.

Theory and Practice of Compositions.

The theory of a composition is that the cash value of the bankrupt's estate is substantially divided among the creditors in proportion to their respective debts. In re Lissburger, 2 Fed. 153. Whether it is expedient to accept the percentage offered by a bankrupt is a question for the creditors primarily to determine. And although the percentage may be very small, when they have determined it, and their action has been approved by the district court, the appellate court will not interfere upon review. In re Joseph, 24 Fed. 137. A bankrupt from whom a composition is received is necessarily at liberty to deal with his assets as he chooses. The creditors have no concern in the matter if their composition be paid and no fraud practiced. He may pledge or sell his stock to one or more of his creditors to raise money to pay the composition, where there is no concealment practiced or unfairness to others. In re Shaw, 9 Fed. 495. An adjudication that the bankrupt is not entitled to a discharge will not bar proceedings for a composition with his creditors. In re Joseph, 24 Fed. 137. See In re Hannahs, 8 Ben. 533, Fed. Cas. No. 6,033. Where a petition in voluntary bankruptcy was filed, but before any adjudication, proceedings in composition were begun, it was held that an adjudication ought not to be made merely because certain creditors asked it, if the debtor did not desire it. In re Alsberg, 9 Ben. 17, Fed. Cas. No. 260. A discharge of a bankrupt in composition proceedings, after a previous refusal to grant him a discharge because of fraud, is binding on all creditors of whom the court had jurisdiction, and is a bar to supplementary proceedings based on a judgment obtained by one of such creditors after the refusal of the discharge, but before the adjudication in the composition proceedings. Leo v. Joseph, 56 Hun, 644, 9 N. Y. Supp. 612.

Objections to Composition.

Where certain creditors objected to the confirmation of a composition, on the ground that it had not been assented to by the requisite number of creditors in accordance with the debtor's statement presented at the creditors' meeting (which appeared to be the fact), but it was claimed by the debtor that the statement was inaccurate, and that an accurate statement would show the composition to have been duly agreed to (which also appeared to be true), it was held that it was too late to amend the statement after the composition had been presented to the court, and the motion must be rejected, but with leave to renew the composition when the statement should have been amended in the manner provided by law. In re Asten, 8 Ben. 350, Fed. Cas. No. 594.

Terms of Composition.

A composition of twenty per cent. payable in money, on time, secured by notes, leaving certain real estate which had passed to the trustee to be converted into money and paid to the creditors in addition, is a lawful composition. In re Wronkow, 15 Blatchf. 38, Fed. Cas. No. 18,105. A resolution of composition, by which the creditors agree to accept payment in *notes*, is bad in substance; but the payments may be in installments, and deferred payments *secured* by notes. In re Langdon, 2 Lowell, 387, Fed. Cas. No. 8,058.

Rights of Secured Creditors.

The provisions of the act relating to compositions design that every creditor should receive the same proportion of his debt; now a secured creditor is a creditor for all that part of his claim which is not covered by the security; hence, whenever it is discovered that there is a deficit, after realizing on the security, that deficit constitutes a charge against the bankrupt of which he must pay the same proportion as he has paid to the unsecured creditors, and it makes no difference that such discovery was not made until after the composition was effected. Paret v. Ticknor, 4 Dill. 111, Fed. Cas. No. 10,711. So where, in the composition proceedings, certain notes were classed as secured debts, but no valuation of the security was made, and it subsequently failed to realize the full amount of the debt, it was held that, as to the deficiency, the creditor was entitled to recover the same percentage as had been paid to the general creditors. Flower v. Greenbaum, 9 Biss. 455, 2 Fed. 897. Composition proceedings do not operate to deprive a secured creditor of the right, after exhausting his own security and ascertaining the amount unpaid, to assert against the bankrupt a claim for the deficiency, and such claim may be enforced through the instrumentality of an execution issued against the property of the debtor upon the deficiency judgment. Cavanna v. Bassett, 3 Fed. 215.

Effect on Creditors not Joining.

An order in composition proceedings, based upon a resolution passed by the requisite majority of the creditors, cannot deprive a non-consenting creditor of a vested right with which the bankruptcy court has no power otherwise to interfere. In re Stowell, 24 Fed. 468. A creditor whose name did not appear in the statement of the debtor or otherwise in composition proceedings, and whose debt is not mentioned, is not bound thereby. In re Blackmore, 11 Fed. 412; Robinson v. Soule, 56 Miss. 549. Where a composition proposed by a bankrupt has been accepted by his creditors and approved by the court, the bankrupt is thereby discharged only from the claims of the creditors whose names, addresses, and debts are placed on the statement produced at the meeting of creditors. In re Becket, 2 Woods, 173, Fed. Cas. No. 1,210.

Proceedings Vitiated by Fraud.

Where, upon a composition in bankruptcy, a particular creditor, by means of a secret bargain, secures to himself an undue advantage over the rest of the creditors, it is a fraud upon the other creditors, and he cannot enforce the agreement. Woodman v. Stow, 11 Ill. App. 613; Russell v. Rogers, 10 Wend. 473; Tinker v. Hurst, 70 Mich. 159, 38 N. W. 16; Carey v. Hess, 112 Ind. 398, 14 N. E. 235; Brownsville Mfg. Co. v. Lockwood, 11 Fed. 705. A bankrupt and the defendant, one of his creditors, agreed that, in consideration that defendant should procure a composition which the bankrupt had offered to his creditors, the bankrupt would pay to the defendant a specified sum in addition to all disbursements. Defendant thereupon bought certain large claims, paying a larger sum for them than the percentage provided for in the composition would amount to, and voted such claims in favor of the composition, as attorney for the original holders of them, concealing the assignment, and, the composition having been thus procured and confirmed, received a transfer of the bankrupt estate. It was held that the agreement and composition were fraudulent, and the assignee could recover the property. Fairbanks v. Amoskeag Nat. Bank, 38 Fed. 630. In another case, it appeared that the bankrupt's book-keeper made an offer of money to two several creditors to induce them to consent to a proposal of composition. One of the creditors accepted the money and agreed to the composition. Of these transactions the bankrupt had no actual knowledge, but the book-keeper was employed generally to procure the consent of the creditors. On this state of facts, it was held that the bankrupt was chargeable with what his representative did in the matter, and that, unfair advantage having been offered to some of the creditors, the whole proceeding was thereby vitiated and the composition must fail. In re Bennett, 8 Ben. 561, Fed. Cas. No. 1,312.

Effect of Composition as a Discharge.

Composition proceedings, duly confirmed by the court, operate as a discharge of the bankrupt. In Re Bjornstad, 11 Biss. 13, 5 Fed. 791. But an action on a debt or claim is not barred by composition proceedings if it would not be barred by the debtor's discharge under the act. Wilmot v. Mudge, 103 U. S. 217; Bayly v. University, 106 U. S. 11, 1 Sup. Ct. 88; Ex parte Halford, L. R. 19 Eq. 436. Such proceedings will not operate to release and discharge one jointly indebted with the bankrupt. Moore v. Stanwood, 98 Ill. 605. Nor will they release the debtor from any fiduciary debt. Succession of Bayly, 30 La. Ann. 75. Composition proceedings do not discharge the bankrupt from a contingent liability unless such liability was included in his schedule of debts, and the creditor holding it was notified that a discharge was sought. Flower v. Greenbaum, 9 Biss. 455, 2 Fed. 897. The acceptance of a composition from the principal debtor does not discharge any party collaterally liable for the same debt. In re Burchell, 4 Fed. 406. If the time has expired for the performance of a composition, and performance has not been made, the creditor may maintain an action on his original claim. Harrison v. Gamble, 69 Mich. 96, 36 N. W. 682; Pupke v. Churchill, 91 Mo. 81, 3 S. W. 829. Composition proceedings are in the nature of accord and satisfaction, and the effect of a resolution duly passed and confirmed is that the creditors bound thereby agree to accept a composition or part of the debt in discharge of the whole. In a suit by a creditor affected by composition proceedings under the bankrupt act brought *before* the expiration of the time for performance of the terms of the composition, the defendant need only plead the proceedings to and including the record of the resolution; but if brought *after* the expiration of such time, and the plaintiff can make out his case without showing the composition, the defendant must not only set up such proceedings in bar, but he must aver performance on his part, or a sufficient excuse for nonperformance. Harrison v. Gamble, 69 Mich. 96, 36 N. W. 682; Browning v. Crouse, 43 Mich. 489, 5 N. W. 664. A composition proceeding not carried out, nor performance of the resolution tendered by the insolvent, is an accord without a satisfaction. It is not a discharge of the debt, and will not prevent a creditor from pursuing his action to recover his debt. Ransom v. Geer, 12 Fed. 607. The bankruptcy court will not issue its injunction to restrain an action brought in the state court by a creditor seeking to recover his whole debt from a bankrupt who has effected a composition. In re Negley, 20 Fed. 499.

Title Revesting in Bankrupt.

The result of a composition is, that the legal title to the effects of the bankrupt remains in him. If the composition is effected before an adjudication and assignment, the title is never divested; if afterwards, it is re-invested in him. Ligon v. Allen, 56 Miss. 632.

COMPOSITIONS, WHEN SET ASIDE.

§ 13. *a* **The judge may, upon the application of parties in interest filed at any time within six months after a composition has been confirmed, set the same aside and reinstate the case if it shall be made to appear upon a trial that fraud was practiced in the procuring of such composition, and that the knowledge thereof has come to the petitioners since the confirmation of such composition.**

Setting Aside Composition.

A creditor who, with full knowledge of the schedule estimates, voted for a composition and received payment under it, is precluded from seeking to set aside the composition for mere inadequacy, or because it ultimately turns out that a larger amount might have been offered and paid, when the schedules show with substantial correctness the situation of the estate. In re Shaw, 9 Fed. 495. Where a composition is set aside, a workman, employed by the debtor during the time when the composition was in force, is entitled to payment of his wages earned during that period. In re Wells, 4 Fed. 68. In a proceeding to set aside a composition in bankruptcy after it has been fully executed, a sale of the bankrupt's stock and fixtures, made prior to the adjudication in bankruptcy, will not be disturbed on the ground of the inadequacy of price in a doubtful case, nor upon other grounds known to the creditors accepting the composition, although it might probably have been avoided by an assignee in bankruptcy. In re Shaw, 9 Fed. 495.

DISCHARGES, WHEN GRANTED.

§ 14. *a* Any person may, after the expiration of one month and within the next twelve months subsequent to being adjudged a bankrupt, file an application for a discharge in the court of bankruptcy in which the proceedings are pending; if it shall be made to appear to the judge that the bankrupt was unavoidably prevented from filing it within such time, it may be filed within but not after the expiration of the next six months.

***b* The judge shall hear the application for a discharge, and such proofs and pleas as may be made in opposition thereto by parties in interest, at such time as will give parties in interest a reasonable opportunity to be fully heard, and investigate the merits of the application and discharge the applicant unless he has (1) committed an offense punishable by imprisonment as herein provided; or (2) with fraudulent intent to conceal his true financial condition and in contemplation of bankruptcy, destroyed, concealed, or failed to keep books of account or records from which his true condition might be ascertained.**

***c* The confirmation of a composition shall discharge the bankrupt from his debts, other than those agreed to be paid by the terms of the composition and those not affected by a discharge.**

Application for Discharge.

Under the former bankrupt law, in cases where no debts had been proved against the bankrupt, or if no assets had come to the hands of the assignee, the court might grant a discharge to the bankrupt, although not applied for within a year, where the delay was satisfactorily excused. In re Donaldson, 2 Dill. 546, Fed. Cas. No. 3,982; In re Lowenstein, 3 Dill. 145, Fed. Cas. No. 8,573; In re Canady, 2 Biss. 75, Fed. Cas. No. 2,377. See, also, In re Sloan, 13 Blatchf. 67, Fed. Cas. No. 12,945. But it will be perceived that the present act makes no such exception, and allows the filing of an application, after the prescribed limitation of twelve months has expired, only in case the bankrupt was "unavoidably prevented" from making his application within that time. Proceedings in bankruptcy, it is held, amount to an injunction against any proceedings against the bankrupt to enforce his contracts in the courts, but if he delays for an unreasonable time to apply for his discharge, the right of action against him upon his contracts or debts, which was suspended by the commencement of proceedings in bankruptcy, revives, and during the time that the right of action was suspended by the bankruptcy proceedings the statute of limitations will not run in his favor. Greenwald v. Appell, 17 Fed. 140. See, also, In re Kelly, 3 Fed. 219. The fact that the trustee in bankruptcy has been discharged, will not necessarily deprive the bankrupt of the right subsequently to apply for his own discharge. In re Forsyth, 4 Fed. 629. The court has authority to allow a bankrupt to withdraw his petition for discharge, no adjudication having passed upon it, and to file a new one at a later day. In re Svenson, 9 Biss. 69, Fed. Cas. No. 13,659. The first petition of a bankrupt for his discharge having been denied, but not upon the merits, upon a subsequent application and a hearing before the register thereon, upon the objections first filed, the testimony of a witness taken on the hearing on the first petition is competent evidence on the second proceeding, the witness having in the mean time died. In re Brockway, 12 Fed. 69. Where the bankrupt dies after his application for discharge has been favorably reported by the master, the court has power to order the discharge to be entered nunc pro tunc as of the date when the master's report was first filed. Young v. Ridenbaugh, 3 Dill. 239, Fed. Cas. No. 18,173. The law, in relation to the granting of discharges, applies both to cases of voluntary and involuntary bankruptcy. In re Clark, 2 Biss. 73, Fed. Cas. No. 2,800. Any creditor who has a provable debt against a bankrupt may apply to the court to require the bankrupt to have the question of his discharge determined. In re Fowler, 2 Low. 122, Fed. Cas. No. 4,999.

Essentials to Validity of Discharge.

In order to the validity of a discharge in bankruptcy it is essential that the court should have acquired jurisdiction of the bankrupt by his residence (or his doing business) within the district. Stiles v. Lay, 9 Ala. 795. And creditors may oppose the bankrupt's application for discharge on the ground that the court never acquired jurisdiction of the case. In re Penn, 4 Ben. 99, Fed. Cas. No. 10,926. The act further provides (section 58) that "creditors shall have at least ten days' notice by mail, to their respective addresses as they appear in the list of creditors of the bankrupt, or as afterwards filed with the papers in the case by the creditors, of * * * all hearings upon applications for the discharge of bankrupts." Under a similar provision in the former law, it was held that, if no such notice was given to creditors, as required, the certificate of discharge should be vacated. Allen v. Thompson, 10 Fed. 116. But it is not essential to the debtor's discharge that the trustee in bankruptcy should have given due notice of his appointment. In re Littlefield, 1 Low. 331, Fed. Cas. No. 8,398.

Opposition to Discharge; Who may Oppose.

A creditor whose debt is provable, though not proved, may oppose the discharge of the bankrupt. In Re Murdock, 1 Low. 362, Fed. Cas. No. 9,939. But creditors who have not proved their claims until after the day fixed for showing cause against the bankrupt's discharge, cannot then make objection to the discharge upon any other ground than fraud distinctly and specifically charged. In Re Balmer, 3 Hughes, 637, Fed. Cas. No. 820; Hester v. Baldwin, 2 Woods, 433, Fed. Cas. No. 6,438. If a preferred creditor abandons his security, and is admitted to prove his debt, the preference is condoned and cannot be set up by way of opposition to the bankrupt's discharge. In re Connor, 1 Low. 532, Fed. Cas. No. 3,118; In re Donnelly, 5 Fed. 783. The acceptance of a dividend under an unlawful assignment does not estop a creditor from objecting to the discharge of the assignor under subsequent proceedings in bankruptcy, where such creditor had no power to dissent from, repudiate, or avoid such assignment. In re Kraft, 3 Fed. 892. Although it is good ground of objection to the discharge that the debtor concealed or removed his property with intent to defraud his creditors, yet a person who was not a creditor of the bankrupt at the time of such concealment or removal, or whose debt was then barred by lapse of time, could not have been defrauded thereby, and therefore cannot make that objection. In re Burk, Deady, 425, Fed. Cas. No. 2,156. It is well settled that the burden of sustaining specifications of objection to the discharge of a bankrupt rests upon the opposing creditors. In re Herdic, 1 Fed. 242.

Same; Pleadings.

Allegations in opposition to a discharge are not sufficient when they simply follow the words of the statute; they must be as exact as the specifications in an indictment, and no intendment will be made in favor of the pleader. In re Butterfield, 5 Biss. 120, Fed. Cas. No. 2,247; In re Hill, 2 Ben. 136, Fed. Cas. No. 6,482; In re Freeman, 4 Ben. 245, Fed. Cas. No. 5,082. Where the specifications of objection to the bankrupt's discharge are insufficient in law to prevent such discharge, the bankrupt may take advantage thereof by demurrer. In re Burk, Deady, 425, Fed. Cas. No. 2,156. After issue has been joined on the specifications filed in opposition to the discharge, and evidence taken, without any allegation that the charges are insufficient, it is too late to permit an amendment of the specifications which would introduce an entirely new ground of objection and present a separate and distinct issue for the consideration of the court. In re Graves, 24 Fed. 550.

Grounds for Refusing Discharge; Omission of Assets from Schedules.

A mere omission to include all his property in his schedule is not of itself cause for refusing a bankrupt his discharge; the omission must be for the purpose of concealment or to mislead or defraud. In re Smith, 1 Woods, 478, Fed. Cas. No. 12,995; In re Boynton, 10 Fed. 277. And the fact that a bankrupt has omitted to state in his schedule certain obsolete and worthless demands, upon which no action could be maintained, does not tend to prove him guilty of fraud so as to bar his discharge. In re Pearce, 21 Vt. 611. So where the bankrupt omits from his schedule the names of certain persons to whom he is indebted, but with their consent, and for the reason that they do not intend to take dividends in competition with the trade creditors, and do not wish to be considered creditors of his estate, and no fraud or injury to the rights of the other creditors is shown, this will not be sufficient to bar his discharge. In re Needham, 1 Low. 309, Fed. Cas. No. 10,081. But a *wilful* omission to state a debt due by the bankrupt to another in his schedule is good ground for refusing a discharge. In re Kallish, Deady, 575, Fed. Cas. No. 7,599; In re Whetmore, Deady, 585, Fed. Cas. No. 17,508. Though if such omission is made in consequence of a private arrangement with the creditor, that particular creditor will not be allowed to oppose the bankrupt's discharge on that ground. In re Whetmore, supra.

Same; Preferences and Fraudulent Conveyances.

Payments of money, or transfers or conveyances of property, by one in insolvent circumstances, and with the open purpose of preferring a part of his creditors, but made prior to the passage of the bankrupt act, are indeed fraudulent, when he is afterwards adjudicated a bankrupt, but they are not a bar to his discharge. In re Hollenshade, 2 Bond, 210, Fed. Cas. No. 6,610. Same point in Re Rosenfield, 7 Am. Law Reg. N. S. 620, Fed. Cas. No. 12,058, where Field, J., says, "To have held that acts committed before its passage were offenses against the bankrupt law, would have been to make that law, if not an ex post facto law, in the strict sense of the term, yet at least a law retroactive or retrospective in its character." And see In re Wolfskill, 5 Sawy. 385, Fed. Cas. No. 17,930. So, however obnoxious to the bankrupt act may be a general assignment for the benefit of creditors made prior to the petition in bankruptcy, such assignment cannot be urged in opposition to the bankrupt's discharge by any creditors who chose, at that time, to ratify it and take action under it for the protection of their claims; this on the principle of equitable estoppel. In re Schuyler, 3 Ben. 200, Fed. Cas. No. 12,494.

Same; Other Grounds of Refusal.

The right of a bankrupt to a discharge depends upon his own acts. Unless a party thereto, he is not bound by the acts of commission or omission of his former partner. In re Heller, 9 Fed. 373. And the fraud contemplated by the statute as a bar to the bankrupt's discharge is fraud *in fact*, involving moral turpitude,—intentional wrong. In re Warne, 10 Fed. 377. Gifts by a bankrupt to his wife and daughter, previous to the bankruptcy, although they may be voidable by his creditors, do not necessarily involve such moral turpitude as would justify the refusal of a discharge. In re Warne, 12 Fed. 431. But where a merchant, being insolvent, permitted and authorized certain of his creditors to take away his goods in payment of their debts, it was held that he could not be discharged; not only were the preferences fraudulent, but it was his duty to protect his assets against such losses. In re Vernia, 5 Fed. 723. A false statement made by the bankrupt upon his examination, as to the existence of books of account, will not prevent his discharge, if it appears that such statement was against his own interest, and apparently without motive, and the circumstances indicate that it was innocently and not wilfully made. In re Warne, 12 Fed. 431. Under the terms of the bankrupt law of 1867 (Rev. St. § 5110, cl. 5), it was made a bar to the bankrupt's discharge if he had lost any part of his estate in "gaming." And it was held that property acquired in gaming was assets, which if the bankrupt spent in gaming, he would lose his discharge. In re Marshall, 1 Low. 462, Fed. Cas. No. 9,123. And see In re Hunt, 26 Fed. 739. But the present statute contains no such provision.

Keeping Books of Account.

The question what are proper books of account to be kept by a merchant, is in each case a question of evidence. In re Newman, 3 Ben. 20, Fed. Cas. No. 10,175. But if, from such books as were kept by the bankrupt, his financial condition and an intelligible account of his business can be ascertained with substantial accuracy, the requirements of the bankrupt law have been complied with. In re Frey, 9 Fed. 376; In re Keach, 1 Low. 335, Fed. Cas. No. 7,629; In re Smith, 16 Fed. 465. It is held to be indispensable that traders should keep a cash-book. In re Bellis, 4 Ben. 53, Fed. Cas. No. 1,275; In re Gay, 2 N. B. R. 358, Fed. Cas. No. 5,279. And the same is true of a stock or invoice book. In re Brockway, 12 Fed. 69; In re White, 2 N. B. R. 590, Fed. Cas. No. 17,532. As to the manner of keeping the books, it is said: "Congress has not attempted to prescribe any particular system or principle of book-keeping. If a competent person, upon an examination of the books and papers kept by the merchant, is able to reach a substantially correct conclusion as to the state of the merchant's affairs, it is enough." In re Graves, 24 Fed. 550. Hence it is no reason to refuse a discharge to a bankrupt because there are obscurities in his books which need explanation, when those obscurities are explained and there is no evidence of fraud or deceit in the entries. In re Townsend, 2 Fed. 559. But where the bankrupt kept no books except a small pocket memorandum-book, in which he entered each day his cash received and cash paid out, a blotter, in which he entered his daily credit sales, and a book in which he kept credit accounts, all of which were imperfectly kept, it was held that he was not entitled to a discharge, even though from these books and his invoices kept on file, it may have been possible, with such memoranda, to make up proper accounts. In re Vernia, 5 Fed. 723. It has been said: "A temporary, accidental omission, in good faith and for a reasonable time, to make the entries, would not be a failure to keep the books. But a cessation to keep them, on purpose, or for an unreasonable time, would be. I cannot rule, as requested by the bankrupt's counsel, that if they employed a clerk whom they considered competent, and left the whole charge of the books to him, they are to be discharged. The law does not require traders to keep a book-keeper, but to keep books, and they are responsible to see that it is done. * * * Nor can I rule that entries on numerous slips of paper, each entry on a separate slip, is a keeping of books under the law. As I have before ruled, it might do for a short time in the absence of the books; but as a system or policy of a permanent character, no." Lowell, J., in re Hammond, 1 Low. 381, Fed. Cas. No. 5,999. Where a merchant drew large sums of money from his business, from time to time, to use in stock speculation, and put slips of paper, with the amounts so withdrawn, in the money-drawer, as memoranda for his book-keeper, so that, when he failed, his cash-book showed a balance of several thousand dollars which did not exist, his discharge as a bankrupt was refused, on the ground that he did not keep proper books of account. In re Hunt, 26 Fed. 739. But in a case where the accounts of exceptional transactions for borrowed money were kept on separate papers, which were preserved and turned over to the assignee with the books, this was considered a sufficient compliance with the law. In re Smith, 16 Fed. 465. But where the debtor had carried on a small trade entirely for cash, but had discontinued it for some months before his bankruptcy, and there was nothing in the way of debts, assets, or capital outstanding, it was held that his failure to keep proper books of that trade would not prevent his discharge. In re Keach, 1 Low. 335, Fed. Cas. No. 7,629. On the hearing of an application for discharge, general objections that the bankrupt did not keep proper books of account, are only available in showing that he did not keep some necessary books, or that the books kept were not as a whole sufficient to show the course or condition of the bankrupt's business. If the objection be merely that some particular transactions were not entered, the objection, to be available, must indicate the omissions or irregularities complained of. In re Smith, 16 Fed. 465; In re Frey, 9 Fed. 376. The burden of showing to the court that the bankrupt's books of account were not properly kept lies upon the creditors, who allege it in their specifications, when it appears that full sets of books were kept by regular book-keepers, hired and kept for that purpose; that such books were all regularly turned over by the bankrupt, with the other property, to the trustee in bankruptcy, and by him, in his office, throughout the pendency of the bankruptcy proceedings, kept subject to examination and inspection by the creditors; and that when the proceedings were closed, the books were turned over to a person who purchased all the property. In re Jewett, 3 Fed. 503. See further, on the general subject, In re Herdic, 1 Fed. 242; In re Williams, 13 Fed. 30; In re Reed, 12 N. B. R. 390, Fed. Cas. No. 11,639.

Under the bankruptcy act of 1867, it was held to be no defense to an objection to the bankrupt's discharge on this ground, to allege that no fraud was intended, but that the failure to keep accounts was due to mere carelessness, for the law was explicit. In re Jorey, 2 Bond, 336, Fed. Cas. No. 7,530. But it is important to notice that the present statute makes this a ground for refusing the discharge only when the failure to keep books was "with fraudulent intent to conceal his true financial condition and in contemplation of bankruptcy."

"Contemplation of Bankruptcy."

In regard to the interpretation of these words, as used in the act, there is some conflict of opinion. It has been held that the phrase means a contemplation of a state of bankruptcy merely, and not necessarily an intention to take the benefit of the bankruptcy law; but that this means more than an inability to pay debts promptly; it contemplates a thorough breaking up of business. McLean v. Lafayette Bank, 3 McLean, 587, Fed. Cas. No. 8,888; Everett v. Stone, 3 Story, 446, Fed. Cas. No. 4,577. But the better opinion appears to be that the phrase in question means either (1) that the debtor contemplates the commission of an act which is, by the statute, made an act of bankruptcy, or (2) that he contemplates being adjudged a bankrupt on his own petition. Buckingham v. McLean, 13 How. 151; In re Craft, 6 Blatchf. 177, Fed. Cas. No. 3,317; Morgan v. Brundrett, 5 Barn. & Adol. 289. Compare In re Wolfskill, 5 Sawy. 385, Fed. Cas. No. 17,930.

Buying Assent of Creditors.

Where one of the creditors, knowing facts sufficient to bar the bankrupt's discharge, is about to file opposition thereto, and the bankrupt, with knowledge thereof, pays money to such creditor to induce him to forbear opposing the discharge, the discharge, when granted, is invalid, and may be impeached on that ground. Coates v. Blush, 1 Cush. 564. And see In re Palmer, 2 Hughes, 177, Fed. Cas. No. 10,678; In re Svenson, 9 Biss. 69, Fed. Cas. No. 13,659; In re Ekings, 6 Fed. 170. So where the bankrupt's wife executes a mortgage on her separate property, at his request, in pursuance of an agreement by which he was to pay the debt of his creditor in full if the latter would assent to his discharge, the mortgage is without consideration and tainted with the illegality of the transaction, notwithstanding it was executed after the discharge and although the wife did not know of the agreement. Blasdel v. Fowle, 120 Mass. 447. It is to be observed that the creditor whose assent to the bankrupt's discharge was procured by the promise of a pecuniary consideration, is estopped from afterwards setting up the fraud as a ground of objection to the discharge; but other creditors, upon learning of the fraud, may object to the discharge on that ground. In re Bright, 9 Fed. 491. Where a surety of the bankrupt pays the debt of a creditor who is opposing the bankrupt's discharge, merely for his own purposes, and without consulting with the bankrupt or informing him of the transaction until long afterwards, and the latter had no part in it, nor made any promise to repay the amount, this will not vitiate his discharge. Ex parte Briggs, 2 Low. 389, Fed. Cas. No. 1,868. And there is nothing in the bankrupt law which forbids a creditor, before any proceedings in bankruptcy have been commenced, to take from a third person a contract or security for the payment of money as an inducement to refrain from throwing his debtor into bankruptcy. Ecker v. Bohn, 45 Md. 278.

Effect of Discharge in Bankruptcy.

No recovery can be had in a state court on a debt that was provable against an estate in bankruptcy, after the debtor has obtained a discharge under the national bankrupt law, unless the debt in question belonged to one of the excepted classes. Talbot v. Suit, 68 Md. 443, 13 Atl. 356. And by a subsequent discharge in bankruptcy, if a judgment is obtained in a state court by a creditor upon a claim provable under the bankrupt law, in an action begun before or after the commencement of the bankruptcy proceedings, and pending such proceedings, the bankrupt is discharged from the judgment itself the same as from the claim upon which it was founded. Leonard v. Yohuk, 68 Wis. 587, 32 N. W. 702; Pine Hill Coal Co. v. Harris, 86 Ky. 421, 6 S. W. 24; Boynton v. Ball, 121 U. S. 457, 7 Sup. Ct. 981. The debtor having been adjudged a bankrupt and received his discharge, after giving a security deed which was void on account of usury, the debt was thereby discharged. Broach v. Smith, 75 Ga. 159. But a discharge in bankruptcy, like the statute of limitations, does not annul the original debt or liability of the bankrupt, but merely suspends the right of action for its recovery. It therefore follows that no one but the bankrupt can plead his discharge in avoidance of his liability. He may, if he chooses, treat his covenants and obligations as still binding upon him. Bush v. Stanley, 122 Ill. 406, 13 N. E. 249.

Conclusiveness of Discharge.

Where a creditor's name is innocently or accidentally (not fraudulently) omitted from the bankrupt's schedule, the discharge and certificate are conclusive evidence in the bankrupt's favor, and a complete bar to a suit against him by the omitted creditor. Hoffman v. Haight, 3 Mackey, D. C. 21; Hubbell v. Cramp, 11 Paige, 310; Graves v. Wright, 53 Mich. 425, 19 N. W. 129. And a discharge in bankruptcy, under the national law is a bar to the claim of an alien creditor suing in the courts of this country, the same as though he were a citizen of the United States. Ruiz v. Eickerman, 2 McCrary, 259, 5 Fed. 790; Murray v. De Rottenham, 6 Johns. Ch. 52. All creditors, whether notified of the proceedings or not, are concluded by the bankrupt's discharge unless they appear within the time limited and assail it for the causes specified in the act. Thurmond v. Andrews, 10 Bush. 400. So a creditor who has unsuccessfully opposed the bankrupt's discharge, is thereby estopped, in a suit which he afterwards brings to recover his debt, and to which the defendant pleads his discharge, from showing that the discharge was fraudulently obtained. Wales v. Lyon, 2 Mich. 276. And an order refusing a discharge is a bar to any second application for discharge in the same proceedings; it is a final determination on the merits of the controversy and must be regarded as res judicata as to the matters involved. In re Brockway, 21 Blatchf. 136, 23 Fed. 583.

Collateral Impeachment of Discharge.

A state court can neither set aside nor disregard a discharge granted by a court of bankruptcy, nor allow it to be impeached collaterally, for fraud or any other cause such as would authorize that court to vacate it; it can only be impeached in a direct proceeding for that purpose in the bankruptcy court itself. Thurmond v. Andrews, 10 Bush, 400; Alston v. Robinett, 37 Tex. 56; Stetson v. Bangor, 56 Me. 286; Fuller v. Pease, 144 Mass. 390, 11 N. E. 694; State v. Gaston, 52 N. J. Law, 321, 19 Atl. 608; Corey v. Ripley, 57 Me. 69; Howland v. Carson, 28 Ohio St. 625; Smith v. Ramsey, 27 Ohio St. 339; Seymour v. Street, 5 Neb. 85; Milhous v. Aicardi, 51 Ala. 594; Oates v. Parish, 47 Ala. 157; Parker v. Atwood, 52 N. H. 181; Stevens v. Brown, 49 Miss. 597; Thomas v. Jones, 39 Wis. 124; Brady v. Brady, 71 Ga. 71. But it is stated in Hennessee v. Mills, 1 Baxt. 38, that the discharge can be attacked in a state court for want of jurisdiction in the court granting it; and in Beardsley v. Hall, 36 Conn. 270, that it may be attacked collaterally if it be absolutely *void*, in consequence of the bankrupt's commission of one of the acts forbidden by the bankrupt law.

Discharge must be Pleaded.

A discharge in bankruptcy will not avail a defendant, either at law or in equity, unless pleaded. Manwarring v. Kouns, 35 Tex. 171; Ludeling v. Felton, 29 La. Ann. 719; Goodrich v. Hunton, 2 Woods, 137, Fed. Cas. No. 5,544. Hence it is not error to exclude a certificate of discharge offered in evidence when the same has not been pleaded. Horner v. Spelman, 78 Ill. 206. But of course if the defendant has no opportunity to plead it, he may set it up in defense whenever the occasion is given. Sanderson v. Daily, 83 N. C. 67; Parks v. Goodwin, 1 Mich. 34. Where the record of a decree shows an absolute discharge in bankruptcy, and that the bankrupt was authorized to receive a certificate, it is sufficient without producing the certificate itself. Viele v. Blanchard, 4 G. Greene, 299.

Second Bankruptcy.

A bankrupt who has not been discharged, or to whom a discharge has been refused, and who has contracted new debts sufficient in amount to give the court jurisdiction, may file a new petition in bankruptcy; but a discharge under such new petition would apply only to new debts, and to such old debts as had been proved anew. In re Drisko, 2 Low. 430, Fed. Cas. No. 4,090; Fisher v. Currier, 7 Metc. (Mass.) 424.

DISCHARGES, WHEN REVOKED.

§ 15. *a* **The judge may, upon the application of parties in interest who have not been guilty of undue laches, filed at any time within one year after a discharge shall have been granted, revoke it upon a trial if it shall be made to appear that it was obtained through the fraud of the bankrupt, and that the knowledge of the fraud has come to the petitioners since the granting of the discharge, and that the actual facts did not warrant the discharge.**

Revoking Discharge; Remedy Exclusive.

The bankrupt act itself having prescribed the forum, the mode, and the time for the direct impeachment of a discharge on the ground of fraud or perjury perpetrated in obtaining it, the remedy thus given is *exclusive.* Neither in the federal nor in the state courts can it be questioned or attacked collaterally. It is conclusively presumed to be valid and effective unless revoked or annulled in the manner prescribed by the act. Smith v. Ramsey, 27 Ohio St. 339; Ray v. Lapham, Id. 452; May v. Howe, 108 Mass. 111; Black v. Blazo, 117 Mass. 17; Seymour v. Street, 5 Neb. 85.

Jurisdiction and Practice.

The jurisdiction of a proceeding to annul a discharge pertains alone to the district court which granted the discharge, and it seems that such proceeding must be brought by the creditor, and will not lie at the instance of his representative the trustee. Nicholas v. Murray, 5 Sawy. 320, Fed. Cas. No. 10,223. In the case of Allen v. Thompson, 10 Fed. 116, an application to vacate the certificate of discharge for want of jurisdiction, because one of the members of the firm did not reside, nor did the firm do business, within the district, was denied. Jurisdictional facts will be presumed in favor of the jurisdiction. Costs may be awarded to the prevailing party in a proceeding to annul a discharge under this provision of the law. In re Holgate, 8 Ben. 355, Fed. Cas. No. 6,601.

Knowledge of Creditors.

A discharge in bankruptcy not being voidable for causes previously known to the creditor, no order to take testimony should be made upon a petition to vacate the discharge unless the petition shows affirmatively reasonable cause to believe that the creditor was ignorant of the ground specified when the discharge was granted. In re Bates, 27 Fed. 604. A discharge will not be set aside when the fraudulent acts relied upon by the petitioning creditors to annul it were suspected and believed to exist before the discharge, and when the after-discovered evidence is incompetent and inadmissible. Marionneaux's Case, 1 Woods, 37, Fed. Cas. No. 9,088. Where specifications in opposition to a discharge were filed by certain creditors, and, after pending in court for a year, were withdrawn, and the bankrupt discharged, another creditor, who was represented in the bankruptcy proceedings by the same solicitor who acted for the objecting creditors, will not be heard to assert personal ignorance before the granting of the discharge of the matters contained in said specifications, nor permitted to set them up as grounds for avoiding the discharge. In re Douglass, 11 Fed. 403.

Limitation as to Time.

The period of one year within which a petition to vacate the discharge of a bankrupt for fraud must be filed, begins to run from the date of the discharge, and not from the discovery of the fraud. Mall v. Ullrich, 37 Fed. 653. An application for leave to contest the validity of a discharge cannot be amended, after the expiration of two years from the date of the discharge, by adding another of the acts mentioned in the statute as cause for withholding a discharge, to those already specified in the application. In re Sims, 9 Fed. 440. In a case where the interest of the creditors who petitioned for a review of the discharge was small in comparison with the aggregate of debts, and the bankrupt had resumed his business on the faith of the discharge, and entered into extensive contracts, it was held that five months was too unreasonable a delay on the part of the creditors, no sufficient excuse being offered, and the petition must be dismissed. In re Murray, 14 Blatchf. 43, Fed. Cas. No. 9,953. Where a discharge was inadvertently granted to a bankrupt, although there were specifications of opposition on file, and no ruling or trial was ever had on such specifications, and the bankrupt, on the faith of his discharge, had borrowed money and resumed business, and the creditor who filed the specifications moved to vacate the discharge, but after such a lapse of time as to make him guilty of laches, it was held that the motion must be denied. In re Buchstein, 9 Ben. 215, Fed. Cas. No. 2,076.

Grounds for Revoking Discharge.

A bankrupt's discharge will be set aside and annulled for fraud practiced in obtaining it. In re Augenstein, 2 MacArthur, 322. The provision of the act relating to the annulling of a discharge does not authorize a rehearing or new trial upon specifications already filed in opposition to the discharge and which were heard and determined before the discharge, even if the opposing creditor can adduce new facts, happening since the discharge, which would be competent evidence if a new trial were authorized by the statute. In re Corwin, 1 Fed. 847.

Buying Assent of Creditors.

Where one of the creditors, knowing facts sufficient to bar the bankrupt's discharge, is about to file opposition thereto, and the bankrupt, with knowledge thereof, pays money to such creditor to induce him to forbear opposing the discharge, the discharge, when granted, is invalid and may be impeached on these grounds. Coates v. Blush, 1 Cush. 564. So where the bankrupt's wife executes a note and mortgage on her separate property, at his request, in pursuance of an agreement by which he was to pay the debt of his creditor in full if the latter would assent to his discharge, the securities are without consideration and are tainted with the illegality of the transaction, notwithstanding they were executed after the discharge, and although the wife did not know of the agreement. Blasdel v. Fowle, 120 Mass. 447. But the rule does not apply to the payment by the bankrupt of the fees of attorney, notary, and register in making proof of claims against his estate, though his sole motive in doing so was to obtain the consent of creditors to his discharge. In re Svenson, 9 Biss. 69, Fed. Cas. No. 13,659. And where a surety of the bankrupt paid the debt of a creditor who was opposing the bankrupt's discharge, merely for his own purposes, and without consulting with the bankrupt or informing him of the transaction until long afterwards, and the latter had no part in it, nor made any promise to repay the amount, it was held that this would not vitiate his discharge. Ex parte Briggs, 2 Low. 389, Fed. Cas. No. 1,868. If the assent of a creditor to the discharge was corruptly procured, and this is assigned as a ground for annulling the same, it is no answer to say that the assent of that creditor was altogether unnecessary. In re Douglass, 11 Fed. 403.

CO-DEBTORS OF BANKRUPTS.

§ 16. *a* **The liability of a person who is a co-debtor with, or guarantor or in any manner a surety for, a bankrupt shall not be altered by the discharge of such bankrupt.**

DEBTS NOT AFFECTED BY A DISCHARGE.

§ 17. *a* **A discharge in bankruptcy shall release a bankrupt from all of his provable debts, except such as (1) are due as a tax levied by the United States, the state, county, district, or municipality in which he resides; (2) are judgments in actions for frauds, or obtaining property by false pretenses or false representations, or for willful and malicious injuries to the person or property of another; (3) have not been duly scheduled in time for proof and allowance, with the name of the creditor if known to the bankrupt, unless such creditor had notice or actual knowledge of the proceedings in bankruptcy; or (4) were created by his fraud, embezzlement, misappropriation, or defalcation while acting as an officer or in any fiduciary capacity.**

Debts due the Sovereign.

Under the English bankruptcy laws, a discharge will not release the debtor from a debt due the crown; because the king is not expressly named in the clauses relating to discharge of debts, and it is familiar law that he is not bound by any statute unless specifically mentioned therein; see 1 Deac. Bankr. p. 784; Rex v. Pixley, Bunb. 202; Ex parte Russell, 19 Ves. 165. Upon the same principle, and for the same reason, it was held, both under the bankrupt act of 1800 and that of 1867, that debts due from the bankrupt to the United States, of any character or description, were not released or affected by his discharge. U. S. v. Herron, 20 Wall. 251; U. S. v. The Rob Roy, 1 Woods, 42, Fed. Cas. No. 16,179; Smith v. Hodson, 50 Wis. 279, 6 N. W. 812; U. S. v. King, Wall. Sr. 13, Fed. Cas. No. 15,536. And by an analogous course of reasoning the conclusion was reached that debts due to a state would not be affected or discharged. Saunders v. Com., 10 Grat. 494; State v. Shelton, 47 Conn. 400; Johnson v. Auditor, 78 Ky. 282; Spalding v. New York, 4 How. 21. But it will be observed that this is entirely changed by the language of the present statute, and all debts to a state or the United States, except only taxes, will be released by a discharge duly granted.

Debts Created by Debtor's Fraud or Embezzlement.

The word "fraud," in this connection, means positive fraud or fraud in fact, involving moral turpitude or intentional wrong, and not implied fraud or fraud in law, which may exist without the imputation of bad faith or immorality. Neal v. Clark, 95 U. S. 704; Allen v. Hickling, 11 Ill. App. 549. And the debt must be tainted with fraud in its inception; for if the contract was fair and honest when made, although the debtor may subsequently be guilty of fraudulent conduct in respect to it, yet such conduct will not destroy the benefit of his discharge. Brown v. Broach, 52 Miss. 536. The recovery of judgment upon a contract induced by a fraud is a waiver of the fraud, and the judgment is not a debt created by fraud so as not to be released by a discharge in bankruptcy. Palmer v. Preston, 45 Vt. 154; per contra, Warner v. Cronkhite, 6 Biss. 453, Fed. Cas. No. 17,180; Donald v. Kell, 111 Ind. 1, 11 N. E. 782. A debt created by fraud is not barred by the bankrupt's discharge even where it was proved against his estate and a dividend received on account. Strang v. Bradner, 114 U. S. 555, 5 Sup. Ct. 1038. An action on the case for deceit is not barred by a discharge in bankruptcy, though the measure of damages was ascertainable by reference to a contract. Hughes v. Oliver, 8 Pa. St. 426. And the joinder, to a count in tort for deceit, of a count in contract for the same cause of action, does not make a discharge in bankruptcy a defense to the count in tort. Morse v. Hutchins, 102 Mass. 439. A discharge in bankruptcy does not release a husband from the obligation to pay alimony decreed by a state court.

In re Garrett, 2 Hughes, 235, Fed. Cas. No. 5,252. If the debtor buys goods for cash on delivery, and obtains possession of them without payment, and immediately ships them beyond the reach of the seller, and then refuses to pay, his conduct is such as to make the debt a fraudulent one within the meaning of the bankrupt law. Classen v. Schoenemann, 80 Ill. 304; Ames v. Moir, 130 Ill. 582, 22 N. E. 535.

Embezzlement.

Embezzlement has been defined as follows: "The fraudulent removing and secreting of personal property with which the party has been intrusted, for the purpose of applying it to his own use." Bouvier, Law Dict. "Embezzlement is a crime unknown to the common law, but depends entirely upon statutory enactments, is a sort of statutory larceny, and may be defined as a fraudulent appropriation to one's own use of the money or goods of another, which were intrusted to his care as servant, bailee, or otherwise." 6 Am. & Eng. Enc. Law, p. 451. "When a clerk, servant, agent, or public officer commits theft by converting to his own use any chattel, money, or valuable security received or taken into possession by him for or in the name or on account of his master, principal, or employer, his offense is called embezzlement." Rapal. & L., Law Dict. For further information as to the nature and definition of embezzlement, and the application of the term to particular acts and relations, the following authorities may be consulted: State v. Wolff, 34 La. Ann. 1153; Chaplin v. Lee, 18 Neb. 440, 25 N. W. 609; State v. Baumhager, 28 Minn. 226, 9 N. W. 704; Reg. v. Rogers, 3 Q. B. Div. 28; Sawin v. Martin, 11 Allen, 439; People v. Burr, 41 How. Prac. 293; Fagnan v. Knox, 40 N. Y. Super. Ct. 41, 49; Com. v. King, 9 Cush. 284; Reed v. Bank of Newburgh, 6 Paige, 337; Ex parte Hedley, 31 Cal. 108; People v. McKinney, 10 Mich. 54; Com. v. Tuckerman, 10 Gray, 173; 2 Bish. Cr. Law, §§ 325–330.

Fiduciary Debts.

The "fiduciary capacity" intended by the bankrupt law relates to cases of technical trusts; not merely such as the law implies from the contract, but actual and expressly constituted; and in like manner the "fraud" intended is an actual or express fraud as distinguished from an implied or constructive fraud founded merely upon some breach of duty. Palmer v. Hussey, 87 N. Y. 303. A sum of money to which a wife was entitled on the sale of certain real estate in partition proceedings was decreed to be paid to her husband, he to apply the interest to his own use, and give bonds for the payment of the principal sum at his death or whenever so required by the court. It was held, in an action to recover such principal sum, that the liability incurred by the husband was incurred while acting in a fiduciary capacity, and was not discharged by proceedings in bankruptcy. Mock v. Howell, 101 N. C. 443, 8 S. E. 167. But a balance due on the bankrupt's subscription to the capital stock of a corporation is not a fiduciary debt. Morrison v. Savage, 56 Md. 142.

Factors.

The question whether or not the liability of a factor or commission merchant for money belonging to his principal, but which he has wrongly converted to his own use, is a debt created by him while acting in a "fiduciary capacity," has been a fruitful source of discussion and has resulted in an almost hopeless conflict of authorities. The leading case on the subject is Chapman v. Forsyth, 2 How. 202, where McLean, J., said "If the act embrace such a debt, it will be difficult to limit its application. It must include all debts arising from agencies, and indeed all cases where the law implies an obligation from the trust reposed in the debtor. Such a construction would have left but few debts on which the law could operate. In almost all the commercial transactions of the country, confidence is reposed in the punctuality and integrity of the debtor, and a violation of these is, in a commercial sense, a disregard of a trust. But this is not the relation spoken of in the act." This decision has been followed in numerous cases; Zeperink v. Card, 3 McCrary, 549, 11 Fed. 295; Owsley v. Cobin, 15 N. B. R. 489, Fed. Cas. No. 10,636 (by Waite, C. J.); In Re Smith, 9 Ben. 494, Fed. Cas. No. 12,976 (citing Neal v. Clark, 95 U. S. 708); Hayman v. Pond, 7 Metc. (Mass.) 328; Scott v. Porter, 93 Pa. St. 38; Falkland v. Bank, 21 Hun, 450; Austill v. Crawford, 7 Ala. 335; Woolsey v. Cade, 54 Ala. 378; Georgia Railroad v. Cubbedge, 75 Ga. 321 (overruling Jones v. Russell, 44 Ga. 460); Maxwell v. Evans, 90 Ind. 596; Du Pont v. Beck, 81 Ind. 271. On the other hand, many respectable authorities hold that a factor *is* one who "acts in a fiduciary character," and that his liability to his principal will not be released by his discharge in bankruptcy. In Re Kimball, 6 Blatchf. 292, Fed. Cas. No. 7,769; Hardenbrook v. Colson, 61 How. Prac. 426; Whitaker v. Chapman, 3 Lans. 155; Banning v. Bleakley, 27 La. Ann. 257; Treadwell v. Holloway, 46 Cal. 547; Lemcke v. Booth, 47 Mo. 385; Brunswig v. Taylor, 2 Mo. App. 351. Upon the whole, we must conclude that the rule announced in Chapman v. Forsyth (that a factor is not a fiduciary) is the true doctrine on the subject, and supported by the proponderance of authority. See an article on this subject in 7 Am. Law Rev. 32.

Bailees.

Where one receives the money or property of another as agent or bailee, the title to which is to remain in the principal, and which is to be paid over or delivered to him, or to be used in a particular way or for a specific purpose for his use, then the money or property is received or held in a fiduciary capacity, or as trustee. Matteson v. Kellogg, 15 Ill. 547. So where grain is stored with a warehouseman, to be returned in kind but not necessarily the identical grain, he does not hold it in a fiduciary capacity. Sumner v. Richie, 54 Iowa, 554, 6 N. W. 752. An agent (not a factor) who retains money of his principal sent to him for a special purpose, is not a fiduciary debtor; this is not a technical trust. Pankey v. Nolan, 6 Humph. 154. So where the bankrupt is under a debt or obligation arising from his appropriating to his own use collateral securities deposited with him as security for the payment of money or the performance of a duty, and his failure or refusal to return the same after the money has been paid or the duty performed, such debt is not created by fraud nor in a fiduciary character in the sense of the bankrupt law. Hennequin v. Clews, 111 U. S. 676, 4 Sup. Ct. 576, affirming S. C. 77 N. Y. 427.

Collecting Agents.

Where the debtor has been employed to collect moneys for the creditor, and the understanding of the parties is such that the debtor may mingle the funds so collected with his own money without being thereby guilty of a breach of trust, and that he is merely to account for the aggregate of collections for a given period, his failure to pay over the funds does not constitute a debt created in a fiduciary character. Guilfoyle v. Anderson, 9 Daly, 64; Kaufman v. Alexander, 53 Tex. 562; Grover & Baker Sewing Mach. Co. v. Clinton, 5 Biss. 324, Fed. Cas. No. 5,845. So it has been held that where the collecting agent of a bank converts to his own use the proceeds of notes and drafts sent to him for collection by the bank, his liability therefor is not a fiduciary debt. Green v. Chilton, 57 Miss. 598. But compare Fulton v. Hammond, 11 Fed. 291. In a case where it appeared that A., for his own accommodation, asked B. to collect money for him, without compensation, and to keep it until A. called for it, and B. collected the money, and without actual fraud or fraudulent intent deposited the proceeds to his own credit with his own funds, and by unexpected reverses he was forced into bankruptcy before he had paid it over, and made a composition with his creditors, it was held that the debt thus incurred by B. to A. was not a debt created by the fraud or embezzlement of the bankrupt, or while he was acting in a fiduciary capacity. Noble v. Hammond, 129 U. S. 65, 9 Sup. Ct. 235.

Attorneys.

The relation of attorney and client is one of trust, and a violation of duty by the attorney (as a failure to pay over money collected for the client) is done in a fiduciary capacity under the bankrupt law. Flanagan v. Pearson, 42 Tex. 1; White v. Platt, 5 Denio, 274; Heffren v. Jayne, 39 Ind. 463; contra, Wolcott v. Hodge, 15 Gray, 547. But a debt created by a person while acting as an attorney in fact is not of this character. Woodward v. Towne, 127 Mass. 41.

Public Officers.

A collector of city taxes is a public officer, and a debt which he owes to the city in consequence of a defalcation in his office of collector is a fiduciary debt and will not be released by his discharge in bankruptcy. Morse v. Lowell, 7 Metc. (Mass.) 152; Richmond v. Brown, 66 Me. 373. But the surety on the official bond of a defaulting constable is entitled to be released, by his discharge in bankruptcy, from his liability for the breach of such bond. McMinn v. Allen, 67 N. C. 131. Where a retiring township trustee gives a note to his successor, in satisfaction of a debt due the township, for funds wrongfully appropriated to his own use, the fiduciary character of the debt is not changed, so as to bring it within the effect of a discharge in bankruptcy. Madison Tp. v. Dunkle, 114 Ind. 262, 16 N. E. 593. On the other hand, where claims are placed in the hands of a public officer for collection, his liability for negligence merely in failing to use due diligence in collecting and paying over the money is not a "defalcation," within the meaning of the bankrupt law. Courtney v. Beale, 84 Va. 692, 5 S. E. 708.

Executors and Administrators.

A sum of money due from an executor to the residuary legatee under the will, as such, is a fiduciary debt. Crisfield v. State, 55 Md. 192. But an agreement by an executor, guaranteeing the payment of a demand against the estate, and admitting the possession of sufficient assets, is not. Amoskeag Co. v. Barnes, 49 N. H. 312. So where an administrator settles up the estate and gives his individual note to the distributees for the balance due, this is not a fiduciary debt. Elliott v. Higgins, 83 N. C. 459.

Sureties on Bonds.

The liability of a surety on a guardian's bond is not a fiduciary debt. "The surety merely guarantees the acts of his principal. No trust or confidence is reposed in him. He has nothing to do with the person or property of the ward, and has no control over the conduct of the guardian. He is liable simply on his contract and according to its terms." Reitz v. People, 72 Ill. 435; McDonald v. State, 77 Ind. 26; Jones v. Knox, 46 Ala. 53. So a debt due by a guardian to his ward in respect of the latter's property is a fiduciary debt; but if the guardian's surety pays it to the ward, and then sues the guardian, this is a debt which will be released by the guardian's discharge in bankruptcy; for the relation of the guardian and surety is that of simple contract. Cromer v. Cromer, 29 Grat. 280; though see Light v. Merriam, 132 Mass. 283. The liability of a surety on an administrator's bond for the default of his principal is not a fiduciary debt. Steele v. Graves, 68 Ala. 21.

Trust-Funds.

Where A. owes B. a debt, and makes an assignment of property, and gives a judgment, to C., in trust to pay such debt to B., such property constitutes, in equity, a trust-fund in the hands of C., and if B. recovers a judgment against him for the amount so received to B.'s use, this is a fiduciary debt. Kingsland v. Spalding, 3 Barb. Ch. 341. In the case of Herman v. Lynch, 26 Kan. 435, it appeared that the defendant received certain money from the plaintiff for the purpose and under an agreement that he should take the money to a designated town and there purchase exchange with it and remit the same to a creditor of the plaintiff; defendant appropriated the money to his own use; it was held that he received and held it in a fiduciary capacity. But in Phillips v. Russell, 42 Me. 360, on an almost identical state of facts, an opposite view was held.

Auctioneers.

An auctioneer acts in a fiduciary character in respect to goods placed in his hands for sale, and his liability for their proceeds will not be released by his discharge in bankruptcy. Jones v. Russell, 44 Ga. 460; In Re Lord, 5 Law Rep. 258; contra, Gibson v. Gorman, 44 N. J. Law, 325.

Rights of Fiduciary Creditor.

"The fiduciary creditor stands on the same footing with other creditors, except that he is unaffected by the discharge. He may prove his debt and share in the distribution, but has no exclusive or superior advantages in the assets over other creditors." Winters v. Claitor, 54 Miss. 349.

Revival of Debt Barred by Discharge;—New Promise.

While the effect of a discharge in bankruptcy is to suspend the right of action against the debtor, upon all provable debts not falling within the excepted classes, yet the debt remains, and the moral obligation to pay it forms a sufficient consideration for a new promise to make such payment; and such promise, if distinct and specific, need not be in writing but may be proved by parol. Worthington v. De Bardlekin, 33 Ark. 651; Apperson v. Stewart, 27 Ark. 619; Barron v. Benedict, 44 Vt. 518; Craig v. Seitz, 63 Mich. 727, 30 N. W. 347; Wislizenus v. O'Fallon, 91 Mo. 184, 3 S. W. 837. But nothing is sufficient to revive a discharged debt unless the jury are authorized by it to say that there is the expression by the debtor of a clear intention to bind himself to the payment of the debt, and the rule is more stringent than in regard to the revival of a debt barred by the statute of limitations. Allen v. Ferguson, 18 Wall. 1. Nothing amounts to a new promise to avoid the effect of the discharge that is not intended distinctly as a recognition and renewal of the debt as binding. Brewer v. Boynton, 71 Mich. 254, 39 N. W. 49; Craig v. Seitz, 63 Mich. 727, 30 N. W. 345; Murphy v. Crawford, 114 Pa. St. 496, 7 Atl. 142. Where a bankrupt, after his discharge, confesses judgment upon an old debt, the debt is a good consideration for the judgment, and the latter is not affected by the discharge. Dewey v. Moyer, 72 N. Y. 70. The majority of the cases hold that when the bankrupt has given a new promise sufficient to revive a debt barred by his discharge in bankruptcy, the creditor, in bringing suit for the recovery of the debt, must declare on the original obligation or engagement, and not on the new promise. Marshall v. Tray, 74 Ill. 379; Apperson v. Stewart, 27 Ark. 619; Badger v. Gilmore, 33 N. H. 361; Fraley v. Kelly, 67 N. C. 78; Riggs v. Roberts, 85 N. C. 151; Clark v. Atkinson, 2 E. D. Smith, 112; Dusenberry v. Hoyt, 53 N. Y. 521. But still the opposite view—that the original debt is absolutely extinguished by the discharge, and the only cause of action is on the new promise—is supported by several decisions, and notably in Pennsylvania. Bolton v. King, 105 Pa. St. 78; Hobough v. Murphy, 114 Pa. St. 358, 7 Atl. 139; Murphy v. Crawford, 114 Pa. St. 496, 7 Atl. 142; Ross v. Jordan, 62

Ga. 298; Fleming v. Lullman, 11 Mo. App. 104; Eckler v. Galbraith, 12 Bush, 71. A discharge in bankruptcy relates back to the adjudication of the fact of bankruptcy; and a subsequent promise to pay a debt is not required to be made after the discharge, but is sufficient if made between the adjudication and the discharge. Griel v. Solomon, 82 Ala. 85, 2 South. 322; Wheeler v. Wheeler, 28 Ill. App. 385. But the original debt is revived only as of the date of the new promise, and where judgment is obtained upon the latter, the debtor is entitled to claim the exemption provided by the law in force at the latter date. Willis v. Cushman, 115 Ind. 100, 17 N. E. 168.

CHAPTER IV.

COURTS AND PROCEDURE THEREIN.

PROCESS, PLEADINGS, AND ADJUDICATIONS.

§ **18.** *a* Upon the filing of a petition for involuntary bankruptcy, service thereof, with a writ of subpœna, shall be made upon the person therein named as defendant in the same manner that service of such process is now had upon the commencement of a suit in equity in the courts of the United States, except that it shall be returnable within fifteen days, unless the judge shall for cause fix a longer time; but in case personal service can not be made, then notice shall be given by publication in the same manner and for the same time as provided by law for notice by publication in suits in equity in courts of the United States.

b The bankrupt, or any creditor, may appear and plead to the petition within ten days after the return day, or within such further time as the court may allow.

c All pleadings setting up matters of fact shall be verified under oath.

d If the bankrupt, or any of his creditors, shall appear, within the time limited, and controvert the facts alleged in the petition, the judge shall determine, as soon as may be, the issues presented by the pleadings, without the intervention of a jury, except in cases where a jury trial is given by this act, and makes the adjudication or dismiss the petition.

_e_ If on the last day within which pleadings may be filed none are filed by the bankrupt or any of his creditors, the judge shall on the next day, if present, or as soon thereafter as practicable, make the adjudication or dismiss the petition.

_f_ If the judge is absent from the district, or the division of the district in which the petition is pending, on the next day after the last day on which pleadings may be filed, and none have been filed by the bankrupt or any of his creditors, the clerk shall forthwith refer the case to the referee.

_g_ Upon the filing of a voluntary petition the judge shall hear the petition and make the adjudication or dismiss the petition. If the judge is absent from the district, or the division of the district in which the petition is filed at the time of the filing, the clerk shall forthwith refer the case to the referee.

PROCEEDINGS IN BANKRUPTCY; ADJUDICATION.

Service of Process.

The thirteenth equity rule provides that "the service of all subpœnas shall be by a delivery of a copy thereof by the officer serving the same to the defendant personally, or by leaving a copy thereof at the dwelling-house or usual place of abode of each defendant, with some adult person who is a member or resident in the family." And the fifteenth rule provides that "the service of all process, mesne and final, shall be by the marshal of the district, or his deputy, or by some other person specially appointed by the court for that purpose, and not otherwise. In the latter case, the person serving the process shall make affidavit thereof." The general appearance of a party to a suit in personam waives all irregularities in the service of the process and confers jurisdiction so far as the person is concerned. Such jurisdiction, when once conferred, cannot be withdrawn by the act of the party who has so appeared, without the consent of the court or of the prosecuting party. In re Ulrich, 3 Ben. 355, Fed. Cas. No. 14,327.

Objections to Jurisdiction.

The creditors, when notified that proceedings in bankruptcy have been commenced, must promptly, by motion or petition, raise any objections they may have to the jurisdiction of the court; if they fail to do so, the objections will be waived. They cannot for the first time object to the jurisdiction in opposition to the application for discharge. Allen v. Thompson, 10 Fed. 116. On the other hand, it is held that an appearance and answer do not waive any question affecting the jurisdiction of the court, for no voluntary act of the defendant can give jurisdiction; and it is never too late, at any stage of the cause, to consider it. Jobbins v. Montague, 6 N. B. R. 509, Fed. Cas. No. 7,330. The proceedings in a court of bankruptcy cannot be attacked collaterally upon questions of jurisdiction. Adams v. Terrell, 4 Fed. 796. A voluntary petition in bankruptcy by a debtor may be received, notwithstanding the fact that a petition for a compulsory decree against him has already been filed, and an order of notice to show cause thereon obtained by a creditor against him, if there has been no adjudication. In re Canfield, 1 N. Y. Leg. Obs. 234, Fed. Cas. No. 2,380.

Requisites of the Petition.

The specific acts of bankruptcy relied upon by the petitioning creditors as justifying an adjudication must be set forth in their petition, and the proofs will be confined to the scope of the petition; that is, evidence of other acts of bankruptcy than those alleged in the petition will not be received. Ex parte Potts, Crabbe, 469, Fed. Cas. No. 11,344. So also, the facts concerning an alleged act of bankruptcy should be stated in the petition with such certainty and detail as to inform the debtor of what he is required to make proof or explanation. In re Randall, Deady, 557, Fed. Cas. No. 11,551. Thus, where the petition contained an allegation that the respondent owed a debt, but no allegation that it was owed to the petitioning creditor, it was held insufficient. In re Western Sav. & T. Co., 4 Sawy. 190, Fed. Cas. No. 17,442. And the nature of the petitioners' debts should be so far stated in the petition that the court may see that they are provable against the estate. In re Hadley, 12 N. B. R. 366, Fed. Cas. No. 5,894. In an anonymous case reported in 15 Pittsb. Leg. J. 81, Fed. Cas. No. 471, permission to file a petition in bankruptcy was refused on account of the illegible manner in which it was written. And in another case, it was stated that if the petition undertakes to name the judge to whom it is to be presented, the name given must be correctly given; it cannot be stricken out as surplusage; and hence if the name is incorrect, permission to file the petition will not be granted. Anonymous, 1 N. B. R. 216, Fed. Cas. No. 459.

Verification of Petition.

It is sufficient if a petition in involuntary bankruptcy be signed and sworn to by an attorney of the petitioning creditor, duly authorized thereto; and it is not necessary that it should be signed or verified by the petitioning creditor in person. In re Raynor, 11 Blatchf. 43, Fed. Cas. No. 11,597. So a voluntary petition in bankruptcy, signed and verified by the agent of the debtor, will be sufficient to sustain the jurisdiction of the bankruptcy court in a collateral proceeding. Wald v. Wehl, 6 Fed. 163. And the fact that the petition in a voluntary proceeding was signed by an attorney who had not, at that time, been admitted to practice in the court in which the petition was filed, is not a ground for dismissing the proceeding, but merely for an order, on notice to the bankrupt and the alleged attorney, that the latter will no longer be recognized as attorney in the case. In re O'Halloran, 8 Ben. 128, Fed. Cas. No. 10,463. Under the act of 1867, it was held that the verification of a petition in involuntary bankruptcy before a notary public was irregular; but the irregularity was a question of practice merely, and not of jurisdiction. In re Getchell, 8 Ben. 256, Fed. Cas. No. 5,371. The failure of a notary to affix his notarial seal to the verification of a creditor's petition and the proofs of debts of such creditor, in a case of involuntary bankruptcy, will not defeat the jurisdiction of the court. In re Donnelly, 5 Fed. 783. And generally, objections to the petition on the ground of the insufficiency of its signature and verification will be considered as waived, where the bankrupt takes issue upon the petition, puts in a denial of its substantive allegations, and demands a trial by jury. In re McNaughton, 8 N. B. R. 44, Fed. Cas. No. 8,912.

Filing and Presenting Petition.

A petition in bankruptcy need not be presented to the court simultaneously with its verification. The fact that the petition was attested nine days before its presentation constitutes no bar to its presentation; and the decree dates back to the application, so that property acquired after the verification of the petition, though before its presentation to the court, passes as assets to the assignee. In re Abrahams, 5 Law Rep. 328, Fed. Cas. No. 20. A petition for adjudication in bankruptcy is to be deemed "filed," within the meaning of the statute, from the time when it is presented to the clerk for the action of the court. The time of filing does not date from the time when the clerk presents it to the judge for his action as to issuing a subpœna or order to show cause. In re Bear, 5 Fed. 53.

Amendment of Petition.

The court of bankruptcy, on a trial before a jury as to the fact of bankruptcy, in an involuntary proceeding, has power to permit an amendment of the creditors' petition. In re Bininger, 7 Blatchf. 262, Fed. Cas. No. 1,420. An amendment to a petition in bankruptcy relates back to the time of the filing of the original petition, and has the same force and effect as though included in the petition itself. Sherman v. International Bank, 8 Biss. 371, Fed. Cas. No. 12,765. But the court, in allowing such amendments, should be governed by substantially the same principles which apply to similar cases in other courts; and hence if the proposed amendments would introduce into the petition entirely new acts of bankruptcy, and are founded upon facts not stated or referred to in the original petition, leave to amend should not be granted, unless, perhaps, where the debtor consents thereto. Reed v. Cowley, 1 N. B. R. 516, Fed. Cas. No. 11,644; In re Leonard, 4 N. B. R. 562, Fed. Cas. No. 8,255. But it has been held that, where the proofs disclose acts of bankruptcy not averred in the petition of the creditor, the petition may be amended so as to conform to the proofs. In re Gallinger, 1 Sawy. 224, Fed. Cas. No. 5,202. And an amendment to the petition, charging that the conveyances which were specifically set forth in the petition, and which were therein alleged to be fraudulent and without consideration, were also made, if there was any consideration, with intent to prefer certain persons to whom the conveyances were made, does not charge a new act of bankruptcy, and should be allowed. In re Henderson, 9 Fed. 196. But it is the design of the law that proceedings in bankruptcy should be summary, and that they should go on without delay; and where an order to show cause was denied on the day the petition was filed, because it appeared on the face thereof that the bankrupt did not reside within the jurisdiction of the court, the petitioners cannot, after delaying for nearly a year without sufficient excuse, have the petition amended so as to show that the bankrupt did in fact reside within the jurisdiction. In re Freudenfels, Fed. Cas. No. 5,112a. A creditor who has joined in an involuntary petition cannot afterwards object to an amendment thereof which is necessary to the prosecution thereof to final effect. In re Sargent, 13 N. B. R. 144, Fed. Cas. No. 12,361.

Plea or Answer of Debtor.

Under the bankruptcy act of 1867, it was doubtful whether any answer was necessary in proceedings in involuntary bankruptcy to a rule upon a debtor to show cause why he should not be adjudged a bankrupt. It was said that a paper simply denying the acts of bankruptcy charged, and demanding a trial by jury, was a proper and sufficient response on the part of the debtor to such a rule. Phelps v. Clasen, Woolw. 204, Fed. Cas. No. 11,074. And in another case it was said that that statute did not require that the answer to the creditors' petition, to entitle the debtor to demand and have a hearing by the court or a trial by jury, should be verified or even in writing. It was held to be sufficient if he appeared before the court and alleged that the facts set forth were not true. But, at the same time, it was said to be the better practice to put the whole answer in writing, and allege in express terms that the facts set forth in the petition are not true, and then conclude with a demand for a hearing by the court or a trial by jury; and this answer should be signed by the respondent in person or by attorney. In re Heydette, 8 N. B. R. 332, Fed. Cas. No. 6,444. The present statute, while it does not expressly require a written plea or answer by the respondent, evidently contemplates a formal answer or traverse of the petition. For it declares that the bankrupt "may appear and plead to the petition;" that "all pleadings setting up matters of fact shall be verified under oath;" that the pleadings shall be "filed;" and that the bankrupt may have a trial by jury "upon filing a written application therefor at or before the time within which an answer may be filed." In proceedings in involuntary bankruptcy, no replication is necessary to the denial by the debtor of the allegations of the petition, for such denial amounts to the general issue. In re Dunham, 2 Ben. 488, Fed. Cas. No. 4,143.

Defenses to Petition in Involuntary Proceedings.

In a proceeding in involuntary bankruptcy, the alleged debtor may deny that the petitioner for an adjudication is his creditor, and if he maintains such denial by proof, he may have the petition dismissed. In re Cornwall, 9 Blatchf. 114, Fed. Cas. No. 3,250. The general rule of pleading being that answers must be specific, and the true object of pleading in any case being to narrow the controversy to the point really in dispute, no greater latitude ought to be allowed the defense in bankruptcy in this respect than in ordinary actions and suits. In re Sutherland, Deady, 344, Fed. Cas. No. 13,638; In re Findlay, 5 Biss. 480, Fed. Cas. No. 4,789. A mere general denial of the intent with which an act is alleged to have been done is not a good defense to a charge of having committed an act of bankruptcy; the respondent must also allege and prove the actual intent with which he did the act mentioned. In re Silverman, 1 Sawy. 410, Fed. Cas. No. 12,855. Where the debtor denies that the requisite number and amount of creditors have joined in the petition against him, and presents a list of his creditors in support of his denial, it seems that such list should be sworn to. In re Steinman, 6 Biss. 166, Fed. Cas. No. 13,357.

Tender and Payment.

Under no circumstances can a plea of tender be a good defense to a petition for adjudication in bankruptcy. For if the debtor is insolvent, he would have no right to offer payment, nor the creditor to accept it, as it would amount to a preference; and if he is not insolvent, or has not committed an act of bankruptcy, that is the question to be determined, and the plea of tender is entirely outside the controversy and extraneous to the issue. In re Ouimette, 1 Sawy. 47, Fed. Cas. No. 10,622; In re Williams, 1 Lowell, 406, Fed. Cas. No. 17,703. Payments made to petitioning creditors, after the petition, and before the trial on an issue raised by a denial of bankruptcy, are material facts on such trial, and if such payments are shown to an amount sufficient to reduce the indebtedness of the alleged bankrupt below the minimum established by the act, the court loses jurisdiction to adjudge the debtor a bankrupt; the receipt of such payments, to that amount, by the petitioning creditors must be considered a waiver of the alleged act of bankruptcy. In re Skelley, 3 Biss. 260, Fed. Cas. No. 12,921.

Burden of Proof.

In some cases arising under the bankruptcy act of 1867, it was held that, by the express terms of the law, the burden was upon the debtor to prove to the satisfaction of the court that the facts set forth in the petition filed against him for an adjudication of bankruptcy were not true, and that, unless he did so, the petitioner was entitled to an adjudication. In re Price, 8 N. B. R. 514, Fed. Cas. No. 11,411. But other cases took the more reasonable view that, although the letter of the statute might seem to throw the burden of proof upon the debtor, yet the creditors ought to be compelled to make out their case as in any other issue; and that the burden was on them to establish the indebtedness of the respondent and the alleged acts of bankruptcy. Brock v. Hoppock, 2 N. B. R. 7, Fed. Cas. No. 1,912; In re Oregon Bulletin Co., 13 N. B. R. 503, Fed. Cas. No. 10,559. But see section 3 of the present act, as to cases in which the burden of proving his solvency is cast on the debtor.

Who May Oppose the Adjudication.

A voluntary petition in bankruptcy may be opposed by creditors, and will be defeated if they can show that the petitioner is not entitled to the benefit of the act, or that he is attempting to defraud them. Thus, the adjudication will be refused if creditors show that the petitioner had property at the time of his application which he knowingly and intentionally omitted to state in his inventory. In re Bailey, 1 N. Y. Leg. Obs. 18, Fed. Cas. No. 726. In an involuntary proceeding, any person who is able to satisfy the court that he is a creditor of the respondent and has an interest to protect, and that his purpose is a meritorious one, and not purely officious, should be allowed to come in and oppose the adjudication. In re Boston, H. & E. R. Co., 9 Blatchf. 101, Fed. Cas. No. 1,677; In re Jack, 13 N. B. R. 296, Fed. Cas. No. 7,119. So, an attaching creditor, though not originally a party to the proceedings, has a right to appear and contest the adjudication on the ground that the requisite number of creditors have not joined (In re Hatje, 6 Biss. 436, Fed. Cas. No. 6,215), or on the ground of fraud and collusion between the petitioner and the debtor. In re Mendelsohn, 3 Sawy. 342, Fed. Cas. No. 9,420; In re Scrafford, 14 N. B. R. 184, Fed. Cas. No. 12,557; In re Jack, 13 N. B. R. 296, Fed. Cas. No. 7,119.

Discontinuance and Dismissal of Proceedings.

When the court is satisfied that a petition in involuntary bankruptcy was not presented in good faith, but for sinister, oppressive, and vexatious purposes, it has power to dismiss the proceedings. In re Hamlin, 8 Biss. 122, Fed. Cas. No. 5,994. Such is also the practice of the English courts. See Ex parte Harcourt, 2 Rose, 203; Ex parte Ashworth, L. R. 18 Eq. 705; In re Davies, 3 Ch. Div. 461; Ex parte Bourne, 2 Glyn & J. 137. If the petition in involuntary proceedings was presented by a single creditor, and he desires to discontinue the proceeding and have his petition dismissed, he may do so before the adjudication, without giving notice to other creditors of the alleged bankrupt. In re Camden Rolling-Mill Co., 3 N. B. R. 590, Fed. Cas. No. 2,338. But where, as is usually the case, several creditors join in the petition, the rule is somewhat different. A creditor who has in good faith joined in an involuntary petition, cannot withdraw, against the objection of the rest, unless in a case where he was induced to join by misrepresentation or misunderstanding, in which event he may be allowed to withdraw at any time before adjudication. In re Sargent, 13 N. B. R. 144, Fed. Cas. No. 12,361; In re Philadelphia Axle Works, 1 Wkly. Notes Cas. 126, Fed. Cas. No. 11,091. But where a majority of the creditors desire a dismissal of the proceedings, and will give proper security for the payment of the objecting creditors, the dismissal should be allowed. In re Indianapolis, C. & L. R. Co., 5 Biss. 287, Fed. Cas. No. 7,023. When an adjudication of bankruptcy is proved, the party who alleges that the proceedings have been dismissed must prove the time of such dismissal. Wills v. Claflin, 92 U. S. 135. A voluntary petition may be withdrawn, and all further proceedings stayed, on the application of the petitioner, before a decree has been made, upon proper cause shown and the payment of costs. Ex parte Randall, 5 Law Rep. 115, Fed. Cas. No. 11,550. Compare Ex parte Harris, 3 N. Y. Leg. Obs. 152, Fed. Cas. No. 6,110.

Conclusiveness of Adjudication.

A decree of the federal district court sitting in bankruptcy, upon a petition in involuntary proceedings, whereby the debtor is adjudged and declared a bankrupt, is in the nature of a decree in rem, since it determines his legal status in that respect, and is therefore notice, of itself, to all creditors, and is conclusive evidence that all the facts necessary to sustain the decree were proved before the court. Shawhan v. Wherritt, 7 How. 627; In re Wallace, Deady, 433, Fed. Cas. No. 17,094; In re Banks, 1 N. Y. Leg. Obs. 274, Fed. Cas. No. 958; Morse v. Godfrey,

3 Story, 391, Fed. Cas. No. 9,856; Rayl v. Lapham, 27 Ohio St. 452; Lewis v. Sloan, 68 N. C. 557; Thornton v. Hogan, 63 Mo. 143. As a consequence of the proposition that the adjudication is in rem, it follows that actual notice to the creditors is not essential to the jurisdiction of the court. Rayl v. Lapham, supra. And when the court had jurisdiction of the person and the subject-matter, and the adjudication is correct in form, it is conclusive of the fact decreed, and it cannot be attacked or impeached in any collateral proceeding, unless it be for fraud in obtaining it. Chapman v. Brewer, 114 U. S. 158, 5 Sup. Ct. 799; Graham v. Boston, H. & E. R. Co., 14 Fed. 753; In re McKinley, 7 Ben. 562, Fed. Cas. No. 8,864; Lewis v. Sloan, 68 N. C. 557; Mount v. Manhattan Co., 41 N. J. Eq. 211, 3 Atl. 726; Michaels v. Post, 21 Wall. 398. The adjudication is a judgment, and is as effective as any other judgment to cure irregularities in practice which do not touch the jurisdiction of the court. In re Getchell, 8 Ben. 256, Fed. Cas. No. 5,371. Moreover, the decree is conclusive as to the jurisdiction of the court rendering it, at least if the record shows the necessary jurisdictional facts. In re Ives, 5 Dill. 146, Fed. Cas. No. 7,115. And it is also beyond legislative control. In re Raffauf, 6 Biss. 150, Fed. Cas. No. 11,525. A shareholder in a railroad corporation is a party to proceedings in involuntary bankruptcy against the company, and therefore cannot collaterally impeach the proceedings. His remedy is to apply to the bankruptcy court, or to seek a review in the court having appellate jurisdiction. Graham v. Boston, H. & E. R. Co., 118 U. S. 161, 6 Sup. Ct. 1009. The fact that the debtor gave his aid to the signing, presenting, and filing of the petition, by soliciting some of the creditors to join in it, furnishes no ground for setting aside the adjudication. In re Duncan, 8 Ben. 365, Fed. Cas. No. 4,131. An adjudication of bankruptcy passing by default against the bankrupt will not be opened to allow him to file an answer and contest the petition, where the answer proposed does not deny the act of bankruptcy charged,

but merely denies that the petitioners are creditors, or are sufficient in number and amount. In re Le Favour, 8 Ben. 43, Fed. Cas. No. 8,208. An adjudication in bankruptcy relates back to the filing of the original petition, and not to the time of an ancillary petition filed to correct an irregularity; and a levy after the filing of the original petition gives no lien. In re Bear, Fed. Cas. No. 1,177.

Malicious Prosecution of Bankruptcy Proceedings.

Proceedings to put a debtor into bankruptcy should never be resorted to as proceedings in terrorem to collect a debt; and if such action is taken by the creditor maliciously and without probable cause, and the petition is dismissed, the debtor is entitled to recover, in an action brought for that purpose, the damages he has sustained by reason of the attempt to throw him into bankruptcy, and, if actual malice is proved, exemplary damages also. Sonneborn v. Stewart, 2 Woods, 599, Fed. Cas. No. 13,176. This case contains an elaborate and most able discussion of the whole topic by Mr. Justice Bradley. And see Cooley, Torts, 187; Add. Torts, § 867.

JURY TRIALS.

§ 19. *a* **A person against whom an involuntary petition has been filed shall be entitled to have a trial by jury, in respect to the question of his insolvency, except as herein otherwise provided, and any act of bankruptcy alleged in such petition to have been committed, upon filing a written application therefor at or before the time within which an answer may be filed. If such application is not filed within such time, a trial by jury shall be deemed to have been waived.**

b **If a jury is not in attendance upon the court, one may be specially summoned for the trial, or the**

case may be postponed, or, if the case is pending in one of the district courts within the jurisdiction of a circuit court of the United States, it may be certified for trial to the circuit court sitting at the same place, or by consent of parties when sitting at any other place in the same district, if such circuit court has or is to have a jury first in attendance.

c **The right to submit matters in controversy, or an alleged offense under this act, to a jury, shall be determined and enjoyed, except as provided by this act, according to the United States laws now in force or such as may be hereafter enacted in relation to trials by jury.**

OATHS, AFFIRMATIONS.

§ 20. *a* **Oaths required by this act, except upon hearings in court, may be administered by (1) referees; (2) officers authorized to administer oaths in proceedings before the courts of the United States, or under the laws of the state where the same are to be taken; and (3) diplomatic or consular officers of the United States in any foreign country.**

b **Any person conscientiously opposed to taking an oath may, in lieu thereof, affirm. Any person who shall affirm falsely shall be punished as for the making of a false oath.**

Who may Administer Oaths.

The language of the above section is comprehensive enough to include almost any domestic officer; still, it has been held that a creditor must not verify his proof of debt before his own attorney, though the latter be a notary public. In re Nebe,

11 N. B. R. 289, Fed. Cas. No. 10,073. And a proof of debt made by an officer of a corporation organized and existing under the laws of one state before a register in bankruptcy in another state, was rejected as insufficient. Ansonia Brass Co. v. Babbitt, 8 Hun (N. Y.) 157.

EVIDENCE.

§ 21. *a* **A court of bankruptcy may, upon application of any officer, bankrupt, or creditor, by order require any designated person, including the bankrupt, who is a competent witness under the laws of the state in which the proceedings are pending, to appear in court or before a referee or the judge of any state court, to be examined concerning the acts, conduct, or property of a bankrupt whose estate is in process of administration under this act.**

b **The right to take depositions in proceedings under this act shall be determined and enjoyed according to the United States laws now in force, or such as may be hereafter enacted relating to the taking of depositions, except as herein provided.**

c **Notice of the taking of depositions shall be filed with the referee in every case. When depositions are to be taken in opposition to the allowance of a claim notice shall also be served upon the claimant, and when in opposition to a discharge notice shall also be served upon the bankrupt.**

d **Certified copies of proceedings before a referee, or of papers, when issued by the clerk or referee, shall be admitted as evidence with like force and effect as certified copies of the records of district**

courts of the United States are now or may hereafter be admitted as evidence.

e **A certified copy of the order approving the bond of a trustee shall constitute conclusive evidence of the vesting in him of the title to the property of the bankrupt, and if recorded shall impart the same notice that a deed from the bankrupt to the trustee if recorded would have imparted had not bankruptcy proceedings intervened.**

f **A certified copy of an order confirming or setting aside a composition, or granting or setting aside a discharge, not revoked, shall be evidence of the jurisdiction of the court, the regularity of the proceedings, and of the fact that the order was made.**

g **A certified copy of an order confirming a composition shall constitute evidence of the revesting of the title of his property in the bankrupt, and if recorded shall impart the same notice that a deed from the trustee to the bankrupt if recorded would impart.**

Examination of Witnesses.

As to the examination of the bankrupt at the first meeting of creditors, and at other times as ordered by the court, see § 7, supra. The wife of the bankrupt, if a competent witness by the laws of the state, may be required to testify as to all facts or transactions to which she was either a party or a witness, but not to mere confessions or admissions of the husband in regard to his dealings with third persons; there is nothing in the act to destroy the privilege of such confidences. In re Gilbert, 1 Low. 340, Fed. Cas. No. 5,410. If she refuses to answer a proper question she may be punished for contempt. In re Woolford, 4 Ben. 9, Fed. Cas. No. 18,-

029. A witness summoned under this section is not a party to the proceeding and is not entitled to be attended or represented by counsel during his examination; neither is a creditor of the bankrupt a party to the proceeding, and therefore he is not entitled to interfere with it or be represented in it by counsel. In Re Comstock, 3 Sawy. 517, Fed. Cas. No. 3,080. In the matter of securing the attendance of a witness in bankruptcy proceedings, the court may exercise all the power conferred upon it in ordinary civil cases (Rev. St. § 876); hence the process may run into another district. In Re Woodward, 8 Ben. 112, Fed. Cas. No. 18,000.

REFERENCE OF CASES AFTER ADJUDICATION.

§ 22. *a* **After a person has been adjudged a bankrupt the judge may cause the trustee to proceed with the administration of the estate, or refer it (1) generally to the referee or specially with only limited authority to act in the premises or to consider and report upon specified issues; or (2) to any referee within the territorial jurisdiction of the court, if the convenience of parties in interest will be served thereby, or for cause, or if the bankrupt does not do business, reside, or have his domicile in the district.**

b **The judge may, at any time, for the convenience of parties or for cause, transfer a case from one referee to another.**

JURISDICTION OF UNITED STATES AND STATE COURTS.

§ 23. *a* **The United States circuit courts shall have jurisdiction of all controversies at law and in equity, as distinguished from proceedings in bankruptcy, between trustees as such and adverse claimants concerning the property acquired or claimed by the trustees, in the same manner and to the same extent only as though bankruptcy proceedings had not been instituted and such controversies had been between the bankrupts and such adverse claimants.**

b **Suits by the trustee shall only be brought or prosecuted in the courts where the bankrupt, whose estate is being administered by such trustee, might have brought or prosecuted them if proceedings in bankruptcy had not been instituted, unless by consent of the proposed defendant.**

c **The United States circuit courts shall have concurrent jurisdiction with the courts of bankruptcy, within their respective territorial limits, of the offenses enumerated in this act.**

Jurisdiction of Federal and State Courts.

Cases which involve the construction and application of a national bankruptcy law, such as those which arise between a trustee in bankruptcy and a person claiming an adverse interest touching any property or rights of property transferable to or vested in such trustee, are cases "arising under the laws of the United States," and therefore, under the prior acts of congress and independently of the foregoing provisions of the bankruptcy law, would be originally cognizable in the United States circuit courts, or removable thereto from the state courts, on the ground of involving a federal question, without regard to the citizenship of the parties. Burbank v. Bigelow, 92 U. S. 179; Claflin v. Houseman, 93 U. S. 130; Woolridge v. McKenna, 8 Fed. 650; Atkinson v. Purdy, Crabbe, 551, Fed. Cas. No. 616; Connor v. Scott, 4 Dill. 242, Fed. Cas. No. 3,119; Payson v. Dietz, 2 Dill. 504, Fed. Cas. No. 10,861; Wehl v. Wald, 17 Blatchf. 342, Fed. Cas. No. 17,356. But the act, it will be observed, provides that the federal circuit courts shall have jurisdiction of such controversies only "in the same manner and to the same extent as though bankruptcy proceedings had not been instituted and such controversies had been between the bankrupts and such adverse claimants." This is equivalent to declaring that those courts shall not take cognizance of such controversies unless the bankrupt and the adverse claimant are citizens of different states and the amount in controversy exceeds two thousand dollars. But the jurisdiction of the United States district courts, sitting as courts of bankruptcy, is superior to and exclusive of the jurisdiction of the state courts in all matters arising under the bankruptcy law. In re Barrow, 1 N. B. R. 481, Fed. Cas. No. 1,057.

The bankruptcy act of 1867 contained no provisions conferring or recognizing jurisdiction in the state courts to entertain controversies between the assignee in bankruptcy and adverse claimants. The foregoing provisions of the present act were probably suggested to its framers by the decided conflict of judicial opinion which existed in regard to the question whether state courts had jurisdiction of suits by trustees in bankruptcy for the recovery of assets or for other purposes. The difficulty arose from the construction of Rev. St. U. S. § 711, which gives to the federal courts exclusive jurisdiction "of all matters and proceedings in bankruptcy." The true principle was authoritatively stated by the supreme court of the United States in Eyster v. Gaff, 91 U. S. 521, where Mr. Justice Miller declared that: "The debtor of a bankrupt, or the man who contests the right to real or personal property with him, loses none of those rights by the bankruptcy of his adversary. The same courts remain open to him in such contests, and the statute has nót divested those courts of jurisdiction in such actions. If it has, for certain classes of actions, conferred a jurisdiction for the benefit of the assignee in the circuit and district courts of the United States, it is concurrent with, and does not divest, that of the state courts." And see Burbank v. Bigelow, 92 U. S. 179; Clark v. Ewing, 9 Biss. 440, 3 Fed. 83; In re Davis, 1 Sawy. 260, Fed. Cas. No. 3,620; Scott v. Kelly, 22 Wall. 57; In re Miller, 6 Biss. 30, Fed. Cas. No. 9,551. But the state courts have no jurisdiction, for fraud or any other cause, to interfere with or set aside a sale of the bankrupt's property by the trustee. Akins v. Stradley, 51 Iowa, 414, 1 N. W. 609. But if a trustee voluntarily submits himself to the jurisdiction of the state court, and that court renders a judgment against him, it is then too late for him to allege that the federal courts have exclusive jurisdiction in bankruptcy. Scott v. Kelly, 22 Wall. 57.

Concurrent Jurisdiction.

Under the act of 1867, as already stated, there was considerable conflict of opinion as to whether the state courts had concurrent jurisdiction with the federal tribunals of actions brought by trustees in bankruptcy for the recovery of assets of the estate. The question was answered in the affirmative in the following cases: Boone v. Hall, 7 Bush, 66; Mann v. Flower, 25 Minn. 500; Wooldbridge v. Rickert, 33 La. Ann. 234; Barton v. Geiler, 3 Lea, 296; McLean v. St. John, 10 Ill. App. 367; Isett v. Stuart, 80 Ill. 404; Peiper v. Harmer, 8 Phila. 100; Clark v. Ewing, 3 Fed. 83; Jordan v. Downey, 40 Md. 401; Cogdell v. Exum, 69 N. C. 464; Lathrop v. Drake, 91 U. S. 516; Kidder v. Horrobin, 72 N. Y. 159; and in the negative in Sherwood v. Burns, 58 Ind. 502; Seavey v. Maples, 94 Ind. 205, and some others. But while Rev. St.

U. S. § 711, does indeed confer upon the federal courts exclusive jurisdiction of "all matters and proceedings in bankruptcy," yet the true construction of that section is undoubtedly the one which confines this exclusive jurisdiction to proceedings which are essentially peculiar to the bankruptcy law and to actions which could not be maintained by any person independently of that law. In entertaining jurisdiction of the trustee's suit to recover assets, the state court is not proceeding under the bankruptcy act, but simply recognizes that act as the source of the trustee's title, in the same manner as it would if he derived his title from a deed or contract. These views were suggested in Jordan v. Downey, 40 Md. 401. And see, to the same effect, Eyster v. Gaff, 91 U. S. 521; Burbank v. Bigelow, 92 U. S. 179. But when the object of the trustee's action is to set aside a conveyance made by the bankrupt in fraud of the act, or by way of illegal preference, it has been held that the state court has no jurisdiction, because (1) such a suit can be maintained only under the bankruptcy law, and (2) a court of equity will not entertain a bill unless it has complete control over all the matters in controversy, directly or by coercion of the parties, and this does not exist in the case of the trustee in bankruptcy. Voorhies v. Frisbie, 25 Mich. 476; Brigham v. Claflin, 31 Wis. 607. A contrary view, however, prevails in some of the states (Otis v. Hadley, 112 Mass. 100; Goodrich v. Wilson, 119 Mass. 429; Rison v. Powell, 28 Ark. 427) and is clearly sanctioned by the decision of the United States supreme court in McKenna v. Simpson, 129 U. S. 507, 9 Sup. Ct. 365. A state court has no jurisdiction of a suit to enjoin the collection of assets by a trustee in bankruptcy. Southern v. Fisher, 6 S. C. 345. The jurisdiction of all matters in bankruptcy vested in the federal courts is not exclusive of that of the state courts to entertain an action for the abatement of a liquor nuisance on property belonging to the bankrupt's estate, that being a matter of police regulation, which does not interfere with the bankruptcy jurisdiction of the federal courts. Radford v. Thornell, 81 Iowa, 709, 45 N. W. 890. That mortgaged property is subject to be administered in bankruptcy will not entitle the mortgagor to resist the administration of it by foreclosure and sale under proceedings in the appropriate court of the state. Broach v. Powell, 79 Ga. 79, 3 S. E. 763.

Actions Against Trustees.

A purchase of goods on credit by one in insolvent circumstances, with the intention to use their proceeds in paying other creditors, and with no intention of paying for them, is fraudulent, and if the vendor can identify the goods, and acts within a reasonable time, he can recover them from the trustee in bankruptcy of the vendee. Donaldson v. Farwell, 5 Biss. 451, Fed. Cas. No. 3,983. So, the principal of a bankrupt factor may recover from the trustee any of the goods remaining unsold, or any proceeds of the sale of such goods which the trustee himself has received, or which remain specifically distinguishable from the mass of the bankrupt's property. Nutter v. Wheeler, 2 Low. 346, Fed. Cas. No. 10,384. But the estate of the bankrupt is not answerable for the tortious acts of the trustee. Adams v. Meyers, 1 Sawy. 306, Fed. Cas. No. 62. But an action will lie in a state court against a trustee in bankruptcy, to recover the amount of a dividend declared and due to a creditor of the estate, which the trustee has fraudulently withheld and converted to his own use. Berford v. Barnes, 45 Hun, 253. It has been held that the assignee of a bankrupt cannot, either voluntarily or by service of process, become a party to a suit in a state court to enforce a lien against the bankrupt's lands, except by express authority from the bankruptcy court, as that court, under the statute, has exclusive jurisdiction over the entire estate. Price v. Price, 4 Hughes, 438, 48 Fed. 823.

Conflicting Jurisdiction of Federal and State Courts.

It is a well-settled general rule that, when property is seized and held under mesne or final process of either a state court or a court of the United States, it is in the custody of the law and within the exclusive jurisdiction of the court from which the process has issued, for the purposes of the writ, and the possession of the officer having it in custody cannot be disturbed by another court of co-ordinate jurisdiction, or its officers, by attachment, levy of execution, replevin, or otherwise; and also that, as between a federal and a state court, when the one court has appointed a receiver of property and he has taken possession, the other court will not interfere with his custody and control of the property, by the appointment of another receiver or otherwise. Wallace v. McConnell, 13 Pet. 136; Taylor v. Carryl, 20 How. 583; Covell v. Heyman, 111 U. S. 176, 4 Sup. Ct. 355; Peale v. Phipps, 14 How. 368; Porter v. Sabin, 149 U. S. 473, 13 Sup. Ct. 1008; Shields v. Coleman, 157 U. S. 168, 15 Sup. Ct. 570. But difficulty arises in the application of these rules when the contest for the possession of property is between an assignee under the federal bankruptcy law and a receiver or other officer of a state court. Several cases are found in the reports of the inferior federal courts wherein it is held that, although an insolvent corporation is in the hands of a receiver appointed by a state court, this will not deprive the national courts of jurisdiction in proceedings against the corporation under the bankruptcy law; for, it is said, any other construction would entirely defeat the operation of that law. In re Green Pond R. Co., 13 N. B. R. 118, Fed. Cas. No. 5,786; In re Safe Deposit & Sav. Inst., 7 N. B. R. 392, Fed. Cas. No. 12,211; In re Washington Marine Ins. Co., 2 Ben. 292, Fed. Cas. No. 17,246; In re Merchants' Ins. Co., 3 Biss. 162, Fed. Cas. No. 9,441; In re National Life Ins. Co., 6 Biss. 25, Fed. Cas. No. 10,046. And in another case, it was ruled that proceedings in bankruptcy supersede a creditors' bill in a state court; and that a receiver appointed by the state court may be compelled to deliver the property over to the assignee in bankruptcy, subject to all the rights which the creditors whom he specifically represents have obtained, and to all the priorities which they have secured by their diligence. In re Whipple, 6 Biss. 516, Fed. Cas. No. 17,512. But this view is contradicted by a considerable body of authorities. See Goodrich v. Remington, 6 Blatchf. 515, Fed. Cas. No. 5,546; In re Clark, 4 Ben. 88, Fed. Cas. No. 2,798; Sedgwick v. Menck, 6 Blatchf. 156, Fed. Cas. No. 12,616. In another case, property was forcibly taken by the marshal, under a warrant issued in bankruptcy proceedings, from the possession of a receiver appointed by a state court in proceedings supplementary to execution against the bankrupt, and was by the marshal handed over to the assignee when appointed. The assignee applied for an order to sell the property. But it was held that the court would not summarily order a sale of property so taken, against the protest of the receiver; the title of the assignee to the property must be enforced by a plenary suit. In re Hulst, 7 Ben. 17, Fed. Cas. No. 6,863. In the case of Alden v. Boston, H. & E. R. Co., 5 N. B. R. 230, Fed. Cas. No. 152, it was said that the federal court in bankruptcy will not interfere with the possession of receivers appointed by the state courts to take charge of the property of a railroad, until their title is impeached for some cause for which it is impeachable under the bankruptcy act; nor is it for the bankruptcy court, before such title is thus impeached, to interfere with the management or control of such railroad or other property by the state court or its receivers. So, again, in Davis v. Railroad Co., 1 Woods, 661, Fed. Cas. No. 3,648, it is ruled that a receiver in possession of mortgaged premises under order of a state court of chancery, in proceedings for foreclosure, prior to the commencement of proceedings in bankruptcy, cannot be dispossessed by order of the federal court in the bankruptcy proceedings. Such possession is a lawful one under a specific and vested lien, and can only be interfered with by the assignee in bankruptcy by payment and redemption of the mortgage. An assignee in bankruptcy cannot maintain an action in a federal court to recover property of the bankrupt from the possession of a state sheriff, who has taken it upon attachment or other process duly issued to him out of a state court before the proceedings in bankruptcy were commenced. Johnson v. Bishop, Woolw. 324, Fed. Cas. No. 7,373; Townsend v. Leonard, 3 Dill. 370, Fed. Cas. No. 14,-117. And, on similar principles, where one of two partners has died, and, under the statute of the state, the partnership property is placed in the hands of the executor of the deceased partner to be administered, the bankruptcy court will not, on a petition against the surviving partner, take the estate out of the hands of such executor. In re Daggett, 8 N. B. R. 287, Fed. Cas. No. 3,535. Where petitions for adjudication are filed in two or more district courts, each having jurisdiction, the court in which the petition is first filed ought to be accorded exclusive jurisdiction over the case. In re Boston, H. & E. R. Co., 9 Blatchf. 409, Fed. Cas. No. 1,678.

JURISDICTION OF APPELLATE COURTS.

§ 24. *a* The supreme court of the United States, the circuit courts of appeals of the United States, and the supreme courts of the territories, in vacation in chambers and during their respective terms, as now or as they may be hereafter held, are hereby invested with appellate jurisdiction of controversies arising in bankruptcy proceedings from the courts of bankruptcy from which they have appellate jurisdiction in other cases. The supreme court of the United States shall exercise a like jurisdiction from courts of bankruptcy not within any organized circuit of the United States and from the supreme court of the District of Columbia.

b The several circuit courts of appeal shall have jurisdiction in equity, either interlocutory or final, to superintend and revise in matter of law the proceedings of the several inferior courts of bankruptcy within their jurisdiction. Such power shall be exercised on due notice and petition by any party aggrieved.

APPEALS AND WRITS OF ERROR.

§ 25. *a* That appeals, as in equity cases, may be taken in bankruptcy proceedings from the courts of bankruptcy to the circuit court of appeals of the United States, and to the supreme court of the territories, in the following cases, to wit, (1) from a judgment adjudging or refusing to adjudge the defendant a bankrupt; (2) from a judgment granting or denying a discharge; and (3) from a judgment allowing or rejecting a debt or claim of five hundred dollars or over. Such appeal shall be taken within ten days after the judgment appealed from has been rendered, and may be heard and determined by the appellate court in term or vacation, as the case may be.

b From any final decision of a court of appeals, allowing or rejecting a claim under this act, an appeal may be had under such rules and within such time as may be prescribed by the supreme court of the United States, in the following cases and no other:

1. Where the amount in controversy exceeds the sum of two thousand dollars, and the question involved is one which might have been taken on appeal or writ of error from the highest court of a state to the supreme court of the United States; or

2. Where some justice of the supreme court of the United States shall certify that in his opinion the determination of the question or questions involved in the allowance or rejection of such claim is essential to a uniform construction of this act throughout the United States.

c Trustees shall not be required to give bond when they take appeals or sue out writs of error.

d Controversies may be certified to the supreme court of the United States from other courts of the United States, and the former court may exercise jurisdiction thereof and issue writs of certiorari pursuant to the provisions of the United States laws now in force or such as may be hereafter enacted.

APPELLATE JURISDICTION.

Jurisdiction of Circuit Court of Appeals.

The language of the foregoing sections (which is substantially similar to that of the corresponding section of the act of 1867) evidently contemplates that an appeal should not be allowed from an interlocutory order or decree made in the progress of the bankruptcy proceedings, except only in the cases specified; apart from these, the decision, to be appealable, must be final as to all the matters within its scope. Clark v. Iselin, 9 Blatchf. 196, Fed. Cas. No. 2,824; Platt v. Stewart, 47 How. Prac. 206. The action of the district court in the exercise of its summary jurisdiction cannot be brought before the appellate court under this section. In re Clark, 9 Blatchf. 372, Fed. Cas. No. 2,801. And under the former statute, an appeal could not be taken for the purpose of obtaining a revision of the decision of the district court granting or refusing a discharge to the bankrupt. Coit v. Robinson, 19 Wall. 274; Ruddick v. Billings, Woolw. 330, Fed. Cas. No. 12,110. But this is one of the cases in which the present act specifically allows an appeal. An appeal will lie in a suit by a trustee in bankruptcy to set aside a claim, and its lien, as against the estate, (Barron v. Morris, 14 N. B. R. 371, Fed. Cas. No. 1,055) and from a decision allowing or rejecting a claim. Wiswall v. Campbell, 15 N. B. R. 421.

Upon Writ of Error.

When this form of procedure is employed, it is always the law decided that is subject to review, and not the facts. Ruddick v. Billings, Woolw. 330, Fed. Cas. No. 12,110. Hence, when the decision of the district court is based upon the report of a referee, the findings of fact made by him are conclusive in the appellate court, and only his conclusions of law can be questioned, and that only so far as they are challenged by exceptions filed in the district court. Sicard v. Buffalo, N. Y. & P. R. Co., 15 Blatchf. 525, Fed. Cas. No. 12,831. And a bill of exceptions is insufficient if it shows on its face that it could not have been taken at the trial. Strain v. Gourdin, 2 Woods, 380, Fed. Cas. No. 13,521. So, a writ of error will not lie when the case is tried by the district court without a jury. Blair v. Allen, 3 Dill. 101, Fed. Cas. No. 1,483. And a denial of a motion for a nonsuit is not reviewable on error. Miller v. Jones, 15 N. B. R. 150, Fed. Cas. No. 9,576.

Practice on Appeal.

In case of an appeal under this section, failure on the part of the appellant or plaintiff in error to give the required notice within the time limited is fatal. Wood v. Bailey, 21 Wall. 640; In re York, 4 N. B. R. 479, Fed. Cas. No. 18,139; In re Place, 4 N. B. R. 541, Fed. Cas. No. 11,200; Hawkins v. Hastings Bank, 1 Dill. 453, Fed. Cas. No. 6,245. But where the omission to take the appeal in time arose from a mistake in the selection of the remedy, the court suggested that perhaps the district court would grant a review of its decree, in order that a regular appeal might, if necessary, be taken. Stickney v. Wilt, 23 Wall. 150.

ARBITRATION OF CONTROVERSIES.

§ 26. *a* **The trustee may, pursuant to the direction of the court, submit to arbitration any controversy arising in the settlement of the estate.**

b **Three arbitrators shall be chosen by mutual consent, or one by the trustee, one by the other party to the controversy, and the third by the two so chosen, or if they fail to agree in five days after their appointment the court shall appoint the third arbitrator.**

c The written finding of the arbitrators, or a majority of them, as to the issues presented, may be filed in court and shall have like force and effect as the verdict of a jury.

COMPROMISES.

§ 27. *a* The trustee may, with the approval of the court, compromise any controversy arising in the administration of the estate upon such terms as he may deem for the best interests of the estate.

Compromises.

Under the general orders in bankruptcy promulgated pursuant to the law of 1867, a bankruptcy court could not authorize a compromise except upon testimony, and upon a petition clearly and distinctly setting forth "the subject-matter of the controversy and the reasons why the assignee thinks it proper, and most for the interest of the creditors, that it should be settled." In re Hoole, 3 Fed. 496. It was held that the court could not empower the assignee to "compound all doubtful claims with the consent and approbation of a committee of creditors." In re Dibblee, 3 Ben. 354, Fed. Cas. No. 3,885. A bankruptcy court has power to vacate an order authorizing the surrender of certain life insurance policies to a creditor, to whom they had been pledged, upon the release of the debt which they had been given to secure, where such order was procured by a material misrepresentation of the facts, although the misrepresentations were not necessarily fraudulent, where the court would not have originally made such order if the real facts had been known. In re Hoole, 3 Fed. 496.

DESIGNATION OF NEWSPAPERS.

§ 28. *a* Courts of bankruptcy shall by order designate a newspaper published within their respective territorial districts, and in the county in which the bankrupt resides or the major part of his property is situated, in which notices required to be published by this act and orders which the court may direct to be published shall be inserted. Any court may in a particular case, for the convenience of parties in interest, designate some additional newspaper in which notices and orders in such case shall be published.

OFFENSES.

§ 29. *a* A person shall be punished, by imprisonment for a period not to exceed five years, upon conviction of the offense of having knowingly and fraudulently appropriated to his own use, embezzled, spent, or unlawfully transferred any property or secreted or destroyed any document belonging to a bankrupt estate which came into his charge as trustee.

b A person shall be punished, by imprisonment for a period not to exceed two years, upon conviction of the offense of having knowingly and fraudulently (1) concealed while a bankrupt, or after his discharge, from his trustee any of the property belonging to his estate in bankruptcy; or (2) made a false oath or account in, or in relation to, any proceeding in bankruptcy; (3) presented under oath any false claim for proof against the estate of a bankrupt, or used any such claim in composition

personally or by agent, proxy, or attorney, or as agent, proxy, or attorney; or (4) received any material amount of property from a bankrupt after the filing of the petition, with intent to defeat this act; or (5) extorted or attempted to extort any money or property from any person as a consideration for acting or forbearing to act in bankruptcy proceedings.

c **A person shall be punished by fine, not to exceed five hundred dollars, and forfeit his office, and the same shall thereupon become vacant, upon conviction of the offense of having knowingly (1) acted as a referee in a case in which he is directly or indirectly interested; or (2) purchased, while a referee, directly or indirectly, any property of the estate in bankruptcy of which he is referee; or (3) refused, while a referee or trustee, to permit a reasonable opportunity for the inspection of the accounts relating to the affairs of, and the papers and records of, estates in his charge by parties in interest when directed by the court so to do.**

d **A person shall not be prosecuted for any offense arising under this act unless the indictment is found or the information is filed in court within one year after the commission of the offense.**

Crimes and Criminal Procedure.

A bankrupt who wilfully and fraudulently omits some of his assets from his inventory or schedule, contrary to the provisions of the statute, may be prosecuted by information. The offense is not an infamous crime, within the meaning of that term at common law and as used in the fifth amendment to the constitution. U. S. v. Block, 15 N. B. R. 325, Fed. Cas. No. 14,609. It has been held that bankrupts are not competent witnesses in proceedings against them under the criminal clauses of the act. U. S. v. Black, 12 N. B. R. 340, Fed. Cas. No. 14,602. But on the other hand, it has been declared (in a criminal case founded on a different statute) that the laws of the United States permit a person charged with crime or misdemeanor to be a witness in his own behalf, and such weight is to be given to his testimony as, under all the circumstances, it is fairly entitled to. U. S. v. Houghton, 14 Fed. 544.

It is provided by Rev. St. U. S. § 5440, that "if two or more persons conspire to commit any offense against the United States in any manner or for any purpose * * * all the parties to such conspiracy shall be liable to a penalty." Under this section, it has been held that persons may be indicted for conspiring with the bankrupt to commit the acts made criminal by the bankruptcy law, although no one but the bankrupt himself is mentioned in that connection. U. S. v. Bayer, 4 Dill. 407, Fed. Cas. No. 14,547.

Crimes After Adjudication.

Where a bankrupt omitted to state in his schedule the amount of money in the hands of a receiver appointed by a state court in a suit between him and his co-partner in relation to partnership property, but stated that the partnership assets would no more than pay the expenses of their litigation, and that he was not able to state their exact amount, it was held that the omission was no ground for refusing a discharge, and that an affidavit to the truth of the schedule was not prima facie perjury. In re Shoemaker, 4 Biss. 245, Fed. Cas. No. 12,799. Where an indictment under the bankrupt law for wilful and fraudulent concealment of his goods by a bankrupt alleged such concealment some months after the adjudication, "all then and there the property" of him the said bankrupt, it was held, that the failure to allege specifically that the property concealed was the property of the bankrupt, at the time of the adjudication in bankruptcy, was a formal defect. U. S. v. Jackson, 2 Fed. 502.

RULES, FORMS, AND ORDERS.

§ 30. *a* **All necessary rules, forms, and orders as to procedure and for carrying this act into force and effect shall be prescribed, and may be amended from time to time, by the supreme court of the United States.**

COMPUTATION OF TIME.

§ 31. *a* **Whenever time is enumerated by days in this act, or in any proceeding in bankruptcy, the number of days shall be computed by excluding the first and including the last, unless the last fall on a Sunday or holiday, in which event the day last included shall be the next day thereafter which is not a Sunday or a legal holiday.**

Computation of Time.

Unless Sunday is especially excepted in the statute, it is to be counted; and it has been held that the fair and unavoidable inference from this section is that when Sunday is not the last day it is not to be excluded. In re York, 4 N. B. R. 479, Fed. Cas. No. 18,139. Although the filing of the petition is the commencement of the bankruptcy proceedings, yet they are not to be deemed commenced until the petition is actually filed, although it was previously made, signed, and verified. Wells v. Brackett, 30 Me. 61. And it is not the filing of every petition that is deemed the commencement of proceedings, but the filing of a petition upon which an order of adjudication may be made by the court. In re Rogers, 10 N. B. R. 444, Fed. Cas. No. 12,003.

TRANSFER OF CASES.

§ 32. *a* In the event petitions are filed against the same person, or against different members of a partnership, in different courts of bankruptcy each of which has jurisdiction, the cases shall be transferred, by order of the courts relinquishing jurisdiction, to and be consolidated by the one of such courts which can proceed with the same for the greatest convenience of parties in interest.

CHAPTER V.

OFFICERS, THEIR DUTIES AND COMPENSATION.

CREATION OF TWO OFFICES.

§ 33. *a* The offices of referee and trustee are hereby created.

APPOINTMENT, REMOVAL, AND DISTRICTS OF REFEREES.

§ 34. *a* Courts of bankruptcy shall, within the territorial limits of which they respectively have jurisdiction, (1) appoint referees, each for a term of two years, and may, in their discretion, remove them because their services are not needed or for other cause; and (2) designate, and from time to time change, the limits of the districts of referees, so that each county, where the services of a referee are needed, may constitute at least one district.

QUALIFICATIONS OF REFEREES.

§ 35. *a* Individuals shall not be eligible to appointment as referees unless they are respectively (1) competent to perform the duties of that office; (2) not holding any office of profit or emolument under the laws of the United States or of any state other than commissioners of deeds, justices of the peace, masters in chancery, or notaries public; (3) not related by consanguinity or affinity, within the third degree as determined by the common law, to any of the judges of the courts of bankruptcy

or circuit courts of the United States, or of the justices or judges of the appellate courts of the districts wherein they may be appointed; and (4) residents of, or have their offices in, the territorial districts for which they are to be appointed.

Qualifications of Referees.

The bankruptcy act of 1867 provided that no person should be eligible to the office of register in bankruptcy unless he was an attorney or counselor at law. In explanation of the phrase "office of profit or emolument," we append certain definitions and decisions which may be found useful. "Emolument" is defined by Webster as "the profit arising from office or employment; that which is received as a compensation for services, or which is annexed to the possession of an office as salary, fees, and perquisites; advantage; gain, public or private." This definition is adopted in Apple v. Crawford Co., 105 Pa. St. 300. The office of postmaster is an office both of profit and trust under the authority of congress. McGregor v. Balch, 14 Vt. 434. A member of the state legislature holds an office of profit as well as of honor. State v. Valle, 41 Mo. 29. The offices of county recorder and county commissioner are lucrative offices within the meaning of the state constitution. Dailey v. State, 8 Blackf. 329. So is the office of inspector of customs. Crawford v. Dunbar, 52 Cal. 36. And so is the federal office of surveyor general. People v. Whitman, 10 Cal. 38.

OATHS OF OFFICE OF REFEREES.

§ 36. *a* **Referees shall take the same oath of office as that prescribed for judges of the United States courts.**

NUMBER OF REFEREES.

§ 37. *a* Such number of referees shall be appointed as may be necessary to assist in expeditiously transacting the bankruptcy business pending in the various courts of bankruptcy.

JURISDICTION OF REFEREES.

§ 38. *a* Referees respectively are hereby invested, subject always to a review by the judge, within the limits of their districts as established from time to time, with jurisdiction to (1) consider all petitions referred to them by the clerks and make the adjudications or dismiss the petitions; (2) exercise the powers vested in courts of bankruptcy for the administering of oaths to and the examination of persons as witnesses and for requiring the production of documents in proceedings before them, except the power of commitment; (3) exercise the powers of the judge for the taking possession and releasing of the property of the bankrupt in the event of the issuance by the clerk of a certificate showing the absence of a judge from the judicial district, or the division of the district, or his sickness, or inability to act; (4) perform such part of the duties, except as to questions arising out of the applications of bankrupts for compositions or discharges, as are by this act conferred on courts of bankruptcy and as shall be prescribed by rules or orders of the courts of bankruptcy of their respective districts, except as herein otherwise provided; and (5) upon the application of the trustee during the examination of the bankrupts, or other proceedings, author-

ize the employment of stenographers at the expense of the estates at a compensation not to exceed ten cents per folio for reporting and transcribing the proceedings.

Powers of Referees.

The proceedings before a referee in bankruptcy are to be conducted by him with the exercise of proper legal discretion, and, subject to that rule, are entirely within his control. In re Hyman, 2 N. B. R. 333, Fed. Cas. No. 6,984. The validity of an order made by a register in bankruptcy, except such as the judge alone has power to make, cannot be collaterally questioned in the absence of any showing that it was disapproved by the court. Geisreiter v. Sevier, 33 Ark. 522. On the adjudication of bankruptcy, the register is authorized and required to receive the surrender of the bankrupt's estate, and to keep the property safely until it can be turned over to the trustee. In re Hasbrouck, 1 Ben. 402, Fed. Cas. No. 6,189. In a proper case the register may appoint a watchman to take charge of the property. In re Bogert, 2 N. B. R. 585, Fed. Cas. No. 1,599. The register has no power, on the mere application of creditors, to issue a summons for the examination of a trustee, or for the production by him of the books and papers mentioned in the summons, where such trustee has been duly appointed by the creditors (pursuant to section 43 of the act of 1867) to settle up the estate. In re Hicks, 2 Fed. 851.

DUTIES OF REFEREES.

§ 39. *a* Referees shall (1) declare dividends and prepare and deliver to trustees dividend sheets showing the dividends declared and to whom payable; (2) examine all schedules of property and lists of creditors filed by bankrupts and cause such as are incomplete or defective to be amended; (3) furnish such information concerning the estates in process of administration before them as may be requested by the parties in interest; (4) give notices to creditors as herein provided; (5) make up records embodying the evidence, or the substance thereof, as agreed upon by the parties in all contested matters arising before them, whenever requested to do so by either of the parties thereto, together with their findings therein, and transmit them to the judges; (6) prepare and file the schedules of property and lists of creditors required to be filed by the bankrupts, or cause the same to be done, when the bankrupts fail, refuse, or neglect to do so; (7) safely keep, perfect, and transmit to the clerks the records, herein required to be kept by them, when the cases are concluded; (8) transmit to the clerks such papers as may be on file before them whenever the same are needed in any proceedings in courts, and in like manner secure the return of such papers after they have been used, or, if it be impracticable to transmit the original papers, transmit certified copies thereof by mail; (9) upon application of any party in interest, preserve the evidence taken or the substance thereof as agreed upon by the parties before them when a stenographer is not in attendance; and (10) whenever their respective offices are in the same cities or towns where the courts of bankruptcy convene, call upon and receive from the clerks all papers filed in courts of bankruptcy which have been referred to them.

b Referees shall not (1) act in cases in which they are directly or indirectly interested; (2) practice as attorneys and counselors at law in any bankruptcy proceedings; or (3) purchase, directly or indirectly, any property of an estate in bankruptcy.

COMPENSATION OF REFEREES.

§ 40. *a* Referees shall receive as full compensation for their services, payable after they are rendered, a fee of ten dollars deposited with the clerk at the time the petition is filed in each case, except when a fee is not required from a voluntary bankrupt, and from estates which have been administered before them one per centum commissions on sums to be paid as dividends and commissions, or one-half of one per centum on the amount to be paid to creditors upon the confirmation of a composition.

b Whenever a case is transferred from one referee to another the judge shall determine the proportion in which the fee and commissions therefor shall be divided between the referees.

c In the event of the reference of a case being revoked before it is concluded, and when the case is specially referred, the judge shall determine what part of the fee and commissions shall be paid to the referee.

CONTEMPTS BEFORE REFEREES.

§ **41.** *a* A person shall not, in proceedings before a referee, (1) disobey or resist any lawful order, process, or writ; (2) misbehave during a hearing or so near the place thereof as to obstruct the same; (3) neglect to produce, after having been ordered to do so, any pertinent document; or (4) refuse to appear after having been subpœnaed, or, upon appearing, refuse to take the oath as a witness, or, after having taken the oath, refuse to be examined according to law: provided, that no person shall be required to attend as a witness before a referee at a place outside of the state of his residence, and more than one hundred miles from such place of residence, and only in case his lawful mileage and fee for one day's attendance shall be first paid or tendered to him.

b The referee shall certify the facts to the judge, if any person shall do any of the things forbidden in this section. The judge shall thereupon, in a summary manner, hear the evidence as to the acts complained of, and, if it is such as to warrant him in so doing, punish such person in the same manner and to the same extent as for a contempt committed before the court of bankruptcy, or commit such person upon the same conditions as if the doing of the forbidden act had occurred with reference to the process of, or in the presence of, the court.

RECORDS OF REFEREES.

§ 42. *a* The records of all proceedings in each case before a referee shall be kept as nearly as may be in the same manner as records are now kept in equity cases in circuit courts of the United States.

b A record of the proceedings in each case shall be kept in a separate book or books, and shall, together with the papers on file, constitute the records of the case.

c The book or books containing a record of the proceedings shall, when the case is concluded before the referee, be certified to by him, and, together with such papers as are on file before him, be transmitted to the court of bankruptcy and shall there remain as a part of the records of the court.

REFEREE'S ABSENCE OR DISABILITY.

§ 43. *a* Whenever the office of a referee is vacant, or its occupant is absent or disqualified to act, the judge may act, or may appoint another referee, or another referee holding an appointment under the same court may, by order of the judge, temporarily fill the vacancy.

APPOINTMENT OF TRUSTEES.

§ 44. *a* **The creditors of a bankrupt estate shall, at their first meeting after the adjudication or after a vacancy has occurred in the office of trustee, or after an estate has been reopened, or after a composition has been set aside or a discharge revoked, or if there is a vacancy in the office of trustee, appoint one trustee or three trustees of such estate. If the creditors do not appoint a trustee or trustees as herein provided, the court shall do so.**

Appointment of Trustee.

It is provided by the present act that the creditors, at their first meeting, are to appoint either *one* or *three* trustees for the estate. And the 47th section directs that when the number of trustees shall be three, "the concurrence of two shall be necessary to the validity of any act." In regard to the qualifications of persons offering to vote at a meeting of creditors, and the majority necessary to the settlement of any matter before them, the directions of the statute are to be found in section 56. It seems that creditors may vote in person or by proxy. But the cases hold that an agent, or attorney at law, cannot vote without showing a power of attorney. In re Purvis, 1 N. B. R. 163, Fed. Cas. No. 11,476. Corporations may vote by their officers or by any person specially and duly authorized. Ex parte Bank of England, 1 Swanst. 10. And one partner may prove the claim and cast the vote of his firm, but the firm's vote will only count as one vote. In re Purvis, 1 N. B. R. 163, Fed. Cas. No. 11,476; Ex parte Mitchell, 14 Ves. 597. A preferred creditor may surrender his preference (whereby he becomes entitled to prove his claim) and vote for trustee. In re Saunders, 13 N. B. R. 164, Fed. Cas. No. 12,371. Where only a single creditor appears at the first meeting and proves his debt, the right to choose a trustee belongs to him. In re Haynes, 2 N. B. R. 227, Fed. Cas. No. 6,269. In the case of the bankruptcy of a co-partnership, it is provided by section 5 of the present act that the trustee or trustees shall be chosen by the creditors of the firm.

Conduct of the Election.

"No particular mode or manner of voting is prescribed by the act. It may be assumed, therefore, that any mode or manner of voting by which the choice of each creditor entitled to vote is clearly expressed is sufficient. It may, no doubt, be taken by ballot or viva voce. It may be taken by calling the name of each creditor, or by calling upon the person or persons representing creditors by power of attorney to name the choice of the creditor or creditors represented by him;" Longyear, J., in Re Lake Superior Ship Canal, Railroad & Iron Co., 7 N. B. R. 387, Fed. Cas. No. 7,997. There is no such thing known to the law as an informal vote; an expression of opinion by the creditors as to their preference is a vote. In re Pearson, 2 N. B. R. 477, Fed. Cas. No. 10,878. Where one creditor objects to the votes of certain other creditors, on the ground that such votes have been influenced by the bankrupt and are collusive and fraudulent, the referee has no power to entertain such objections. In re Noble, 3 Ben. 332, Fed. Cas. No. 10,282.

Who is Eligible as Trustee.

The attorney for one of the petitioning creditors may be chosen trustee of the bankrupt's estate. In re Barrett, 2 Hughes, 444, Fed. Cas. No. 1,043. So may also a person who has been counsel for the bankrupt, it being understood that he cannot occupy the position of counsel and trustee at the same time. In re Clairmont, 1 N. B. R. 276, Fed. Cas. No. 2,781. But the election of a near relative of the bankrupt as trustee is not proper. In re Zinn, 4 N. B. R. 370,

Fed. Cas. No. 18,216; In re Powell, 2 N. B. R. 45, Fed. Cas. No. 11,354. The trustee must reside in the district in which the proceedings are being carried on. In re Havens, 1 N. B. R. 485, Fed. Cas. No. 6,231.

Confirmation of Trustee.

Under the act of 1867 the choice of an assignee by the creditors was made subject to the approval and confirmation of the judge. No such provision is explicitly contained in the present statute. But as it is yet uncertain whether the bankruptcy courts may not feel justified in revising the creditors' action in this respect, we append some of the decisions made under the former law. The proper rule for the exercise of the judge's discretion in this matter is thus stated by Lowell, J.; "The person whom the majority in number and value of the creditors choose to be the assignee ought to be confirmed, unless disqualified by residence out of the district, by personal character, or by some interest adverse to that of the body of creditors." In re Clairmont, 1 Low. 230, Fed. Cas. No. 2,781. But when the register is satisfied that any reasons exist why an assignee elected or appointed should not be approved by the judge, it is his duty to state such reasons fully in submitting to the judge the question of approval. In re Bliss, 1 Ben. 407, Fed. Cas. No. 1,543. The bankrupt has a locus standi in court to object to the confirmation of trustees of his estate chosen at the creditors' meeting. In re McGlynn, 2 Low. 127, Fed. Cas. No. 8,804.

Appointment of Trustee by the Court.

Where a majority of resident creditors who had been represented in a first creditors' meeting, and who had proved their claims by attorney, had voted for one person as trustee, and a majority of creditors who had proved in person had voted for another person as trustee, it was held that there was no election, and the court was at liberty to appoint a trustee. In re Portsmouth Sav. Fund Soc., 2 Hughes, 238, Fed. Cas. No. 11,297. Where no creditor who has proved his debt attends at the place and time specified in the notice for the first meeting of creditors, the court is to appoint a trustee or trustees. In re Cogswell, 1 Ben. 388, Fed. Cas. No. 2,959. Where, after the death of a trustee in bankruptcy, evidence of the existence of unadministered assets is produced, the court will appoint a new trustee, notwithstanding that his right to recover such assets may be doubtful, depending upon several disputed questions of law and fact. A solution of such questions will not be attempted on the motion for appointment of a trustee. Without that, there is sufficient ground to justify the appointment. In re Mahoney, 5 Fed. 518.

QUALIFICATIONS OF TRUSTEES.

§ 45. *a* **Trustees may be (1) individuals who are respectively competent to perform the duties of that office, and reside or have an office in the judicial district within which they are appointed, or (2) corporations authorized by their charters or by law to act in such capacity and having an office in the judicial district within which they are appointed.**

DEATH OR REMOVAL OF TRUSTEES.

§ 46. *a* **The death or removal of a trustee shall not abate any suit or proceeding which he is prosecuting or defending at the time of his death or removal, but the same may be proceeded with or defended by his joint trustee or successor in the same manner as though the same had been commenced or was being defended by such joint trustee alone or by such successor.**

Death of Trustee.

A cause of action against a trustee in bankruptcy, for wrongfully paying the assets in his hands to other creditors of the bankrupt than the plaintiff, in disregard of the latter's right of priority, does not abate by the death of the trustee. U. S. v. Dewey, 39 Fed. 251.

Removal of Trustees.

The second section of the act, regulating the jurisdiction of the courts of bankruptcy, provides that they may remove trustees "for cause," but only after notice to the trustee proposed to be removed and upon a hearing, and only in case complaint is made in that behalf by the creditors.

When a trustee has failed in properly informing creditors in regard to their rights and the value of the assets, and the information has been suppressed in the interest of one class of creditors, it is the duty of the court to remove him. Ex parte Perkins, 5 Biss. 254, Fed. Cas. No. 10,982. A trustee of a bankrupt estate petitioned for an order allowing him to sell certain securities belonging to the estate for the settlement of claims against it. A referee being appointed to take proofs and report, he recommended that the proposed sale and settlement be made. The trustee neglected to obtain an order of confirmation, and allowed the securities to be taken by creditors of the estate, involving a long litigation and delay. It was held that there was sufficient cause for removing the trustee. In re Prouty, 24 Fed. 554. The removal of a trustee in bankruptcy by the district court for a "cause which in its judgment renders such removal necessary or expedient" (as expressed in the act of 1867), is not such a case or question as can be reviewed by the circuit court; it rests wholly in the discretion of the district court. In re Adler, 2 Woods, 571, Fed. Cas. No. 82. See In re Blodget, 5 N. B. R. 472, Fed. Cas. No. 1,552. The court, and not the referee, is the proper party to entertain a motion to remove a trustee. But it seems that a referee may have a rule issued on the trustee to show cause why he should not be removed. In re Price, 4 N. B. R. 406, Fed. Cas. No. 11,409; In re Stokes, 1 N. B. R. 489, Fed. Cas. No. 13,475.

DUTIES OF TRUSTEES.

§ 47. *a* **Trustees shall respectively (1) account for and pay over to the estates under their control all interest received by them upon property of such estates; (2) collect and reduce to money the property of the estates for which they are trustees, under the direction of the court, and close up the estate as expeditiously as is compatible with the best interests of the parties in interest; (3) deposit all money received by them in one of the designated depositories; (4) disburse money only by check or draft on the depositories in which it has been deposited; (5) furnish such information concerning the estates of which they are trustees and their administration as may be requested by parties in interest; (6) keep regular accounts showing all amounts received and from what sources and all**

amounts expended and on what accounts; (7) lay before the final meeting of the creditors detailed statements of the administration of the estates; (8) make final reports and file final accounts with the courts fifteen days before the days fixed for the final meetings of the creditors; (9) pay dividends within ten days after they are declared by the referees; (10) report to the courts, in writing, the condition of the estates and the amounts of money on hand, and such other details as may be required by the courts, within the first month after their appointment and every two months thereafter, unless otherwise ordered by the courts; and (11) set apart the bankrupt's exemptions and report the items and estimated value thereof to the court as soon as practicable after their appointment.

b **Whenever three trustees have been appointed for an estate, the concurrence of at least two of them shall be necessary to the validity of their every act concerning the administration of the estate.**

Suits by Trustees.

There are two limitations upon the right of a trustee in bankruptcy to bring suits; first, that the thing sought to be recovered shall be such as, when recovered, shall be assets of the estate; and second, that the action brought shall not be an action of tort for damages such as at common law is strictly personal and dies with the person. Trustees of Mut. Bldg. Fund & Dollar Sav. Bank v. Bossieux, 4 Hughes, 387, 3 Fed. 817. The trustee represents the rights of the creditors and each of them, as well as the bankrupt, and may therefore maintain or defend proceedings in regard to the bankrupt's estate, which, on grounds of public policy or otherwise, the latter would not be allowed to bring or defend. In re St. Helen Mill Co., 3 Sawy. 88, Fed. Cas. No. 12,222; In re Gurney, 7 Biss. 414, Fed. Cas. No. 5,873. The trustee in bankruptcy of a banking corporation, organized under the laws of a state where, by statute, the stockholders of such corporation are individually liable for its debts to the amount of the stock held by them respectively, cannot maintain a bill in equity to enforce such liability against the stockholders; for such liability is not in any sense a part of the assets of the bankrupt corporation. Dutcher v. Bank, 12 Blatchf. 435, Fed. Cas. No. 4,203.

Appeals and Injunctions.

The trustee may prosecute a writ of error to reverse a judgment or decree rendered against the bankrupt before the appointment of the trustee. Jenkins v. International Bank, 97 Ill. 568. But it seems that if the judgment is rendered before the adjudication, the appeal may be prosecuted either in the name of the bankrupt or of the trustee. O'Neil v. Dougherty, 46 Cal. 575. Where property in the possession of the bankrupt's debtor is claimed by a third person, the trustee may bring a bill in equity against the holder, the claimant, and the bankrupt, to obtain a determination of their respective rights, and to restrain the claimant from prosecuting an action in the state court for the recovery of the property. Wilkinson v. Barnard, 9 Ben. 249, Fed. Cas. No. 17,669. A gift of personalty by an insolvent husband to his wife, without any visible change of possession, does not raise such an adverse interest in the wife as to necessitate a plenary action by the trustee; he may recover possession of the property on summary petition. In re Pierce, 7 Biss. 426, Fed. Cas. No. 11,139.

Pleading and Practice in Actions by Trustees.

In suing for the recovery of assets, the trustee need not aver in his complaint the various steps in the bankruptcy proceedings; they are not ultimate but probative facts; the pleading is good if he alleges ownership in himself, for under such allegation he can prove the bankruptcy and his own appointment. Dambmann v. White, 48 Cal. 439. But if, in suing in trover, he undertakes to set out in detail the manner in which he claims to have become the owner of the property converted, by alleging the proceedings in bankruptcy, it is absolutely fatal to his declaration if he omits to aver the *adjudication*. Wright v. Johnson, 8 Blatchf. 150, Fed. Cas. No. 18,082. But it seems that if he alleges the filing of a voluntary petition by the debtor, and the appointment of the trustee and assignment to him, the adjudication will be understood by necessary implication. Lakin v. Bank, 13 Blatchf. 83, Fed. Cas. No. 7,999. An objection to a bill in equity in which the complainant describes himself as trustee in bankruptcy, to the effect that he is not legally such trustee, must be made by plea and cannot be taken on demurrer. Nicholas v. Murray, 5 Sawy. 320, Fed. Cas. No. 10,223.

To a bill filed by a trustee to set aside a conveyance of real and personal property by the bankrupt, as being a fraud upon creditors, the bankrupt is not a necessary party. Buffington v. Harvey, 95 U. S. 99; Harding v. Crosby, 17 Blatchf. 348, Fed. Cas. No. 6,050; Fry v. Street, 37 Ark. 39; per contra, Verselius v. Verselius, 9 Blatchf. 189, Fed. Cas. No. 16,925. Where two persons jointly purchase property in contravention of the bankrupt act, the recovery by the trustee may be against both for the full value of all the property, though they may have been interested in different proportions. Schulenburg v. Kabureck, 2 Dill. 132, Fed. Cas. No. 12,487.

Although actions in equity by trustees in bankruptcy are not required to be as formal and plenary as equity proceedings usually are, yet the trustee must pursue the appropriate remedies, and not resort to equity where the remedy is at law, nor seek an injunction where the proper course is to bring replevin. In re Oregon Iron Works, 4 Sawy. 169, Fed. Cas. No. 10,562. Where a transfer of property is held void under the bankrupt law as against the trustee, the transferee is to be regarded as holding the property in trust for the bankrupt's estate, and to be held to account in that capacity, and therefore a bill in equity is a proper mode of procedure for the trustee in bankruptcy when he seeks to recover the property. Schrenkeisen v. Miller, 9 Ben. 55, Fed. Cas. No. 12,480. But in another case it is held that such a suit is substantially an action of trover, and that the trustee must either allege a distinct and actual conversion by the creditor, or a demand and refusal to deliver the property, because the receipt of the property by the creditor is not tortious, nor does it amount per se to a conversion. Shuman v. Fleckenstein, 4 Sawy. 174, Fed. Cas. No. 12,826; but see Gaytes v. American, 5 Biss. 86, Fed. Cas. No. 5,286. A trustee in bankruptcy may maintain ejectment. Barstow v. Adams, 2 Day (Conn.) 70. Where there has been a voluntary general assignment for the benefit of creditors, before the adjudication in bankruptcy, the trustee must first take proper steps to disaffirm and avoid such assignment, before he can sustain a claim to money in the hands of a debtor of the bankrupt as against the assignee under that conveyance. Wehl v. Wald, 18 Blatchf. 163, 3 Fed. 93.

The trustee stands in no better position than the bankrupt in respect to assets, except in cases of fraud, preference, etc. When, therefore, the bankrupt would be estopped to deny that a particular chattel in his possession was the property of a third person, so will the trustee be estopped. Ex parte Rockford, R. I. & St. L. R. Co., 1 Low. 345, Fed. Cas. No. 11,978. The rule that one who purchases pendente lite is bound by the subsequent proceedings applies to a trustee in bankruptcy, and to the transfer effected by a bankruptcy proceeding. Kimberling v. Hartly, 1

McCrary, 136, 1 Fed. 571. Although a tenant cannot dispute his landlord's title, yet when the trustee in bankruptcy sues to recover real estate, the tenant of the bankrupt may dispute the assignment. Steadman v. Jones, 65 N. C. 388.

Liability of Trustee for Negligence of His Employes.

In the case of Cardot v. Barney, 63 N. Y. 281, it was held that a trustee in bankruptcy of an insolvent railroad corporation, who, by direction of the court, is operating the road in his official capacity, is not liable to an action for the negligence of an employé resulting in the death of a passenger, where it is not shown that he held himself out as a common carrier otherwise than in his capacity as an officer of the court, and where no personal negligence is imputable to him. But this case, if it decides anything more than that the trustee should not be held answerable in his individual capacity, is of doubtful authority. It is abundantly settled upon the authorities that a receiver in equity, who is operating a railroad in that capacity, is liable, in his official character, to an action for damages caused by the negligence of his own employés; that such an action cannot be brought, during the receivership, against the corporation itself; and that the liability is a liability of the receivership and to be enforced against the funds thereof. Cowderly v. Railroad Co., 93 U. S. 352; Little v. Dusenberry, 46 N. J. Law, 614; Newell v. Smith, 49 Vt. 255; Hicks v. Railroad Co., 62 Tex. 38; Blumenthal v. Brainerd, 38 Vt. 402; Meara v. Holbrook, 20 Ohio St. 137. And the analogy in this respect between trustees in bankruptcy and receivers in equity is so strong and so obvious on its face that the decisions last cited are quite as applicable to the one case as to the other.

Sales by Trustees.

The bankrupt law of 1867 conferred express authority upon assignees in bankruptcy to make sales of the real and personal estate, either on their own motion, in certain cases, or by order and direction of the court, and prescribed the manner and effect of such sales. Rev. St. §§ 5062–5065. In the absence of such provisions in the present act, the *power* of a trustee to sell the property of the estate must probably be derived from the clause requiring him to "collect and reduce to money the property of the estate."

Formalities of the Sale.

The power of the trustee to sell and convey the bankrupt's estate depends wholly upon statute, and a sale in any other manner than as therein prescribed would be a nullity. Wisner v. Brown, 50 Mich. 553, 15 N. W. 901. Under no circumstances can the bankrupt, after filing his petition and schedule, be justified in selling any part of his property without leave of the court. In Re Pryor, 4 Biss. 262, Fed. Cas. No. 11,457. But it is immaterial who may be the purchaser when the sale is properly conducted by the trustee; the bankrupt may himself become the purchaser, and he will take by such purchase all the interest which the trustee had to convey. Gates v. Fraser, 9 Ill. App. 624.

What Interests are not Divested.

A wife's right of dower is not barred by an assignment of the husband's estate under the national bankrupt law and a sale thereof by the trustee in bankruptcy by order of court. Porter v. Lazear, 109 U. S. 84, 3 Sup. Ct. 58, affirming Lazear v. Porter, 87 Pa. St. 513; Smith v. Smith, 5 Ves. 189; In re Angier, 10 Am. Law Reg. (N. S.) 190, Fed. Cas. No. 388; Kelso's Appeal, 102 Pa. St. 7. A sale by the trustee, whether under judicial order or not, does not divest the lien of the state for taxes, unless, in case of a sale ordered by the court, the revenue officer or other proper representative of the state is made a party to such order. Meeks v. Whatley, 48 Miss. 337.

Sale Free of Incumbrances.

As stated by Howe, J., in King v. Bowman, 24 La. An. 506, "an assignee in bankruptcy may sell, without petition to or order of the bankrupt court, any property of the bankrupt incumbered in any manner. But when he so sells, he sells subject to any and all lawful incumbrances, and can convey no better or higher interest than the bankrupt could have done." But the bankruptcy court has power to *order* a sale of incumbered property, belonging to the bankrupt, free of all incumbrances, and such a sale, if regularly made, will discharge all liens and pass an entirely free title to the purchaser. Ray v. Norseworthy, 23 Wall. 128; In re Kahley, 2 Biss. 383, Fed. Cas. No. 7,593. But in order to the regularity of the proceedings it is absolutely essential that the incumbrancer should be notified of the proposed sale, or should, in some other way, be given an opportunity to appear and show cause why his lien should not be discharged; failing this, the purchaser will take subject to the lien. Ray v. Norseworthy, 23 Wall. 128; Factors' & Traders' Ins. Co. v. Murphy, 111 U. S. 738, 4 Sup. Ct. 679; In re McGilton, 3 Biss. 144, Fed. Cas. No. 8,798. An order for such a sale may be made by the court in the exercise of its summary jurisdiction, if the order does not assume to provide for a determination as to the validity of the lien in a summary way and without the consent of the holder. In re Kirtland, 10 Blatchf. 515, Fed. Cas. No. 7,851. If the proceeds of the sale are insufficient to discharge the elder of two mortgages, the purchaser will hold the property free of all incumbrances arising from the junior mortgage. Houston v. City Bank, 6 How. 486. Where the property is sold free of incumbrances, the lien is transferred to the funds in court. In re Kahley, 2 Biss. 383, Fed. Cas. No. 7,593.

Strength of Title Conveyed.

The powers of a trustee in bankruptcy are in no sense judicial, and his acts bind only those whom he represents; in a sale of the bankrupt's estate he acts only for the creditors who prove their claims, and in such matters he can conclude the rights of no one else. Second Nat. Bank of Louisville v. National State Bank of New Jersey, 10 Bush, 367. The purchaser of a bankrupt's real estate at a sale thereof by the trustee will hold the title against a prior unrecorded deed of the bankrupt. Holbrook v. Dickenson, 56 Ill. 497. The purchaser of a *chose in action* from the trustee of a bankrupt estate may maintain an action upon it in the trustee's name. Rogers v. Stone Co., 134 Mass. 31.

Revision of Sale by the Court.

When a public sale of the real estate is made by the trustee under order of court, and the property is struck off to the highest bidder, such sale is subject to the approval of the court, which has a discretion to refuse to confirm it for mere inadequacy of price; it is not necessary that there should be fraud or such gross inadequacy of price as to be evidence of fraud. In re O'Fallon, 2 Dill. 548, Fed. Cas. No. 10,445. So a sale of the bankrupt's estate made to a solicitor of the trustee, retained generally in the bankruptcy, will be set aside as against public policy. Citizens' Bank v. Ober, 1 Woods, 80, Fed. Cas. No. 2,731. And see In re Troy Woolen Co., 8 Blatchf. 465, Fed. Cas. No. 14,201, for other circumstances which will discredit a trustee's sale. The bankruptcy court has power, by summary order, to set aside and order to be surrendered and cancelled deeds given by the official trustee without due authority, or improvidently or irregularly. In re Hyde, 19 Blatchf. 115, 6 Fed. 587. In general, the confirmation by the court of a trustee's sale of land relates back to the time of sale, so that the purchaser is entitled to the intermediate rents and profits as against the trustee; but this rule cannot hold in the face of a statute on the subject, and the opinion is intimated in Lathrop v. Nelson, 4 Dill. 194, Fed. Cas. No. 8,111, that it may yield to countervailing equities arising out of special circumstances.

Deposit of Cash.

A trustee in bankruptcy who disregards the express order of the court in depositing funds of the estate, is liable for the interest which the designated depository would have paid. In re Newcomb, 32 Fed. 826. And he is also liable, in the absence of a reasonable explanation or excuse, for legal interest on money collected by him and not deposited, where the same remains in his hands for a considerable period of time. In re Burt, 27 Fed. 548; In re Thorp, 4 N. Y. Leg. Obs. 337, Fed. Cas. No. 14,002; In re Newcomb, 32 Fed. 826.

Discharge of Trustee.

A step which in effect puts an end to the bankruptcy proceedings ought not to be taken without notice to the creditors. So, where a trustee sought to renounce his trust by making application for his discharge, based on his own affidavit alleging that no tangible assets have come into his hands, and that he has no information of any property belonging to the bankrupt, other than a chose in action in favor of the estate, *held*, that notice to creditors of such application, and the approval of the court or referee in charge of the case, was necessary. In re Savage, 12 Fed. 719.

Criminal Offenses by Trustees.

By reference to section 29 of the act, supra, it will be seen that "a person shall be punished, by imprisonment for a period not to exceed five years, upon conviction of the offense of having knowingly and fraudulently appropriated to his own use, embezzled, spent, or unlawfully transferred any property or secreted or destroyed any document belonging to a bankrupt estate which came into his charge as trustee." Moreover, if a trustee in bankruptcy refuses "to permit a reasonable opportunity for the inspection of the accounts relating to the affairs of, and the papers and records of, estates in his charge by parties in interest when directed by the court so to do," this will constitute an offense which is punishable by fine and by forfeiture of the office. See section 29, supra.

COMPENSATION OF TRUSTEES.

§ 48. *a* **Trustees shall receive, as full compensation for their services, payable after they are rendered, a fee of five dollars deposited with the clerk at the time the petition is filed in each case, except when a fee is not required from a voluntary bankrupt, and from estates which they have administered, such commissions on sums to be paid as dividends and commissions as may be allowed by the courts, not to exceed three per centum on the first five thousand dollars or less, two per centum on the second five thousand dollars or part thereof, and one per centum on such sums in excess of ten thousand dollars.**

b **In the event of an estate being administered by three trustees instead of one trustee or by successive trustees, the court shall apportion the fees and commissions between them according to the services actually rendered, so that there shall not be paid to trustees for the administering of any estate a greater amount than one trustee would be entitled to.**

c **The court may, in its discretion, withhold all compensation from any trustee who has been removed for cause.**

ACCOUNTS AND PAPERS OF TRUSTEES.

§ **49.** *a* The accounts and papers of trustees shall be open to the inspection of officers and all parties in interest.

BONDS OF REFEREES AND TRUSTEES.

§ **50.** *a* Referees, before assuming the duties of their offices, and within such time as the district courts of the United States having jurisdiction shall prescribe, shall respectively qualify by entering into bond to the United States in such sum as shall be fixed by such courts, not to exceed five thousand dollars, with such sureties as shall be approved by such courts, conditioned for the faithful performance of their official duties.

b Trustees, before entering upon the performance of their official duties, and within ten days after their appointment, or within such further time, not to exceed five days, as the court may permit, shall respectively qualify by entering into bond to the United States, with such sureties as shall be approved by the courts, conditioned for the faithful performance of their official duties.

c The creditors of a bankrupt estate, at their first meeting after the adjudication, or after a vacancy has occurred in the office of trustee, or after an estate has been reopened, or after a composition has been set aside or a discharge revoked, if there is a vacancy in the office of trustee, shall fix the amount of the bond of the trustee; they may at any time increase the amount of the bond. If the creditors do not fix the amount of the bond of the trustee as herein provided the court shall do so.

d The court shall require evidence as to the actual value of the property of sureties.

e There shall be at least two sureties upon each bond.

f The actual value of the property of the sureties, over and above their liabilities and exemptions, on each bond shall equal at least the amount of such bond.

g Corporations organized for the purpose of becoming sureties upon bonds, or authorized by law to do so, may be accepted as sureties upon the bonds of referees and trustees whenever the courts are satisfied that the rights of all parties in interest will be thereby amply protected.

h Bonds of referees, trustees, and designated depositories shall be filed of record in the office of the clerk of the court and may be sued upon in the name of the United States for the use of any person injured by a breach of their conditions.

i Trustees shall not be liable, personally or on their bonds, to the United States, for any penalties or forfeitures incurred by the bankrupts under this act, of whose estates they are respectively trustees.

j Joint trustees may give joint or several bonds.

k If any referee or trustee shall fail to give bond, as herein provided and within the time limited, he shall be deemed to have declined his appointment, and such failure shall create a vacancy in his office.

l Suits upon referees' bonds shall not be brought subsequent to two years after the alleged breach of the bond.

m **Suits upon trustees' bonds shall not be brought subsequent to two years after the estate has been closed.**

Bond of Trustee.

In a case where a trustee in bankruptcy had given a bond conditioned for the faithful discharge of his duties in all cases in which he might be appointed trustee, it was held that this was not sufficient; for the law contemplates that he should give a separate and distinct bond for each and every case in which he is appointed. In re McFaden, 3 N. B. R. 104, Fed. Cas. No. 8,785.

DUTIES OF CLERKS.

§ 51. *a* **Clerks shall respectively (1) account for, as for other fees received by them, the clerk's fee paid in each case and such other fees as may be received for certified copies of records which may be prepared for persons other than officers; (2) collect the fees of the clerk, referee, and trustee in each case instituted before filing the petition, except the petition of a proposed voluntary bankrupt which is accompanied by an affidavit stating that the petitioner is without, and cannot obtain, the money with which to pay such fees; (3) deliver to the referees upon application all papers which may be referred to them, or, if the offices of such referees are not in the same cities or towns as the offices of such clerks, transmit such papers by mail, and in like manner return papers which were received from such referees after they have been used; (4) and within ten days after each case has been closed pay to the referee, if the case was re-**

ferred, the fee collected for him, and to the trustee the fee collected for him at the time of filing the petition.

COMPENSATION OF CLERKS AND MARSHALS.

§ 52. *a* Clerks shall respectively receive as full compensation for their service to each estate, a filing fee of ten dollars, except when a fee is not required from a voluntary bankrupt.

b Marshals shall respectively receive from the estate where an adjudication in bankruptcy is made, except as herein otherwise provided, for the performance of their services in proceedings in bankruptcy, the same fees, and account for them in the same way, as they are entitled to receive for the performance of the same or similar services in other cases in accordance with laws now in force, or such as may be hereafter enacted, fixing the compensation of marshals.

DUTIES OF ATTORNEY-GENERAL.

§ 53. *a* The attorney-general shall annually lay before congress statistical tables showing for the whole country, and by states, the number of cases during the year of voluntary and involuntary bankruptcy; the amount of the property of the estates; the dividends paid and the expenses of administering such estates; and such other like information as he may deem important.

STATISTICS OF BANKRUPTCY PROCEEDINGS.

§ 54. *a* **Officers shall furnish in writing and transmit by mail such information as is within their knowledge, and as may be shown by the records and papers in their possession, to the attorney-general, for statistical purposes, within ten days after being requested by him to do so.**

CHAPTER VI.

CREDITORS.

MEETINGS OF CREDITORS.

§ 55. *a* The court shall cause the first meeting of the creditors of a bankrupt to be held, not less than ten nor more than thirty days after the adjudication, at the county seat of the county in which the bankrupt has had his principal place of business, resided, or had his domicile; or if that place would be manifestly inconvenient as a place of meeting for the parties in interest, or if the bankrupt is one who does not do business, reside, or have his domicile within the United States, the court shall fix a place for the meeting which is the most convenient for parties in interest. If such meeting should by any mischance not be held within such time, the court shall fix the date, as soon as may be thereafter, when it shall be held.

b At the first meeting of creditors the judge or referee shall preside, and, before proceeding with the other business, may allow or disallow the claims of creditors there presented, and may publicly examine the bankrupt or cause him to be examined at the instance of any creditor.

c The creditors shall at each meeting take such steps as may be pertinent and necessary for the promotion of the best interests of the estate and the enforcement of this act.

d A meeting of creditors, subsequent to the first one, may be held at any time and place when all of the creditors who have secured the allowance of their claims sign a written consent to hold a meeting at such time and place.

e The court shall call a meeting of creditors whenever one-fourth or more in number of those who have proven their claims shall file a written request to that effect; if such request is signed by a majority of such creditors, which number represents a majority in amount of such claims, and contains a request for such meeting to be held at a designated place, the court shall call such meeting at such place within thirty days after the date of the filing of the request.

f Whenever the affairs of the estate are ready to be closed a final meeting of creditors shall be ordered.

VOTERS AT MEETINGS OF CREDITORS.

§ 56. *a* Creditors shall pass upon matters submitted to them at their meetings by a majority vote in number and amount of claims of all creditors whose claims have been allowed and are present, except as herein otherwise provided.

b Creditors holding claims which are secured or have priority shall not, in respect to such claims, be entitled to vote at creditors' meetings, nor shall such claims be counted in computing either the number of creditors or the amount of their claims, unless the amounts of such claims exceed the values of such securities or priorities, and then only for such excess.

PROOF AND ALLOWANCE OF CLAIMS.

§ **57.** *a* Proof of claims shall consist of a statement under oath, in writing, signed by a creditor, setting forth the claim, the consideration therefor, and whether any, and, if so what, securities are held therefor, and whether any, and, if so what, payments have been made thereon, and that the sum claimed is justly owing from the bankrupt to the creditor.

b Whenever a claim is founded upon an instrument of writing, such instrument, unless lost or destroyed, shall be filed with the proof of claim. If such instrument is lost or destroyed, a statement of such fact and of the circumstances of such loss or destruction shall be filed under oath with the claim. After the claim is allowed or disallowed, such instrument may be withdrawn by permission of the court, upon leaving a copy thereof on file with the claim.

c Claims after being proved may, for the purpose of allowance, be filed by the claimants in the court where the proceedings are pending, or before the referee if the case has been referred.

d Claims which have been duly proved shall be allowed, upon receipt by or upon presentation to the court, unless objection to their allowance shall be made by parties in interest, or their consideration be continued for cause by the court upon its own motion.

e Claims of secured creditors and those who have priority may be allowed to enable such creditors to participate in the proceedings at creditors' meetings held prior to the determination of the value of their securities or priorities, but shall be allowed for such sums only as to the courts seem to be owing over and above the value of their securities or priorities.

f Objections to claims shall be heard and determined as soon as the convenience of the court and the best interests of the estates and the claimants will permit.

g The claims of creditors who have received preferences shall not be allowed unless such creditors shall surrender their preferences.

h The value of securities held by secured creditors shall be determined by converting the same into money according to the terms of the agreement pursuant to which such securities were delivered to such creditors or by such creditors and the trustee, by agreement, arbitration, compromise, or litigation, as the court may direct, and the amount of such value shall be credited upon such claims, and a dividend shall be paid only on the unpaid balance.

i Whenever a creditor, whose claim against a bankrupt estate is secured by the individual undertaking of any person, fails to prove such claim, such person may do so in the creditor's name, and if he discharge such undertaking in whole or in part he shall be subrogated to that extent to the rights of the creditor.

j Debts owing to the United States, a state, a county, a district, or a municipality as a penalty or forfeiture shall not be allowed, except for the amount of the pecuniary loss sustained by the act, transaction, or proceeding out of which the penalty

or forfeiture arose, with reasonable and actual costs occasioned thereby and such interest as may have accrued thereon according to law.

k **Claims which have been allowed may be reconsidered for cause and reallowed or rejected in whole or in part, according to the equities of the case, before but not after the estate has been closed.**

l **Whenever a claim shall have been reconsidered and rejected, in whole or in part, upon which a dividend has been paid, the trustee may recover from the creditor the amount of the dividend received upon the claim if rejected in whole, or the proportional part thereof if rejected only in part.**

m **The claim of any estate which is being administered in bankruptcy against any like estate may be proved by the trustee and allowed by the court in the same manner and upon like terms as the claims of other creditors.**

n **Claims shall not be proved against a bankrupt estate subsequent to one year after the adjudication; or if they are liquidated by litigation and the final judgment therein is rendered within thirty days before or after the expiration of such time, then within sixty days after the rendition of such judgment: provided, that the right of infants and insane persons without guardians, without notice of the proceedings, may continue six months longer.**

Proof of Claims; Formal Requisites of Proof.

The statement of the debt in the schedule is not a proof of it. It may be stated in fraud, and may not exist. The bankrupt may have made payments, or may have counterclaims or offsets. The debt must be proved by the oath of the creditor. This applies to lien creditors as well as unsecured creditors. In re Davis, 2 N. B. R. 392, Fed. Cas. No. 3,618. Similarly, the finding, in a decree of adjudication in involuntary bankruptcy, that the petitioning creditor has a valid and provable claim to the amount of $250, is not conclusive upon the trustee and creditors, so as to dispense with proof of debt of the petitioning creditor, or to preclude questioning his right to participate in the distribution of the estate. In re Cleveland Ins. Co., 22 Fed. 200. A proof of debt cannot be filed unless it is correctly entitled in the cause. In re Walther, 14 N. B. R. 273, Fed. Cas. No. 17,126. A proof against a firm should state that the firm or company, describing it by the firm name and the individuals who composed it, was indebted to the creditor and how and in what amount; it should not be left in uncertainty whether the demand is a firm debt or a joint claim against the individual partners. In re Walton, Deady, 510, Fed. Cas. No. 17,129. "A proof of debt is not open to objection because it appears on its face that the statute of limitations, if set up, would be a good defense to the claim. The proof of claim need not anticipate the defense, or give proof of facts to take the case out of the statute." Blatchford, J., in Re Knoepfel, 1 Ben. 402, Fed. Cas. No. 7,892. Upon proof of a claim in bankruptcy the *particulars* of the consideration must be given in the statement. In re Elder, 1 Sawy. 73, Fed. Cas. No. 4,326. Where the bankrupt is dead, the proving creditor is nevertheless a competent witness in his own behalf to prove the contract out of which his claim arose; the case falls under Rev. St. § 858. In re Merrill, 9 Ben. 165, Fed. Cas. No. 9,466. In making proof of a claim the creditor's Christian name ought to appear in the documents offered in evidence or in the record of the proceeding, and it is not sufficient that the initials of the creditor's name appear. In re Valentine, 4 Biss. 317, Fed. Cas. No. 16,812.

Who May make Proof.

A creditor cannot prove by an attorney testifying upon information and belief, unless the creditor is prevented from making the affidavit as provided in the act. In re Barnes, 1 Low. 560, Fed. Cas. No. 1,012. A proof of debt taken before a notary public who is the attorney and solicitor of record for the bankrupt will not be allowed to be filed. In re Keyser, 9 Ben. 224, Fed. Cas. No. 7,748. The assignee of a non-negotiable *chose in action* may prove it against the estate of the debtor in bankruptcy upon his own deposition, and it is not necessary to the sufficiency of the proof that the deposition of the assignor should be added. Ex parte Davenport, 1 Low. 384, Fed. Cas. No. 3,586. The proof of a claim by a state should be made by the state treasurer or by some officer holding a relation to the state similar to that which a president, cashier, or treasurer bears to the corporation of which he is such officer. In re Corn Exch. Bank, 15 N. B. R. 216, Fed. Cas. No. 3,243. A creditor who resides out of the district where the bankruptcy proceedings are taken, subjects himself to the jurisdiction of the court by proving his debt, and is thereafter bound to obey all the orders of the court touching his alleged debt, and the court, in case he disobeys its orders, can deprive him of all the benefits of the act, and can reject and expunge his claims. In re Kyler, 2 Ben. 414, Fed. Cas. No. 7,956. Where an indorsee of a note has proved his claim against the estate of the maker in bankruptcy, and afterwards, pending the bankruptcy proceedings, receives payment from the indorser, his relation to the liability ceases, he can no longer be considered a creditor of the maker, and he can take no further part in the proceedings; but the indorser is subrogated to his rights in respect to the demand, and it belongs to him to participate, in that capacity, in the further proceedings. In re Broich, 7 Biss. 303, Fed. Cas. No. 1,921.

When Proof must be Made.

A creditor may come in at any time before the hearing of the petition for the bankrupt's discharge and prove his claim. In re Longest, 7 Biss. 477, Fed. Cas. No. 8,485. In a case where, after the third meeting of creditors and the bankrupt's discharge, about five years elapsed, and then some assets were realized unexpectedly, and a fourth meeting was called, it was held that a creditor having a just debt might prove it at this meeting and receive a dividend, not disturbing the former dividends. In re Robinson, 2 Low. 326, Fed. Cas. No. 11,941.

Withdrawal and Amendment of Proofs.

A creditor who has proved his debt in bankruptcy may be permitted to withdraw his proof, if it was made under a mistake of fact or law, provided neither the bankrupt nor the other creditors who have proved will be injured thereby. In re Hubbard, 1 Lowell, 190, Fed. Cas. No. 6,813. It was so held where the attorney, through a mistake of mixed fact and law, had prepared the proofs as unsecured claims. The creditors were permitted to withdraw their proofs upon terms of indemnity to the estate. In Re Baxter, 12 Fed. 72. A secured creditor, who inadvertently proves his debt as an unsecured claim, will not be required to surrender his lien and participate in the general distribution, but may be allowed to withdraw and amend his proofs. In re Brand, 3 N. B. R. 324, Fed. Cas. No. 1,809.

Postponement of Proofs.

When there is a reasonable and substantial doubt in the mind of the referee as to the validity of any claim and as to the right of the alleged creditor to prove it, he may postpone the proof of such claim until after the election of a trustee. In re Jackson, 7 Biss. 280, Fed. Cas. No. 7,123. Where a review by the district judge of the action of the referee in such cases is sought, the better practice on the part of creditors who object to such postponement of their claims is to have the objection noted, obtain a stay of proceedings, and have the case certified before any further action is taken before the referee. Id.; and see In re Stevens, 4 Ben. 513, Fed. Cas. No. 13,391.

Proof by Preferred Creditors.

Under the act of 1867 it was held, that where the trustee sues a preferred creditor to recover property alleged to have been sold or conveyed to him by the bankrupt in fraud of the act, and the creditor denies his liability, resists a recovery, goes to trial, and judgment is rendered against him, such judgment conclusively establishes that the creditor sought to obtain a fraudulent preference, and disentitles him to prove up that claim; and if he pays such judgment under execution, this is not a "surrender" under the act, and will not enable him to prove his debt. In re Richter's Estate, 1 Dill. 544, Fed. Cas. No. 11,803; In re Leland, 7 Ben. 156, Fed. Cas. No. 8,230; In re Drummond, 4 Biss. 149, Fed. Cas. No. 4,094; In re Stephens, 3 Biss. 187, Fed. Cas. No. 13,365, and see In re Graves, 9 Fed. 816. But in a case where the assets were sufficient to pay all the other creditors in full and leave a surplus, it was held that a preferred creditor from whom his advantage had been wrested by compulsion of legal process, might make proof of his debt and be paid out of such surplus; for as between the bankrupt and himself he was entitled to the money. In re McGuire, 8 Ben. 452, Fed. Cas. No. 8,813. And where the fraud is merely constructive, a mortgagee who has taken the mortgaged property and held it until a trial and finding against him in favor of the trustee, but who then, and before judgment, surrenders the property, may be allowed to prove his debt. Burr v. Hopkins, 6 Biss. 355, Fed. Cas. No. 2,192. A creditor who has *never accepted* a deed of trust made to a third person, the enforcement of which would give him a preference, and who disclaims all interest in it, may prove his debt as unsecured. In re Saunders, 2 Lowell, 444, Fed. Cas. No. 12,371. If the principal creditor has lost the right to prove his claim, by reason of accepting a preference and refusing to surrender it, neither can the guarantors prove. In re Ayers, 6 Biss. 48, Fed. Cas. No. 685: "When a creditor has two or more separate and disconnected debts, receiving a fraudulent preference as to some one or more only will not affect his right to prove those as to which no preference has been received, and to receive dividends thereon. So, where a creditor has separate and disconnected debts as to which he has received separate and distinct fraudulent preferences, he may surrender as to some and prove and receive dividends as to them without surrendering as to the others." In re Holland, 8 N. B. R. 190, Fed. Cas. No. 6,604; Longyear, J. A mere repayment to the debtor cannot take the place of a surrender to the trustee. In re Currier, 13 N. B. R. 68, Fed. Cas. No. 3,492. A return of part payments, as a condition of proof of debt, is not required, except upon the concurrence of an intent in the bankrupt, when the payment was made, to create a preference, with knowledge of his unlawful intent by the creditor. In re Baxter, 25 Fed. 700.

Power to Expunge Proofs.

It is the policy of the act to do equal and exact justice between the estate of the bankrupt and the creditors. The court has ample power to investigate a claim at any stage of the proceedings, and to make any correction that equity and justice demand; not only to reduce the amount if it is too large, but also to increase it if, through inadvertence, it is smaller than by right it should be. Questions of amendment address themselves to the equitable consideration of the court, and great discretion is exercised in disposing of them. In re Montgomery, 3 Ben. 567, Fed. Cas. No. 9,727. It is competent for the court to correct any mere mistake, and to allow the proof to stand for any sum that, upon examination, is found to be actually due. In re New Brunswick Carpet Co., 4 Fed. 514. A proof of a judgment which is subsequently set aside should be expunged. In re Bruce, 6 Ben. 515, Fed. Cas. No. 2,044. Where, upon a long re-examination of a creditor's proof of debt, the claim, as made, is disproved in form and substance, it should be expunged. In re Mead, 14 Fed. 287. Where the claim, after being proved, is discovered to have been founded upon an illegal or gaming contract, the proof thereof may be expunged on motion of the trustee. In re Green, 7 Biss. 338, Fed. Cas. No. 5,751. So the court has power to refer to the referee a petition of a creditor praying that a proof of claim of another creditor be expunged on account of matters occurring since the claim was proved. In re Loring, Holmes, 483, Fed. Cas. No. 8,512. The bankrupt himself is a competent party to move the expunction of a creditor's proof. In re McDonald, 14 N. B. R. 477, Fed. Cas. No. 8,753. The burden of showing that a claim, duly proven according to the provisions of the statute, is founded in mistake or fraud, lies upon the trustee or the creditor attacking the proof. After such proof, the claim is prima facie good. In re Felter, 7 Fed. 904. The court has the power to pass an order requiring the creditor to show cause why proof should not be vacated and annulled; but such power does not appertain to the referee. Comstock v. Wheeler, 2 N. B. R. 561, Fed. Cas. No. 3,084. A referee need not give notice to either party of his findings and decision on a proceeding to re-examine and expunge a claim. In re Pease, 29 Fed. 593.

Appeal from Rejection of Claim.

Where a proof of debt is disallowed by the district court, and an appeal taken to the circuit court of appeals, the cause of action prosecuted in the latter court must be the same one that was rejected by the former, and it is not permissible, under cover of an appeal, to transform the claim into a new and distinct cause of action. In re Jaycox, 12 Blatchf. 209, Fed. Cas. No. 7,237.

NOTICES TO CREDITORS.

§ 58. *a* **Creditors shall have at least ten days' notice by mail, to their respective addresses as they appear in the list of creditors of the bankrupt, or as afterwards filed with the papers in the case by the creditors, unless they waive notice in writing, of (1) all examinations of the bankrupt; (2) all hearings upon applications for the confirmation of compositions or the discharge of bankrupts; (3) all meetings of creditors; (4) all proposed sales of property; (5) the declaration and time of payment of dividends; (6) the filing of the final accounts of the trustee, and the time when and the place where they will be examined and passed upon; (7) the proposed compromise of any controversy, and (8) the proposed dismissal of the proceedings.**

b **Notice to creditors of the first meeting shall be published at least once and may be published such number of additional times as the court may direct; the last publication shall be at least one week prior to the date fixed for the meeting. Other notices may be published as the court shall direct.**

c **All notices shall be given by the referee, unless otherwise ordered by the judge.**

WHO MAY FILE AND DISMISS PETITIONS.

§ 59. *a* Any qualified person may file a petition to be adjudged a voluntary bankrupt.

b Three or more creditors who have provable claims against any person which amount in the aggregate, in excess of the value of securities held by them, if any, to five hundred dollars or over; or if all of the creditors of such person are less than twelve in number, then one of such creditors whose claim equals such amount may file a petition to have him adjudged a bankrupt.

c Petitions shall be filed in duplicate, one copy for the clerk and one for service on the bankrupt.

d If it be averred in the petition that the creditors of the bankrupt are less than twelve in number, and less than three creditors have joined as petitioners therein, and the answer avers the existence of a larger number of creditors, there shall be filed with the answer a list under oath of all the creditors, with their addresses, and thereupon the court shall cause all such creditors to be notified of the pendency of such petition and shall delay the hearing upon such petition for a reasonable time, to the end that parties in interest shall have an opportunity to be heard; if upon such hearing it shall appear that a sufficient number have joined in such petition, or if prior to or during such hearing a sufficient number shall join therein, the case may be proceeded with, but otherwise it shall be dismissed.

e In computing the number of creditors of a bankrupt for the purpose of determining how many

creditors must join in the petition, such creditors as were employed by him at the time of the filing of the petition or are related to him by consanguinity or affinity within the third degree, as determined by the common law, and have not joined in the petition, shall not be counted.

f **Creditors other than original petitioners may at any time enter their appearance and join in the petition, or file an answer and be heard in opposition to the prayer of the petition.**

g **A voluntary or involuntary petition shall not be dismissed by the petitioner or petitioners or for want of prosecution or by consent of parties until after notice to the creditors.**

What creditors may petition.

Attaching creditors are not to be counted, nor their claims computed, in ascertaining whether the petition in involuntary bankruptcy is supported by the requisite number and amount of creditors. In re Jewett, 7 Biss. 242, Fed. Cas. No. 7,305; In re Hazens, 4 Dill. 549, Fed. Cas. No. 6,285; In re Scrafford, 4 Dill. 376, Fed. Cas. No. 12,556. A creditor who has been fraudulently preferred cannot proceed for adjudication against his debtor for the very act of preference to which he was a party; he is estopped on every principle of equity; and therefore he ought not to be reckoned in computing the number or amount of creditors who have or have not petitioned. In re Currier, 2 Lowell, 436, Fed. Cas. No. 3,492; In re Israel, 3 Dill. 511, Fed. Cas. No. 7,111; see, however, a somewhat different opinion expressed in Coxe v. Hale, 10 Blatchf. 56, Fed. Cas. No. 3,310. It is important to observe that the present act authorizes secured creditors to be petitioners in respect to the excess of their demand over the security; a permission not accorded by previous statutes. In re Green Pond R. R. Co., 13 N. B. R. 118, Fed. Cas. No. 5,783. Where a creditor has released his debt, but was induced to do so by the fraudulent representations of another creditor, who sought, by this means, to get possession of the whole property and so obtain a preference, which plan was effected, the first creditor may repudiate his own release and file a petition against the common debtor. Michaels v. Post, 21 Wall. 398. It has been held to be no defense to a petition in compulsory bankruptcy that the petitioning creditor is the *only* creditor of the alleged bankrupt. In re Alexander, 1 Lowell, 470, Fed. Cas. No. 161. But where a single creditor, whose debt is fully secured on real estate, presents a petition, this is not regarded as a case coming within the scope and intent of the act, and the court will not take jurisdiction. In re Johann, 2 Biss. 139, Fed. Cas. No. 7,331. Lawful solicitation by a debtor to induce his creditors to sign a petition against him in involuntary bankruptcy is permissible. In re Bouton, 5 Sawy. 427, Fed. Cas. No. 1,706; and see Sanford v. Huxford, 32 Mo. 313. While of course the debtor himself cannot legally bribe his creditors to forbear instituting proceedings against him, yet there is nothing in the bankrupt law which forbids a creditor to take from a *third person* a contract or security for the payment of money as an inducement to refrain from throwing his debtor into bankruptcy. Ecker v. Bohn, 45 Md. 278. And conversely, a party, if he acts in good faith, may purchase a claim in order to join in an involuntary petition and make up the necessary number of creditors. In re Woodford, 13 N. B. R. 575, Fed. Cas. No. 17,972. The same number and amount of creditors must join in a proceeding to force a corporation into bankruptcy as are required in the case of an individual. In re Leavenworth Sav. Bank, 14 N. B. R. 92, Fed. Cas. No. 8,165; In re Oregon B. & P. Co., 10 Pac. Law Rep. 103.

Requisites as to Number and Amount.

There is some conflict of opinion as to whether the sufficiency of the number and amount of creditors joining in the petition is a jurisdictional fact or not. Thus, it was held, in In re Scammon, 6 Biss. 130, Fed. Cas. No. 12,427, that it is so far a jurisdictional fact that the petition must show affirmatively that the requisite number of creditors join therein; that such averment is necessary before the debtor can be required to show cause, or even to file a schedule. And this view is supported by In re Burch, 10 N. B. R. 150, Fed. Cas. No. 2,138, and In re Rosenfields, 11 N. B. R. 86, Fed. Cas. No. 12,061. On the other hand, it is squarely denied in In re Henderson, 9 Fed. 196, and Exparte Jewett, 2 Lowell, 393, Fed. Cas. No. 7,303. Probably the true solution is found in accepting the doctrine of In re Scammon, as above, while yet admitting the force of In re Duncan, 8 Ben. 365, Fed. Cas. No. 4,131, which is to the effect that, the requisite number and amount of creditors appearing on the face of the proceedings to have joined, the fact cannot be re-examined, or the judgment of the court thereon attacked, either directly or collaterally, except for fraud. To same effect see In re Funkenstein, 3 Sawy. 605, Fed. Cas. No. 5,158. The allegation may be upon information and belief. In re Scammon, 6 Biss. 130, Fed. Cas. No. 12,427. Whereas it is required that the demands of the petitioning creditors should amount to a certain sum, it is not necessary that the principal of the debts should reach that sum; interest, evidently due on the face of the petition, may be added in for this purpose. Sloan v. Lewis, 22 Wall. 150. The law does not require the court, in its adjudication of bankruptcy, formally to pass upon the question whether the requisite proportion of creditors, in number and the amount of their claims, have joined in the petition; if the defendant desires to contest this point, he should do it in the manner prescribed in the act. Lastrapes v. Blanc, 3 Woods, 134, Fed. Cas. No. 8,100. It was said that "although the law does not expressly require that the list of creditors presented by the debtor, in denial that the requisite number and amount have joined in the petition, should be sworn to by him, the general intent of the act would seem to indicate that it should be done." In re Steinman, 6 Biss. 166, Fed. Cas. No. 13,357. And this is now expressly required by the act.

Petitioning Creditors cannot Withdraw.

Creditors who have joined in a petition cannot afterwards be allowed to withdraw from the proceedings; because such a practice would lead to underhand and secret negotiations between the debtor and a portion of his creditors at the expense of the others. In re Heffron, 6 Biss. 156, Fed. Cas. No. 6,321; In re Vogel, 9 Ben. 498, Fed. Cas. No. 16,981; In re Sargent, 13 N. B. R. 144, Fed. Cas. No. 12,361. But when a creditor's name has been used in the petition without his knowledge or consent, he may repudiate the proceedings, and the petition will be dismissed as to him. In re Rosenfields, 11 N. B. R. 86, Fed. Cas. No. 12,061; In re Sargent, 13 N. B. R. 144, Fed. Cas. No. 12,361.

Who may intervene.

When, on the return day of a rule to show cause in involuntary bankruptcy, the petitioning creditors fail to appear or to proceed, any creditors to the required amount may intervene, and pray an adjudication on the original petition. In re Sheffer, 4 Sawy. 363, Fed. Cas. No. 12,742; In re Lacey, 12 Blatchf. 322, Fed. Cas. No. 7,965. This right of intervention is secured to creditors, and no settlement or arrangement by which the petitioning creditor seeks to withdraw his petition can defeat it. In re Lacey, supra. But to entitle a creditor to join an involuntary petition he must have a debt provable immediately; a promissory note indorsed by the debtor, not falling due until after the petition is filed, is not such a debt. In re Morse, 17 Blatchf. 72, Fed. Cas. No. 9,851.

PREFERRED CREDITORS.

§ 60. *a* A person shall be deemed to have given a preference if, being insolvent, he has procured or suffered a judgment to be entered against himself in favor of any person, or made a transfer of any of his property, and the effect of the enforcement of such judgment or transfer will be to enable any one of his creditors to obtain a greater percentage of his debt than any other of such creditors of the same class.

b If a bankrupt shall have given a preference within four months before the filing of a petition, or after the filing of the petition and before the adjudication, and the person receiving it, or to be benefited thereby, or his agent acting therein, shall have had reasonable cause to believe that it was intended thereby to give a preference, it shall be voidable by the trustee, and he may recover the property or its value from such person.

c If a creditor has been preferred, and afterwards in good faith gives the debtor further credit without security of any kind for property which becomes a part of the debtor's estates, the amount of such new credit remaining unpaid at the time of the adjudication in bankruptcy may be set off against the amount which would otherwise be recoverable from him.

d If a debtor shall, directly or indirectly, in contemplation of the filing of a petition by or against him, pay money or transfer property to an attorney and counselor at law, solicitor in equity, or proctor in admiralty for services to be rendered,

the transaction shall be reexamined by the court on petition of the trustee or any creditor and shall only be held valid to the extent of a reasonable amount to be determined by the court, and the excess may be recovered by the trustee for the benefit of the estate.

Preferences.

A preference, within the meaning of the bankrupt law, is an advantage in the payment of the debt due him, acquired by one creditor over the other creditors of the same debtor. In re Horton, 5 Ben. 562, Fed. Cas. No. 6,707. Hence a payment, by an insolvent debtor, of a percentage on claims of a part of his creditors, which does not have the effect to lessen the percentage which his other creditors will receive, is not an unlawful preference. In re Hapgood, 2 Low. 200, Fed. Cas. No. 6,044. And a mere promise of security, in which no specific property is pledged, is not sufficient to establish a preference. Southwick v. Whipple, 2 Fed. 773. And a transfer, by one in failing circumstances, of the greater portion of his assets to a creditor, is not void as involving an unlawful preference of such creditor, where all known creditors, and all whom the grantee suspected were creditors, and all the creditors of whose existence he was bound to know, joined in the arrangement under which the transfer was made, though such creditor thereby in fact secured a preference. Judson v. Courier Co., 8 Fed. 422. But the fact that a bankrupt received money or property upon an unlawful contract, under which a creditor sought a preference, which property went to increase the estate, will not render such contract valid. Adams v. Merchants' Bank, 2 Fed. 174. A creditor of a bankrupt cannot obtain a preference of his debt by purchasing the property of the bankrupt through the intervention of an agent, and tendering the notes of the bankrupt in payment. Fleming v. Andrews, 3 Fed. 632.

Deed of Trust.

Under the former bankrupt law it was held to be necessary that the following things should concur in order to render a deed of trust invalid: It must have been executed within two months (now four) of the filing of a petition in bankruptcy against the grantor; the bankrupt must have been insolvent, or it must have been made in contemplation of insolvency; the deed of trust must have been made with a view to give a preference; the party to whom it was made must have had reasonable cause to believe that the bankrupt was insolvent at the time, and must have known that the deed of trust was made in fraud of the bankrupt law. May v. Le Claire, 18 Fed. 164.

Assignments for Creditors.

"An assignment to a trustee of all a trader's property in trust for the benefit of his creditors, which necessarily puts an end to the business of the debtor, and which gives a preference to some creditors over others, is made out of the usual, ordinary course of business, and, if made in contemplation of insolvency, is not only prima facie but conclusive evidence of an intent on the part of the debtor to defeat the operation of the bankrupt act, and is therefore void." Woods, J., in Jackson v. McCulloch, 13 N. B. R. 284, Fed. Cas. No. 7,140. But where the assignment is made in good faith and for the equal and common benefit of all creditors, there is some difference of opinion as to its constituting a preference. The case of Globe Ins. Co. v. Cleveland Ins. Co., 14 N. B. R. 311, Fed. Cas. No. 5,486, may be regarded as settling the question in the affirmative; though see Haas v. O'Brien, 66 N. Y. 597.

Procuring or Suffering Judgment.

In order to constitute a preference under this clause, the debtor must *do some act* to facilitate the proceedings. Submissive inactivity is not enough. The leading case on the subject (Wilson v. City Bank, 17 Wall. 488), says: "Something more than passive non-resistance of an insolvent debtor to regular judicial proceedings, in which a judgment and levy on his property are obtained, when the debt is due and he is without just defense to the action, is necessary to show a preference of a creditor, or a purpose to defeat or delay the operation of the bankrupt act." Wilson v. City Bank, 17 Wall. 488; National Bank v. Warren, 96 U. S. 539; Sage v. Wyncoop, 104 U. S. 319; Loucheim v. Henzey, 86 Pa. St. 350; Henkelman v. Smith, 42 Md. 164. In the case of In re Heller, 3 Biss. 153, Fed. Cas. No. 6,337, it was said to be the duty of an insolvent man, when sued, to take measures to secure the equal distribution of his property among his creditors, and if he makes no defense to the actions, does not notify his other creditors of the suits, nor do anything to prevent the obtaining of a preference, he "suffers" his property to be taken within the meaning of the law. This case, however, undoubtedly goes too far. A much better statement of the principle involved is found in Brown v. Jefferson Co. Nat. Bank, 9 Fed. 258, 19 Blatchf. 315, where Blatchford, J., observed: "The mere existence of a desire on the part of a debtor, however strong such desire, that a particular creditor may succeed by suit, judgment, execution, and levy, in obtaining a preference over other creditors, so that such preference may be maintained even as against proceedings in bankruptcy which mav be subsequently commenced, is not sufficient to establish that the debtor procured or suffered his property to be taken on legal process, with intent to prefer such creditor, if the proceedings of the creditor were the usual proceedings in a suit, unaided by any act of the debtor, either by facilitating the proceedings as to time or method, or by obstructing other creditors who otherwise would obtain priority." Hence it is competent for a creditor to institute a suit against a bankrupt, and obtain judgment by default, and issue execution, and unless the bankrupt does some act by which he has participated in some way in the act of the creditor, the preference thereby acquired is a *valid* preference as against other creditors. In re Runzi, 3 Fed. 790. But although, under a sound construction of the bankrupt law, mere passive non-resistance by the insolvent debtor will not defeat a judgment and levy, where the debt was due and there was no defense to the same, still, very slight evidence of an affirmative character of a desire to prefer a creditor, or of acts done to secure such preference, may be sufficient to invalidate the whole transaction. Parsons v. Caswell, 1 Fed. 74. Where a debtor, being insolvent, gave a confession of judgment to one of his creditors, with the intention of preferring that creditor, on which judgment his property was taken and sold, it was held that this state of facts was sufficient to support a petition in involuntary bankruptcy, although the debtor did not, at the time, actually contemplate bankruptcy, or even know that there was any such law as the bankrupt law. In re Craft, 2 Ben. 214, Fed. Cas. No. 3,316. Where the debtor contributes to the rendition of a judgment at an earlier day than without his aid it could have been rendered, intending a preference, and execution and levy follow, he "procures" his property to be taken on legal process. Rogers v. Palmer, 102 U. S. 263. So where a debtor is sued for a just debt, and interposes a groundless defense, in such a manner that another creditor, who brings a later suit, to which no defense is made, is enabled to obtain a prior judgment and have a receiver appointed, the proper inference is that the debtor intended to prefer the latter creditor. Wight v. Muxlow, 8 Ben. 52, Fed. Cas. No. 17,629. Although the judgment complained of was entered against the bankrupt before the passage of the bankrupt act, yet if it be fraudulent and fictitious, and the debtor has taken no steps to set it aside, and, after the enactment of the law, the judgment being still in force, his property is seized on an execution issued thereunder, this is procuring his property to be taken, etc. In re Schick, 2 Ben. 5, Fed. Cas. No. 12,455.

Exchange of Securities.

The leading case on this point is Sawyer v. Turpin, 91 U. S. 114, where Strong, J., said: "An exchange of securities, within the four months, is not a fraudulent preference within the meaning of the bankrupt law, even when the creditor and the debtor know that the latter is insolvent, if the security given up is a valid one when the exchange is made, and it be undoubtedly of equal value with the security substituted for it. * * * The reason is, that the exchange takes nothing away from the other creditors." The substitution and registration of a chattel mortgage, correcting a mistake in a prior unrecorded mortgage, is not an illegal preference, but simply an exchange of securities. Player v. Lippincott, 4 Dill. 125, Fed. Cas. No. 11,224. So where the bankrupt's debt consists of a sum with accumulated interest, some time overdue, secured by a valid mortgage, and the parties have an accounting and compute the amount due to date for both principal and interest, and a new mortgage is given for the sum so ascertained, upon the same property, the old mortgage being cancelled, this cannot be regarded as an illegal preference. Burnhisel v. Firman, 22 Wall. 170. And see Douglass v. Vogeler, 6 Fed. 53; Hough v. Bank, 4 Biss. 349, Fed. Cas. No. 6,721. Again, where the debtor, as security for a loan of money, gives to the creditor in pledge a number of bills receivable, the pledgee may properly hand them back to the debtor for purposes of collection, or that he may replace them with others; and in doing so, the pledgee does not lose his special property in them, and the pledgor holds them in a fiduciary character; and if the debtor replaces a portion of the collaterals with others, his estate not being thereby impaired, and no purpose to delay or defraud his other creditors being shown, the transaction will not be voidable as a preference. Clark v. Iselin, 21 Wall. 360. Where a bank levied an attachment upon lands owned by its treasurer, who was under liabilities to it far exceeding in amount the value of the lands, and in order to save the trouble of legal proceedings he made a deed of the lands to the bank in lieu of the attachment, it was held that creditors of his who afterwards attached the lands could not avoid the conveyance to the bank. Ashuelot Bank v. Frost, 19 Fed. 237. For a case where a complicated series of transactions was held *not* an exchange of securities, see Upham v. Loan & Trust Co., 76 N. Y. 1.

Cumulative Securities, and Transfer of Property already Incumbered.

A confessed judgment for a debt already secured by a prior valid lien against the bankrupt's real estate to which the judgment creditor had the equitable right of subrogation, is not impeachable as a fraudulent preference, for it takes nothing from the general creditors, and does not impair the value of the bankrupt's estate. Reber v. Gundy, 13 Fed. 53. A mortgage is not a preference, where the debt is secured by a prior mortgage covering goods subsequently acquired, where both mortgages cover the same property. Brett v. Carter, 14 N. B. R. 301, Fed. Cas. No. 1,844. A conveyance by an insolvent debtor to his creditor of property upon which the said creditor has a lien to a greater amount than the value thereof, is not a fraudulent preference. Catlin v. Hoffman, 2 Sawy. 486, Fed. Cas. No. 2,521. Where the bankrupt was a member of a stock exchange, the rules of which provided that when a member became insolvent, he should assign his seat to be sold, and that the proceeds should be first applied to the payment of his debts to members of the exchange, to the exclusion of his other creditors, it was held that a member who became insolvent, complied with this rule, and was afterward adjudged a bankrupt, was not guilty of a preference to those creditors whose debts were, in this manner, first paid. Hyde v. Woods, 94 U. S. 523. Where the creditor holds a valid and subsisting lien on the debtor's property, and the equity of redemption therein is conveyed to him under such circumstances as to make it a fraudulent preference, the conveyance is void, but it does not divest the lien. Avery v. Hackley, 20 Wall. 407. Where the seller of goods to the bankrupt has the right to stop them in transit, and does so, his recovery of possession of them in this manner does not amount to a preference. In re Foot, 11 Blatchf. 530, Fed. Cas. No. 4,907. Under the act of 1841 (5 Stat. 442), it was held by Nelson, J., that payments made by a bankrupt on a judgment recovered under such circumstances as to constitute a valid lien on his property, could not be regarded as fraudulent preferences, because they operated to discharge, for the benefit of his general creditors, an amount of property equal in value to the sum paid. Livingston v. Bruce, 1 Blatchf. 318, Fed. Cas. No. 8,410.

Advances in Good Faith.

The principle is thus stated by Judge Dillon: "An insolvent person may properly make efforts to extricate himself from his embarrassments, and therefore he may borrow money and give *at the time* security therefor, provided always the transaction be free from fraud in fact and upon the bankrupt act. And hence it is a settled principle of bankrupt law, both in England and in this country, that advances made in good faith to a debtor to carry on business, upon security taken at the time, do not violate either the terms or policy of the bankrupt act. This is manifestly right, since the power to raise ready money may save the party from bankruptcy and ruin, and since his creditors are not injured nor his estate impaired, because he gets a present equivalent for the debt he creates and the security he gives." Darby v. Boatman's Sav. Inst., 1 Dill. 141, Fed. Cas. No. 3,571; Gaffney v. Signaigo, 1 Dill. 158, Fed. Cas. No. 5,169; Clark v. Iselin, 10 Blatchf. 204, Fed. Cas. No. 2,825; Ex parte Ames, 1 Low. 561, Fed. Cas. No. 323. A merchant who *does not know* that he is insolvent may pledge his property to another whose money he has unlawfully used, without thereby making a preference. Jenkins v. Mayer, 2 Biss. 303, Fed. Cas. No. 7,272.

Transfers between Partners.

The conveyance of the joint assets of an insolvent firm to a continuing partner is a fraudulent preference under the bankrupt act, and if made within the time limited before a petition in bankruptcy, it may be set aside at the instance of the joint creditors. In re Johnson, 2 Low. 129, Fed. Cas. No. 7,369. Thus, where a firm consisting of an active and a silent partner was insolvent and known to the partners to be so, and was dissolved, the silent partner conveying all his interest to the other, and the latter, on the same day, and as a part of the same transaction, mortgaged the whole stock in trade to secure the pre-existing debt of a separate creditor of each partner, and neither partner had any separate estate, it was held that this transaction was fraudulent throughout as a preference, and both partners were liable to be adjudged bankrupt on the petition of a joint creditor. In re Waite, 1 Low. 207, Fed. Cas. No. 17,044.

Miscellaneous Examples of Preferences.

Under the former bankrupt law it was held that a chattel mortgage given to secure a creditor more than four months before a petition in bankruptcy was filed, but kept off the record until within the four months, was not a fraudulent preference; for the limitation began to run from the time the security was *given*, not from the time when creditors had notice of it. Matthews v. Westphal, 1 McCrary, 446, 48 Fed.

664. This case was rested on the authority of Burnhisel v. Firman, 22 Wall. 170; Sawyer v. Turpin, 91 U. S. 114; Bean v. Brookmire, 1 Dill. 25, Fed. Cas. No. 1,168, and overruled Harris v. Bank, 4 Dill. 133, Fed. Cas. No. 6,119. A transfer of property to a factor, with intent to give him a preference by enabling him to claim a factor's lien thereon, is void. Nudd v. Burrows, 91 U. S. 420. And a mortgage given by a trader under such circumstances as to make it a preference, will not be made valid by the existence of a general parol agreement, entered into when the debt was contracted, that security should be given when required. In re Connor, 1 Low. 532, Fed. Cas. No. 3,118. In a case where a policy of insurance, obtained by a debtor on his own life, was assigned to one of a firm consisting of four members, in trust, as security for a debt due the firm, and two members of the firm subsequently retired, and the firm assets passed to the remaining members, one of whom was the trustee of the policy, and, the last-named firm having become embarrassed and procured an extension of credit from their creditors, the trustee of the policy two months afterwards assigned the policy to his sons in trust for their mother without consideration, and six months later made a general assignment, and shortly after was thrown into bankruptcy, it was held that the assignment of the policy in trust for the mother must be deemed invalid as to creditors, and that the assignee in bankruptcy was entitled to the proceeds. Barnes v. Vetterlein, 16 Fed. 218. But on the other hand, where bankrupts, before insolvency or contemplation thereof, delivered their bill of exchange drawn on a certain firm payable at a future day to certain creditors, and said creditors, after the insolvency and with knowledge that it had occurred, presented the bill to said firm, who accepted it, while ignorant of the insolvency, thereby obtaining an equitable lien for its amount upon property in their hands as consignees of the bankrupts, it was held that the payment of the bill was not an illegal preference, although made after

the bankruptcy was notorious. In re Baxter, 28 Fed. 452. An agreement by a creditor not to prosecute a debtor for a misdemeanor affecting public interests is an illegal consideration, and will not support a transfer of the debtor's property to the creditor with knowledge of his insolvency. Sharp v. Warehouse Co., 10 Fed. 379. Where the obligor in a bond, in order to indemnify his sureties, obtained certain securities from one of his debtors and turned them over to the sureties, the transaction was held a preference. Smith v. Little, 5 Biss. 490, Fed. Cas. No. 13,072. So if, in advance of his liability being fixed, an indorser takes the bankrupt maker's property to meet the note when it shall mature, or to secure himself against loss, he will be liable as accepting a preference. Sill v. Solberg, 10 Biss. 252, 6 Fed. 468; Ahl v. Thorner, 2 Bond, 287, Fed. Cas. No. 103. Where a debtor, knowing that his creditor is insolvent, accepts a draft drawn on him by such creditor, the draft being drawn and accepted with the purpose of giving a preference, the transaction is a fraud on the bankrupt act, and the trustee can recover from the acceptor the amount of the draft. Fox v. Gardner, 21 Wall. 475. The debtor cannot escape the effect of a preference by passing the conveyance through his wife. So held where the debtor, being insolvent, conveyed his real estate to his wife without consideration, and she gave a mortgage thereon to creditors who knew the debtor to be insolvent. Gibson v. Dobie, 5 Biss. 198, Fed. Cas. No. 5,394. But a payment or other disposition of property made by a debtor after the adjudication of bankruptcy against him is not a preference, but simply an unlawful meddling with the property of the trustee and therefore a nullity. In re Randall, 1 Sawy. 56, Fed. Cas. No. 11,552.

Pressure, Solicitation, or Threats.

The doctrine of "pressure" by a creditor to force the giving of a security for the payment of a debt has no application under the bankrupt act, and when a debtor mortgages his property to secure such a debt, it is no defense to an allegation that the preference was fraudulent to say that he was "pressed" to do it. Rison v. Knapp, 1 Dill. 187, Fed. Cas. No. 11,861; Foster v. Hackley, 2 N. B. R. 406 (132), Fed. Cas. No. 4,971; Wilson v. Brinkman, 2 N. B. R. (468) 149, Fed. Cas. No. 17,794; Graham v. Stark, 3 N. B. R. 357 (93), Fed. Cas. No. 5,676. So the fact that a warrant of attorney to confess judgment, given under such circumstances as to make it a preference, was executed under threats of legal process and arrest, and in fear of disgrace, does not shield the debtor; the act is nevertheless voluntary. Campbell v. Bank, 2 Biss. 423, Fed. Cas. No. 2,370. Nor does it alter the case that the debtor was advised by counsel that unless he made the payment he would be liable to a criminal prosecution under the state law. Strain v. Gourdin, 2 Woods, 380, Fed. Cas. No. 13,521. And it is immaterial that the preference was given at the urgent solicitation of the creditor. Clarion Bank v. Jones, 21 Wall. 325.

What Constitutes Insolvency.

Under former bankruptcy laws, where the term "insolvency" was not expressly defined, it was held that this word does not imply an absolute inability to pay one's debts at a future time upon a settlement and winding up of his concerns; but it means that the trader is not in a condition to pay his debts as they mature in the ordinary course of his business, as persons in trade usually do. In re Doyle, Holmes, 61, Fed. Cas. No. 4,050; Bailey v. Schofield, 1 Maule & S. 338; Thompson v. Thompson, 4 Cush. 127; May v. Le Claire, 18 Fed. 164; In re Gay, 2 N. B. R. 358 (114), Fed. Cas. No. 5,279; Toof v. Martin, 13 Wall. 40; Wager v. Hall, 16 Wall. 599; In re Bininger, 7 Blatchf. 262, Fed. Cas. No. 1,420; Warren v. Bank, 10 Blatchf. 493, Fed. Cas. No. 17,202; Sawyer v. Turpin, 2 Low. 29, Fed. Cas. No. 12,410. "A trader is insolvent when he cannot pay his debts in the ordinary course of business, although he may not be compelled to stop business from his inability, and although, on a settlement of his affairs, he may have sufficient to pay in full." Woods, J., in Jackson v. McCulloch, 1 Woods, 433, Fed. Cas. No. 7,140. "Insolvency, within the meaning of the bankrupt act, means inability to pay debts in the ordinary course of business, and unless the debtor is able to pay such debts as they mature, *with money*, he is insolvent in the contemplation of said act, notwithstanding he may have lands and goods sufficient in time to meet all his liabilities." Anshutz v. Hoerr, 1 Fed. 592; Swan v. Robinson, 5 Fed. 287. And the fact that a merchant, in a mercantile community, who has no defense to debts maturing in the course of his business, submits to be sued, to compel payment of such debts, is a very high evidence of his inability to pay them. Mayer v. Hermann, 10 Blatchf. 256, Fed. Cas. No. 9,344. But the first section of the present act (clause 15) provides that "a person shall be deemed insolvent, within the provisions of this act, whenever the aggregate of his property, exclusive of any property which he may have conveyed, transferred, concealed, or removed, or permitted to be concealed or removed, with intent to defraud, hinder, or delay his creditors, shall not, at a fair valuation, be sufficient in amount to pay his debts."

The question whether or not the preference was made at a time when the debtor was insolvent is a question for the jury. Pierce v. Evans, 61 Pa. St. 415.

Notice Imputable to Creditor; What is Reasonable Cause of Belief.

The rule upon this subject, as stated by Mr. Justice Field in the leading case of Toof v. Martin, 13 Wall. 49, is as follows: "The statute, to defeat the conveyances, does not require that the creditors should have had absolute knowledge on the point, nor even that they should, in fact, have had any belief on the subject. It is only required that they should have had reasonable cause to believe that such was the fact. And reasonable cause they must be considered to have had, when such a state of facts was brought to their notice in respect to the affairs and pecuniary condition of the bankrupts as would have led prudent business men to the conclusion that they could not meet their obligations as they matured in the ordinary course of business." And the transferee is not only charged with notice of facts within his knowledge, but of all such as he could have discovered upon inquiry, if reasonable prudence required inquiry. Rice v. Melendy, 41 Iowa, 399; Scammon v. Cole, 3 Cliff. 472, Fed. Cas. No. 12,432; Ex parte Mendell, 1 Low. 506, Fed. Cas. No. 9,418. And although the general business transactions and condition of the bankrupt, at the time of making a deed of preference, may not have been sufficient to raise a reasonable belief that he was insolvent, yet if the especial facts and circumstances passing between the particular parties, and out of which the deed grew, were such as to give a reasonable cause for such belief, the creditor is chargeable with notice. Alderdice v. Bank, 1 Hughes, 47, Fed. Cas. No. 154. Ignorance of the law cannot avail creditors who are possessed of facts that show the insolvency of the debtor, and a preference received under such circumstances is fraudulent and void. Martin v. Toof, 1 Dill. 203, Fed. Cas. No. 9,167. But "it is not enough that a creditor has some cause to *suspect* the insolvency of his debtor; he must have such a knowledge of facts as to induce a reasonable *belief* of his debtor's insolvency, in order to invalidate a security taken for his debt." Grant v. Bank, 97 U. S. 80; Stucky v. Bank, 108 U. S. 74, 2 Sup. Ct. 219; May v. Le Claire, 18 Fed. 164. The reasonable cause must be such as would induce a belief in the mind of an intelligent and capable business man. Otis v. Hadley, 112 Mass. 100; Graham v. Stark, 3 N. B. R. 357, Fed. Cas.

No. 5,676. Hence a preference may be avoided under the bankrupt law whenever the creditor has knowledge of facts calculated not merely to raise a suspicion, but to produce a reasonable belief of the debtor's insolvency. What facts are necessary to produce such belief must be determined in each particular case. Claridge v. Kulmer, 1 Fed. 399. And see Metcalf v. Officer, 2 Fed. 640. When it is sought to affect a second vendee (of the bankrupt's stock in trade) with fraud, such fraud must be shown; and the mere fact, without more, that he knew that the sale by the bankrupt to the first vendee embraced all of the stock of the seller, will not make the purchase of the second vendee fraudulent in law. Babbitt v. Walbrun, 1 Dill. 19, Fed. Cas. No. 694. As in other matters, knowledge may be brought home to the creditor by the possession of information on the part of those who are bound to communicate it to him. Thus, where two members of an insolvent firm are president and cashier of a bank, their knowledge of the insolvency of their firm is the knowledge of the bank. Nesbit v. Macon Co., 12 Fed. 686. Where the creditor employs an attorney to collect his debt by suit, and all the facts made necessary by the bankrupt law to invalidate a preference gained by such suit are made known to the attorney after he enters on such employment, the knowledge of the attorney is the knowledge of the creditor. Mayer v. Hermann, 10 Blatchf. 256, Fed. Cas. No. 9,344; Rogers v. Palmer, 102 U. S. 263. But where the creditor sent an account to a collection agency with directions to collect the debt, and the agency placed the claim in the hands of their attorney (who was not the attorney of the creditor), and the attorney, knowing the debtor to be insolvent, procured a confession of judgment from him, and within four months thereafter the debtor was adjudged a bankrupt, it was held that the knowledge of the attorney was not imputable to the creditor, under these circumstances, so as to make him liable to the trustee in bankruptcy for the money collected on the judgment. Hoover v. Wise, 91 U. S. 308. A banker who allows his drafts to go to protest, suspends payment, and closes his doors against depositors, proclaims to the world that he is insolvent, and a creditor who, with knowledge of these facts, receives payment of his debt, secures an illegal preference. Markson v. Hobson, 2 Dill. 327, Fed. Cas. No. 9,099. So where a merchant stops payment of his commercial paper, and the holder, being compelled to bring suit on the same, encounters no defense, he has reasonable cause to believe that the merchant is insolvent. Dunning v. Perkins, 2 Biss. 421, Fed. Cas. No. 4,180. But the simple fact that a man doing a large business obtains renewals of his commercial paper or pays, under special circumstances, a large discount, is not notice of insolvency to a creditor, it being shown that at that time similar commercial paper was selling at equal rates in the market. Golson v. Niehoff, 2 Biss. 434, Fed. Cas. No. 5,524. As it has been decided repeatedly that inability to meet debts as they mature in the ordinary course of business constitutes insolvency within the meaning of the bankrupt act, a creditor who holds unpaid protested paper of the bankrupt at the time he accepts a preference must be presumed to have actual knowledge of the insolvency of the bankrupt; and any contract by which such preference is attempted to be secured is thereby made void. Swan v. Robinson, 5 Fed. 287. A creditor may also be affected by rumors which he has heard concerning the debtor's embarrassment. Post v. Corbin, 5 N. B. R. 11, Fed. Cas. No. 11,299. And the existence of a financial crisis constitutes of itself reasonable cause for believing doubtful men to be insolvent. In re Clarke, 10 N. B. R. 21, Fed. Cas. No. 2,843. Where an execution must necessarily stop the debtor's business, the execution in general is reasonable cause to believe the debtor insolvent. Hood v. Karper, 5 N. B. R. 358, Fed. Cas. No. 6,664; Zahm v. Fry, 9 N. B. R. 546, Fed. Cas. No. 18,198. So again, the debtor's remonstrance, that the giving of the security demanded will injure his business, is sufficient to put the creditor upon inquiry. Wager v. Hall, 16 Wall. 584. "If it appears that the party making the conveyance was actually insolvent, and that the means of knowledge upon the subject were at hand, and that such facts and circumstances were known to the party receiving the conveyance as clearly put the assignee, transferee, or grantee of the property upon inquiry, it would seem to be just to hold that the party receiving the assignment, transfer, or conveyance, even if he omitted to make inquiries, had reasonable cause to believe that his assignor or grantor was insolvent." Scammon v. Cole, 3 Cliff. 472, Fed. Cas. No. 12,432. Hence it will not do to ask protection on account of ignorance, when a small amount of inquiry would have given all the necessary information. In re Wright, 2 N. B. R. 490, Fed. Cas. No. 18,071. And when the facts and circumstances are such as to put a reasonable man upon inquiry, that duty is not satisfied by an inquiry addressed to the chief actor in the suspected fraud, who has every motive for concealing the truth, when better and reliable sources of information are open to the inquirer. Singer v. Jacobs, 11 Fed. 559.

Meaning of "Transfer."

This section of the act provides that, under certain circumstances, a "transfer" of any of the debtor's property may constitute a preference. That this term is to be taken in a very wide sense is apparent on reference to the first section of the act (clause 25) wherein it is declared that "transfer shall include the sale and every other and different mode of disposing of or parting with property, or the possession of property, absolutely or conditionally, as a payment, pledge, mortgage, gift, or security."

Intention of Debtor.

Under former laws on the subject of bankruptcy, it was not only necessary that the creditor should have had reasonable cause to believe that a preference was intended, but such must have been the actual intention of the debtor. The present statute, however, only makes it necessary that "the effect of the enforcement of such judgment or transfer" should be "to enable any one of his creditors to obtain a greater percentage of his debt than any other of such creditors of the same class." This appears to make the intention of the debtor immaterial, provided a preference actually results; or rather, perhaps, it applies the rule that a man must be presumed to have intended the necessary consequences of his own acts. But since there may be some cases in which the intention of the insolvent may become an actual and material issue, we append notes of the decisions on this point rendered under the former statutes.

When the question at issue is whether a particular thing was given or done with a view to create a preference, it is the intention of the debtor which must be scrutinized, for that is the turning-point of the case. Little v. Alexander, 21 Wall. 500; In re Craft, 2 Ben. 214, Fed. Cas. No. 3,316. If the debtor did not intend to give a preference, and the creditor did not have reasonable cause to believe the debtor to be insolvent, the transfer is valid, although in fact the debtor was then insolvent. Mays v. Fritton, 20 Wall. 414. The motives of the bankrupt, as well as all the peculiar circumstances connected with the transaction, must be taken into consideration in order to determine whether he thereby gave a fraudulent preference to one creditor over others; and if he believed, and such was the fact, that money received by him from such creditor was in the nature of trust-funds, so that it would not create the ordinary relation of debtor and creditor between the parties, but a claim upon which there was a special and peculiar obligation, on his part, in the nature of a trust, to settle, a settlement thereof cannot be considered a fraudulent preference within the meaning of the bankrupt law. In re Frantzen, 20 Fed. 785. But the requisite intent on the part of an insolvent debtor to give, and of a creditor to secure, an illegal preference, may be inferred from circumstances. Vanderhoof v. City Bank, 1 Dill. 476, Fed. Cas. No. 16,842. And when a debtor is insolvent and knows it, any payment then made by him to a creditor in full must be made with an intent to prefer, as the intention of the parties is to be judged from the legal effects of their acts. Traders' Bank v. Campbell, 14 Wall. 87. Where the circumstances tend to show an intent to give and receive a preference, the failure to produce the testimony of the debtor, or of the alleged preferred creditor, as to the intent, will be considered strongly corroborative of the evidence of an intent to prefer. Darling v. Townsend, 5 Fed. 176. Where one had ceased to be a trader years before, and had disposed of all his property, but not settled all his trade debts, and was living on his salary as a clerk, and paid his rent and some other necessary expenses every month, without intending to become bankrupt, it was held that such payments were not fraudulent preferences of which his trade creditors could take advantage in opposing his discharge. In re Locke, 1 Low. 293, Fed. Cas. No. 8,439.

Burden of Proof.

The burden of showing that a creditor of a bankrupt has acquired an illegal preference is upon the trustee in bankruptcy seeking to avail himself of that fact. He must establish, by a fair preponderance of proof, that the debtor was insolvent, or in contemplation of bankruptcy or insolvency, that the security was designed to give a preference, and that the creditor had reasonable cause to believe the fact of insolvency, and knew the security was intended as a preference. Crane v. Penny, 2 Fed. 187; Parsons v. Topliff, 14 N. B. R. 547; Barbour v. Priest, 103 U. S. 293. In the case last cited the court observed: "It has never been denied, so far as we are advised, that it is necessary for the assignee of the bankrupt, in attacking such a conveyance, to prove the existence of this reasonable cause of belief of the debtor's insolvency in the mind of the preferred party." But since one is always presumed to intend the necessary and legitimate consequences of his own acts (2 Whart. Ev. § 1258), "where the act which is made the act of bankruptcy is a passive act, such as that of suffering property to be taken on legal process, when the debtor is insolvent or in contemplation of insolvency, with intent to give a preference to a creditor, if the natural and probable consequence of the act of sufferance is to give the preference to the creditor, it will be inferred that the debtor had such intent, unless he shows the contrary; and the burden will be upon him to show the contrary." Blatchford, J., in In re Black, 2 Ben. 196, Fed. Cas. No. 1,457; Webb v. Sachs, 4 Sawy. 158, Fed. Cas. No. 17,325. The testimony of the parties to a transaction challenged as preferential under the bankrupt law, as to their intentions, though competent, is inherently weak and can rarely avail against the stronger proof which the transaction itself affords. Oxford Iron Co. v. Slafter, 13 Blatchf. 455, Fed. Cas. No. 10,637.

Recovery by Trustee.

Under the provisions of this section, it might appear at first sight that the trustee could not maintain an action to set aside or avoid a transfer of property made by the debtor prior to the time limited by the bankrupt law itself; that if such transfer or conveyance were made more than four months before the filing of the petition in bankruptcy, the trustee would have no authority to recover the property. But this is to be read in connection with section 70 of the act, which provides that there shall vest in the trustee the title to "property transferred by him [the bankrupt] in fraud of his creditors," and that "the trustee may avoid any transfer, by the bankrupt, of his property which any creditor of such bankrupt might have avoided, and may recover the property so transferred, or its value, from the person to whom it was transferred, unless he was a bona fide holder for value prior to the date of the adjudication." And it has been decided, under a substantially similar clause, that this gives to the trustee a right of action to annul any fraudulent conveyance of the bankrupt, whenever made, even before the bankrupt act was passed, so it be not barred by the statute of limitations. Cady v. Whaling, 7 Biss. 430, Fed. Cas. No. 2,285; Cookingham v. Ferguson, 8 Blatchf. 488, Fed. Cas. No. 3,182. Where property has been transferred under such circumstances as to constitute a preference, the trustee may recover possession of the property itself, and the market value of any that has been sold by the transferee, with interest from the time he demanded it. Cookingham v. Morgan, 7 Blatchf. 480, Fed. Cas. No. 3,183. The trustee of one partner cannot set aside a conveyance made by both partners with intent to prefer a joint creditor, the other partner not being bankrupt; for the preference does not become fraudulent and therefore voidable, unless they *both* become bankrupt within the time limited. Forsaith v. Merritt, 1 Low. 336, Fed. Cas. No. 4,946. Where the grantee in a conveyance made by an insolvent debtor, in fraud of the bankrupt act, takes the title merely at the request of and in trust for a third person, and derives no profit from the transaction, he is not liable to the assignee in bankruptcy for the value of the land, unless he not only knew of the insolvency, but also shared the bankrupt's intent to defeat the law. Alleman v. Kneedler, 2 Fed. 671. The amount which the trustee is entitled to recover from a creditor who has received a preference by means of a judgment, is the gross amount obtained on execution, without any deduction for the costs and expenses of the creditor. Traders' Bank v. Campbell, 14 Wall. 27; Street v. Dawson, 4 N. B. R. 207, Fed. Cas. No. 13,533.

CHAPTER VII.

ESTATES.

DEPOSITORIES FOR MONEY.

§ 61. *a* **Courts of bankruptcy shall designate, by order, banking institutions as depositories for the money of bankrupt estates, as convenient as may be to the residences of trustees, and shall require bonds to the United States, subject to their approval, to be given by such banking institutions, and may from time to time as occasion may require, by like order increase the number of depositories or the amount of any bond or change such depositories.**

Depositories.

Under the statute and the rules of court, all sums of money received by assignees in bankruptcy, and by the clerk of the district court were required to be deposited, with a certain bank to be named by the court, to be drawn out upon the checks of the court. The funds so deposited were kept as a unit to the credit of the court, and were paid out on checks signed by the clerk and countersigned by the judge. The clerk failed to make deposit of all the funds received by him, and the bank paid checks drawn on it until it had paid out all the funds deposited, but refused to pay other checks drawn, whereupon suit was brought on a check so refused. It was held that the bank was not liable to the holder of such check. As there was no misappropriation of the funds by the bank, it was not liable for any deficit in the amount due beneficiaries, arising from the neglect of the clerk to deposit all the trust funds that came to his hands as an officer of the court. The bank was not bound to open a separate account as to the several cases in which the deposits were made, nor to take notice of any memoranda either on the margin or in the body of any check drawn upon it, for such memoranda are to be regarded as having been made for the convenience of the drawers, and not as an order or direction to the bank. State Nat. Bank v. Reilly, 124 Ill. 464, 14 N. E. 657.

EXPENSES OF ADMINISTERING ESTATES.

§ 62. *a* **The actual and necessary expenses incurred by officers in the administration of estates shall, except where other provisions are made for their payment, be reported in detail, under oath, and examined and approved or disapproved by the court. If approved, they shall be paid or allowed out of the estates in which they were incurred.**

Allowance for Expenses.

On a trustee's accounting in bankruptcy, charges for the employment of a book-keeper will not be passed, beyond what is proved to have been necessary in the administration of the estate, nor for a longer period than the exigencies required. And where charges are made for a book-keeper employed partly in the personal business of the trustee, and partly for the estate, no apportionment of charges by the trustee will be approved except upon proof of the services rendered, their necessity, and their reasonable value. In re Barnes, 18 Fed. 158. And the same rule applies to rent for offices used for both purposes. Id. The court may, in proper cases, authorize the trustee to expend money of the estate in finishing goods for sale, when it is clear that benefit will result to the estate, and that the work can be done within a reasonable time. Foster v. Ames, 1 Low. 313, Fed. Cas. No. 4,965. A trustee is not at liberty to charge the assets of the estate in his hands for professional and clerical services rendered him in the execution of his trust, unless the same shall have been first duly allowed by the court. In re Noyes, 6 N. B. R. 277, Fed. Cas. No. 10,371. This allowance for services cannot be made until after the services have been rendered, because, until the court is advised what the services have been, it cannot determine whether any particular amount of compensation is or is not reasonable. In re Hughes, 2 Ben. 85, Fed. Cas. No. 6,841. Fees for the assistance of an attorney will not be allowed without the most satisfactory evidence going to show the necessity for legal aid on the part of the trustee and the actual rendition of the services charged for. In re Tulley, 3 N. B. R. 82, Fed. Cas. No. 14,235. A trustee's account for money paid to an attorney for services not authorized by the court cannot be allowed beyond what the evidence shows to be reasonable, having reference to the amount and circumstances of the estate. In re Cook, 17 Fed. 328. A trustee cannot be permitted to expend the chief part of the money collected by him in the employment of an attorney to search for additional property, which results in nothing. Id. The attorneys having charge of proceedings in behalf of the trustee are bound to take steps to procure indemnity from the general creditors, in whose interest proceedings for the remission of a forfeiture were instituted by them, before incurring large expenses therein; and not having done so, and the proceedings being fruitless and without benefit to the estate, neither they nor the trustee have any claim for their services in the remission proceedings, as against the fund. In re Barnes, 18 Fed. 158. The court, in its discretion, may allow to the trustee additional compensation for his own services as an attorney at law in the conduct of necessary litigation for the preservation of the estate. In re Welge, 1 McCrary, 46, 1 Fed. 216. Where creditors have in good faith brought suit against the trustee, and have been defeated, and the estate is insufficient to pay both their costs and the costs and counsel fees of the trustee, the latter is entitled to preference. Gazin v. Norton, 38 Fed. 200. A voluntary assignee in insolvency under a void assignment will not be reimbursed his expenses incurred under the assignment, nor is he entitled to compensation for services as assignee. For such services and disbursements, however, as benefit the general body of creditors, either by reason of the preservation of the fund to their use, by advantageous collection of assets, or by conversion of property into money, he will be allowed what is reasonable and just. Hunker v. Bing, 9 Fed. 277. In a case of involuntary bankruptcy, the creditor on whose petition the debtor is adjudged bankrupt, and who pays his attorney a reasonable fee for prosecuting the proceeding, is entitled to receive the amount so paid out of the assets of the estate before a dividend is declared. But he is not entitled to reimbursement for time and money spent in traveling to and from the court and in attending the trial of the case. In re King, 4 Biss. 319, Fed. Cas. No. 7,780. See, also, In re New York Mail S. S. Co., 7 Blatchf. 178, Fed. Cas. No. 10,208.

Fees of Successive Trustees.

A former trustee of a bankrupt estate has not a prior claim for his compensation to that of a subsequent trustee in whose hands there are not sufficient funds to pay the charges of both. And it seems that in such a case the amount should be divided pro rata between the two trustees. In re Schneider, 15 Fed. 913.

DEBTS WHICH MAY BE PROVED.

§ 63. *a* Debts of the bankrupt may be proved and allowed against his estate which are (1) a fixed liability, as evidenced by a judgment or an instrument in writing, absolutely owing at the time of the filing of the petition against him, whether then payable or not, with any interest thereon which would have been recoverable at that date or with a rebate of interest upon such as were not then payable and did not bear interest; (2) due as costs taxable against an involuntary bankrupt who was at the time of the filing of the petition against him plaintiff in a cause of action which would pass to the trustee and which the trustee declines to prosecute after notice; (3) founded upon a claim for taxable costs incurred in good faith by a creditor before the filing of the petition in an action to recover a provable debt; (4) founded upon an open account, or upon a contract express or implied; and (5) founded upon provable debts reduced to judgments after the filing of the petition and before the consideration of the bankrupt's application for a discharge, less costs incurred and interests accrued after the filing of the petition and up to the time of the entry of such judgments.

b Unliquidated claims against the bankrupt may, pursuant to application to the court, be liquidated in such manner as it shall direct, and may thereafter be proved and allowed against his estate.

Provable Debts.

As a general rule, every debt recoverable either at law or in equity is provable in bankruptcy. In re Jordan, 2 Fed. 319. But a debt contracted by the bankrupt subsequent to the commencement of the proceedings against him cannot be proved in bankruptcy. In re Merrell, 19 Fed. 874. The fees of an attorney for resisting an involuntary adjudication and preparing the schedules cannot be proved as a debt against the bankrupt unless the retainer was prior to the date of the filing of the bankruptcy petition. In re Ward, 12 Fed. 325.

Debts Payable in the Future.

The law provides that debts which are owing at the time of the petition shall be provable, whether they are immediately payable or payable in the future. The test is the fixed and certain character of the liability. Thus, one who holds the bankrupt's note not yet due, has a good right to petition, for his claim is provable. In re Alexander, 1 Low. 470, Fed. Cas. No. 161. So the liability of a subscriber to corporate stock for his unpaid subscription is a provable debt in bankruptcy against the estate of such subscriber, although no assessment has yet been made, because the debt, although not yet due, is fixed and ascertainable. Glenn v. Abell, 39 Fed. 10. But compare, as to the last point, Sayre v. Glenn, 87 Ala. 631, 6 South. 45, where a contrary ruling was made.

Equitable Demands.

A debt, in order to be provable in bankruptcy, need not be enforceable at law, but may be of an equitable character. Sigsby v. Willis, 3 Ben. 371, Fed. Cas. No. 12,849. Where an assignee in bankruptcy made a demand for certain wagons belonging to the bankrupt which were stored in the petitioner's barn, and delivery was refused on the ground of a lien claimed on them for storage, it was held that the refusal to deliver to the assignee on demand was in the petitioner's own wrong, and debarred her from any claim for subsequent storage while held under that refusal. But it was also held that the petitioner was entitled to an equitable compensation for the storage of the goods from the time of the proceedings in bankruptcy up to the time of the demand and refusal. In re Kelly, 18 Fed. 528. And see, on a somewhat similar state of facts, In re Secor, Id. 319. The costs of an attachment, laid by the wife of the bankrupt in a libel for divorce, are not provable in the bankruptcy, and are not an equitable charge against the assets in the hands of the trustee. In re Foye, 2 Low. 399, Fed. Cas. No. 5,021.

Breaches of Covenant.

A covenant against incumbrances, in a deed of land, is broken, immediately upon the conveyance, by an outstanding and unpaid mortgage; and the damages from such breach constitute a debt provable against the grantor in bankruptcy. Reed v. Pierce, 36 Me. 455; Parker v. Bradford, 45 Iowa, 311; Williams v. Harkins, 55 Ga. 172. So a demand arising from the breach of a covenant for quiet enjoyment contained in a deed, is a contingent debt provable in bankruptcy. Jemison v. Blowers, 5 Barb. 686. A claim arising in damages for breach of a warranty of a piece of machinery is provable when the breach occurred before the petition in bankruptcy was filed. Merrill v. Schwartz, 68 Me. 514. And a claim founded upon a covenant to repay part of the premium paid for a policy of insurance issued by a stock company, upon cancellation of the policy, is provable in bankruptcy. In re Independent Ins. Co., 2 Low. 187, Fed. Cas. No. 7,019.

Judgments.

A judgment is a provable debt in bankruptcy. But a verdict, without a judgment upon it is not a provable debt; it does not come within the category of claims whose payment is postponed to a future day. Black v. McClelland, 12 N. B. R. 481, Fed. Cas. No. 1,462. Where a judgment debt is offered for proof against the estate of a bankrupt, whose petition was filed after the rendition of the judgment, it may be objected to by the other creditors on the ground of fraud or irregularity, including fraudulent preference, for they, not being parties or privies to the judgment, are not prohibited from subjecting it to collateral impeachment when it conflicts with their interests. Ex parte O'Neil, 1 Low. 163, Fed. Cas. No. 10,527.

Liability of Bankrupt as Drawer, Indorser, or Surety.

Where a party, previous to becoming a bankrupt, was liable on a bond, by the terms of which he became a continuing guarantor of notes discounted by a certain bank for a company of which he was the president, and at the time of his bankruptcy the bank held a note so discounted, indorsed by him, the fact that a renewal note was given after the filing of his petition, will not prevent the debt from being proved as a claim against the estate. In re Letchworth, 19 Fed. 873. A claim of this character, against the bankrupt, under this clause of the act, cannot be proved until the liability has become fixed. Until that time it is not regarded as a debt due and payable, or even as a debt existing but not payable until a future day, in such sense as to be provable. In re Loder, 4 N. B. R. 190, Fed. Cas. No. 8,457. And in order to charge the bankrupt as indorser upon a demand note, the note must be presented for payment within a reasonable time; a demand after four years is not sufficient. In re Crawford, 5 N. B. R. 301, Fed. Cas. No. 3,364. The act includes indorsers who are liable in the second instance only. McNeil v. Knott, 11 Ga. 142. The guarantors of a note, the holder of which has forfeited his claim against the bankrupt estate, have no right to prove against the estate, for their liability has been already discharged by the act of the principal. In re Ayers, 6 Biss. 48, Fed. Cas. No. 685. So where an indorsee of a note has proved his claim against the estate of the maker in bankruptcy, and afterwards, pending the bankruptcy proceedings, receives payment from the indorser, his relation to the liability ceases, he can no longer be considered a creditor of the maker, and he can take no further part in the proceedings; but the indorser is subrogated to his rights in respect of the demand, and it belongs to him to participate, in that capacity, in the future proceedings. In re Broich, 7 Biss. 303, Fed. Cas. No. 1,921. The bona fide holder for value of an accommodation bill is entitled, on the bankruptcy of the parties thereto, to prove as to all parties against whom the holder could have supported an action on the bill. Downing v. Traders' Bank, 2 Dill. 136, Fed. Cas. No. 4,046. Where the bankrupt is the indorser of a note, and the maker has paid a part thereof to the holder, the latter can prove against the bankrupt's estate only for the balance unpaid. In re Pulsifer, 9 Biss. 487, 14 Fed. 247. The estates of five out of the seven sureties on an official bond are not released by the acceptance of the individual bonds of their co-sureties, since become insolvent, but the city (the obligee) may prove against their estates for the whole debt. In re Blumer, 13 Fed. 623.

Interest.

The accrued interest constitutes part of a debt provable against the bankrupt's estate. Sloan v. Lewis, 22 Wall. 150. But interest accruing subsequently to the time of adjudication is not provable. In re Haake, 2 Sawy. 231, Fed. Cas. No. 5,883. If the contract is silent as to interest after maturity, the creditor is entitled to interest from that time to the date of adjudication by operation of law, and not by any provision of the contract. In re Bartenbach, 11 N. B. R. 61, Fed. Cas. No. 1,068. But a creditor seeking to prove his claim against the debtor's estate in bankruptcy stands in the position of a plaintiff at law, and the trustee may set up usury in defense; hence if, by the state law, the taking of usury causes a forfeiture of all interest when the debt is put in suit, the same consequence attends the presentation in bankruptcy of a claim on which usury has been exacted. In re Prescott, 5 Biss. 523, Fed. Cas. No. 11,389.

Debts Barred by Limitation.

A debt or claim against which the statute of limitations has run can no longer be said to be "due," "owing," or "payable" by the debtor. And hence if a debt (otherwise provable) is barred by the statute of limitations of the state where the debtor resides, at the time of the adjudication, it cannot be proved against his estate in bankruptcy. In re Kingsley, 1 Low. 216, Fed. Cas. No. 7,819; In re Hardin, 1 N. B. R. 396, Fed. Cas. No. 6,048; In re Reed, 6 Biss. 250, Fed. Cas. No. 11,635; In re Noesen, 6 Biss. 443, Fed. Cas. No. 10,288; In re Cornwall, 9 Blatchf. 114, Fed. Cas. No. 3,250. This is also the English rule. Ex parte Dewdney, 15 Ves. 479. But on the other hand, it is held in Re Ray, 2 Ben. 53, Fed. Cas. No. 11,589, and In re Shepard, 1 N. B. R. 439, Fed. Cas. No. 12,753, that a debt, to be barred by limitation so as not to be provable in bankruptcy, must be shown to be so barred throughout the limits of the United States. In accordance with the doctrine of the majority of the cases, it is held that a debt which is barred by the statutes of the state where the debtor resides and where the petition is filed cannot be proved against his estate in bankruptcy, though not barred by the statutes of the state where the creditor resides and where both parties resided when the contract was made. In re Kingsley, 1 Low. 216, Fed. Cas. No. 7,819. In the case of Nicholas v. Murray, 5 Sawy. 320, Fed. Cas. No. 10,223, Judge Deady thought that if the debt was not barred at the time of the adjudication, still the statute is not suspended by the bankruptcy proceedings, but continues to run against the debt, and after the term has expired it is no longer provable. But the opposite view is supported by the greater weight of authority. In re Wright, 6 Biss. 317, Fed. Cas. No. 18,068; In re Eldridge, 12 N. B. R. 540, Fed. Cas. No. 4,331; Wofford v. Unger, 53 Tex. 634. These last cases hold that a debt which was not barred at the time when the petition was filed will remain valid against the trustee throughout the bankruptcy proceedings, and will be provable at any time when offered, notwithstanding the whole time limited by the statute has then expired, for the institution of the bankruptcy proceedings stops the running of the statute.

Rights of Creditor where Several Parties are Liable.

A creditor who holds commercial paper signed by a firm in bankruptcy and indorsed by an individual member of the firm, a bankrupt, may prove his debt against both estates and share in the dividends of each; because he would have had a right of action against each, though entitled to but one satisfaction. Emery v. Bank, 3 Cliff. 507, Fed. Cas. No. 4,446; In re Bigelow, 2 N. B. R. 121, Fed. Cas. No. 1,397; In re Howard, 4 N. B. R. 185, Fed. Cas. No. 6,750; Mead v. Bank of Fayetteville, 6 Blatchf. 185, 7 Am. Law Reg. (N. S.) 818, Fed. Cas. No. 9,366. Out of a firm consisting of four partners, two were insolvent, one was a bankrupt, and the fourth paid off and discharged all the firm debts out of his separate estate; it was held that he was entitled to prove against the separate estate of the bankrupt one-half of the amount so paid by him. In re Dell, 5 Sawy. 344, Fed. Cas. No. 3,774. Where the firm of A. & B. was indebted to the firm of B. & C., and the former firm became bankrupt, it was held that C., as the remaining member of the latter firm, settling its affairs, could prove the debt against the assets of A. & B. In re Buckhause, 2 Low. 331, Fed. Cas. No. 2,086.

Who are Creditors within the Act.

Any person who is authorized to give an acquittance of a debt is entitled to prove that debt in bankruptcy. Ex parte Norwood, 3 Biss. 504, Fed. Cas. No. 10,364. The bankrupt's *wife* may prove as a creditor against his estate for money realized by him out of property which she held as her separate estate, if it clearly appears that the transaction was intended as a loan and not as a gift. In re Blandin, 1 Low. 543, Fed. Cas. No. 1,527. A creditor who resides out of the district where the bankruptcy proceedings are taken, subjects himself to the jurisdiction of the court by proving his debt, and is thereafter bound to obey all the orders of the court touching his alleged debt, and the court, in case he disobeys its orders, can deprive him of all the benefits of the act, and can reject and expunge his claims. In re Kyler, 2 Ben. 414, Fed. Cas. No. 7,956. The government, in the capacity of a creditor, may prove its claims. Where, before the commencement of bankruptcy proceedings, the United States brought an action against the bankrupts to recover the value of goods which had been forfeited for violation of the customs revenue laws, and after the adjudication the bankrupts admitted the right of the government to recover, and a judgment was rendered, it was held that this was a provable debt. In re Vetterlein, 13 Blatchf. 44, Fed. Cas. No. 16,929. See also Barnes v. U. S., 12 N. B. R. 526, Fed. Cas. No. 1,023. A court of bankruptcy may permit the bankrupts themselves, acting in a representative capacity as the administrators of an estate, to prove an equitable debt, arising from a loan of funds borrowed from the estate of their intestate, whether such loan was lawful or not. Warner v. Spooner, 3 Fed. 890. Services rendered by counsel for the benefit of particular creditors only, and not for all the creditors of the bankrupt, are not allowable against the estate of such bankrupt. In re Baxter, 28 Fed. 452.

Rights of Bankrupt's Surety.

The surety has a provable claim against the principal's estate in bankruptcy, although he has not yet paid the debt for which he is liable. Lipscomb v. Grace, 26 Ark. 231; Mace v. Wells, 7 How. 272; Kyle v. Bostick, 10 Ala. 589; Fulwood v. Bushfield, 14 Pa. St. 90; Tubbs v. Williams, 9 Ired. 1; Morse v. Hovey, 1 Sandf. Ch. 187; Post v. Losey, 111 Ind. 74, 12 N. E. 121; Liddell v. Wiswell, 59 Vt. 365, 8 Atl. 680. See, per contra, Ecker v. Bohn, 45 Md. 278. The claim of an indorser against the principal debtor is a provable debt, notwithstanding the indorser does not pay the note until after the commencement of the bankruptcy proceedings. Hardy v. Carter, 8 Humph. 153. Rev. St. § 5070 settles the question that the payment of a part of a debt by a surety does not entitle him to prove the same as a debt against the principal until the creditor is paid in full. In re Hollister, 3 Fed. 452, distinguishing Downing v. Traders' Bank, 2 Dill. 136, Fed. Cas. No. 4,046.

Fraudulent Conduct or Laches of Creditor bars Proof of Claim.

Where the creditor included in his proof claims a part of which were invalid and some valid, and made his claim in this manner intentionally, knowing that only part of it was legal, and supported the claim for the whole amount by a false oath, it was held that this fraudulent conduct would disentitle him to any dividends whatever on any part of his claim. Marrett v. Atterbury, 3 Dill. 444, Fed. Cas. No. 9,-102. So a claim for money loaned to a debtor to aid him in the commission of an act of bankruptcy is not a provable debt; to admit it, would simply give legal effect to a fraud. In re Hatje, 6 Biss. 436, Fed. Cas. No. 6,215. Where the bankrupt's brokers were carrying stocks on a margin, and, at the commencement of the bankruptcy proceedings, could have sold them out at a profit, but carried the stocks until a decline and finally sold at a loss, all without application to the court, it was held that they could not prove their claim for differences against the estate. In re Daniels, 6 Biss. 405, Fed. Cas. No. 3,566. On the other hand, where a party whose estate will pay fifty cents on the dollar, intending to go into bankruptcy, gets a friend to buy up all or a part of his indebtedness at ten cents on the dollar, upon false statements of fact as to the amount of dividend his estate will pay, no court of bankruptcy would hesitate to hold that an indebtedness thus obliterated by fraud could be proven against the bankrupt's estate. In re State Ins. Co., 16 Fed. 756.

Contingent Demands and Liabilities.

So long as it remains wholly uncertain whether a contract or engagement will ever give rise to an actual duty or liability, and there is no means of removing the uncertainty by calculation, such contract or engagement is not provable in bankruptcy. It was so held in regard to a claim for breach of a covenant that the grantor had an indefeasible estate in fee, the claim arising from the grantor's wife's right of dower, both husband and wife being yet alive. Riggin v. Magwire, 15 Wall. 549; Mills v. Auriol, 1 Smith's Lead. Cas. (8th Ed.) pt. II, p. 1266, American note. The fact that the accounts of a guardian with his ward are in course of settlement in the probate court does not preclude the ward from proving her claim against the guardian's estate in bankruptcy. Bourne v. Maybin, 3 Woods, 724, Fed. Cas. No. 1,700. Where a judgment-creditor issues process of garnishment, and obtains a judgment and makes demand against the garnishee long after the latter's bankruptcy, such judgment is not a debt provable ex parte against the garnishee's estate. Ex parte Columbian Ins. Co., 2 Low. 5, Fed. Cas. No. 3,037. Every joint debtor has a demand against his co-debtor contingent upon his being compelled to pay more than his share of the debt, and such a demand is provable in bankruptcy.

Dean v. Speakman, 7 Blackf. 317. A loss on a policy of fire insurance is a provable debt against the estate of the company in bankruptcy, although the loss occurred after the adjudication, if proof is made before a final dividend. In Re American Plate Glass Co., 12 N. B. R. 56, Fed. Cas. No. 314. A note deposited with a third person for the sole purpose of enabling the creditor to determine whether he will elect to abide by a certain contract and receive the note, is a contingent demand. Spalding v. Dixon, 21 Vt. 45. A liability as bail is a provable claim against the bankrupt's estate, if the liability became fixed before the final dividend was declared. Houston v. State, 34 Tex. 542. The contingent liability of a surety on a guardian's bond is provable against him. Davis v. McCurdy, 50 Wis. 569, 7 N. W. 665.

Privileges of an Unexpired Contract.

A lessee, whose goods were under distraint for rent, made an assignment for the benefit of creditors. The assignee, while disclaiming any interest in the lease, made an arrangement with the lessor by which the distress was withdrawn, he promising to pay the rent then in arrear, and all rent which should accrue during his occupancy of the premises, and to inform the lessor when he would vacate. About two months afterwards he vacated the premises, sending the key to the lessor and paying the rent up to that day. The lessor thereupon re-entered and rented the premises to other parties for a less rent. On this state of facts it was held that there was neither an eviction of the tenant nor a surrender of the lease, and that the lessor was entitled to prove against the lessee's estate in bankruptcy for damages for the breach of the covenant in the lease to pay the subsequently accruing rent. In re Orne, 12 Fed. 779.

Landlord's Rights and Remedies.

A landlord cannot prove, as a claim against the bankrupt's estate, a demand for rent which accrued after the bankruptcy; but if either the bankrupt or the trustee continues to occupy the leased premises after the bankruptcy, he is personally liable for the rent, and the lessor has the usual lien on goods on the premises. In Re Commercial Bulletin Co., 2 Woods, 220, Fed. Cas. No. 3,060. If the trustee elects to take a term belonging to the bankrupt under a lease, he takes it with the burden of the accruing rent, and not merely with the obligation to pay from the time he begins to occupy. Ex parte Faxon, 1 Low. 404, Fed. Cas. No. 4,704. An express provision in a lease whereby the lessee gives to the lessor a lien on specified personal property used by the former upon the demised premises, when not in conflict with any statute, is valid against the lessee and his trustee in bankruptcy. McLean v. Klein, 3 Dill. 113, Fed. Cas. No. 8,884. So also a lease which, by its terms, cannot be assigned without the written consent of the landlord, is cancelled by the bankruptcy. In re Breck, 8 Ben. 93, Fed. Cas. No. 1,822.

Claims for Torts and Penalties.

The present statute provides that "unliquidated claims" against the bankrupt may be proved in bankruptcy, after being liquidated by the court. It was otherwise under the bankrupt act of 1867. Under that statute it was held that a claim for damages for a tort of a purely personal character, such as assault, slander, or deceit, was not a debt provable in bankruptcy. In re Hennocksburgh, 6 Ben. 150, Fed. Cas. No. 6,367; In re Schuchardt, 8 Ben. 585, Fed. Cas. No. 12,483. In the case of the Boston & Fairhaven Iron Works, 29 Fed. 783, it was held that a claim for an account of profits against an infringer of a patent-right was provable against his estate in bankruptcy. This decision was reversed in the circuit court (23 Fed. 880) by Colt, J., on the ground that the claim was one for unliquidated damages for a tort, and therefore not provable. But under the present state of the law, the original decision must now be regarded as good, and not the ruling of the circuit court. See also Watson v. Holliday, 20 Ch. Div. 780. A judgment in favor of the state for a fine imposed upon the bankrupt as a punishment for the commission of a crime of which he had been duly convicted was not a provable debt. In Re Sutherland, Deady, 416, Fed. Cas. No. 13,639. If, however, a claim sounding in tort has been reduced to judgment before the institution of bankruptcy proceedings against the defendant, it is so far merged in the judgment as to be no longer excluded from proof against his estate. In other words, a judgment existing against the bankrupt at the time the petition is filed is a provable debt against his estate, irrespective of whether the cause of action upon which the judgment was founded arose out of a tort or a contract. Howland v. Carson, 28 Ohio St. 625; Hays v. Ford, 55 Ind. 52. But if the adjudication in bankruptcy intervenes between the rendition of a verdict and the entry of judgment upon it, the debt was held not provable. Zimmer v. Schleehauf, 115 Mass. 52; Ex parte Charles, 14 East, 197; Black v. McClelland, 12 N. B. R. 481, Fed. Cas. No. 1,462. "Where a claim originates in contract, although fraudulently induced, and is prosecuted in an action sounding in damages, it continues to constitute a provable debt, even though the fraud must be proved to entitle the plaintiff to a recovery." In re Schwartz, 14 Blatch. 196, Fed. Cas. No. 12,502. But a liability by reason of the wrongful conversion of chattels by the bankrupt is provable. Cole v. Roach, 37 Tex. 413.

DEBTS WHICH HAVE PRIORITY.

§ **64.** *a* The court shall order the trustee to pay all taxes legally due and owing by the bankrupt to the United States, state, county, district, or municipality in advance of the payment of dividends to creditors, and upon filing the receipts of the proper public officers for such payment he shall be credited with the amount thereof, and in case any question arises as to the amount or legality of any such tax the same shall be heard and determined by the court.

b The debts to have priority, except as herein provided, and to be paid in full out of bankrupt estates, and the order of payment shall be (1) the actual and necessary cost of preserving the estate subsequent to filing the petition; (2) the filing fees paid by creditors in involuntary cases; (3) the cost of administration, including the fees and mileage payable to witnesses as now or hereafter provided by the laws of the United States, and one reasonable attorney's fee, for the professional services actually rendered, irrespective of the number of attorneys employed, to the petitioning creditors in involuntary cases, to the bankrupt in involuntary cases while performing the duties herein prescribed, and to the bankrupt in voluntary cases, as the court may allow; (4) wages due to workmen, clerks, or servants which have been earned within three months before the date of the commencement of proceedings, not to exceed three hundred dollars to each claimant; and (5) debts owing to any per-

son who by the laws of the states or the United States is entitled to priority.

c In the event of the confirmation of a composition being set aside, or a discharge revoked, the property acquired by the bankrupt in addition to his estate at the time the composition was confirmed or the adjudication was made shall be applied to the payment in full of the claims of creditors for property sold to him on credit, in good faith, while such composition or discharge was in force, and the residue, if any, shall be applied to the payment of the debts which were owing at the time of the adjudication.

Priority of the United States.

The present bankruptcy law, it will be observed, does not expressly grant a priority of payment to debts due the United States, except in the case of taxes. But it accords such a priority to "debts owing to any person who by the laws of the states or the United States is entitled to priority." Now an earlier act of congress provides that, whenever any person indebted to the United States is insolvent, or whenever the estate of any deceased debtor, in the hands of the executors or administrators, is not sufficient to pay all the debts due from the deceased, the debts due to the United States shall be first satisfied, and the priority thereby established shall extend as well to cases in which a debtor, not having sufficient property to pay all his debts, makes a voluntary assignment thereof, or in which the estate and effects of an absconding, concealed, or absent debtor are attached by process of law, as to cases in which an act of bankruptcy is committed. Rev. St. U. S. § 3466. And see Lewis v. U. S., 92 U. S. 618. The courts are not likely to hold that this statute is repealed, by implication, by the bankruptcy law. On the contrary, the two acts are to be read together as in pari materia; and the priority of debts due the government should be regarded as established by law, to the same extent as if the provisions of the earlier statute were incorporated in this section of the bankruptcy law.

Where a bankrupt firm, through fraudulent undervaluations of goods entered at the custom-house, has incurred a forfeiture of their value to the United States, the claim of the latter against the firm for the tort is joint and several; and upon proof of the debt, containing a statement of the facts, the United States is entitled, under sections 5501 and 3466 of the Revised Statutes, to priority of payment out of any of the proceeds of either the joint or several estates, without reference to what may be the particular claim of priority in its proof of debt. In re Vetterlein, 20 Fed. 109. The right of priority of the United States extends to debts of every kind, including the indorsement of a bill of exchange of which the government is the holder. U. S. v. Fisher, 2 Cranch, 358, Fed. Cas. No. 14,720. It extends as well to equitable as to legal debts. Howe v. Sheppard, 2 Sumn. 133, Fed. Cas. No. 6,772. It includes a penalty incurred for a violation of the internal revenue laws. In Re Rosey, 6 Ben. 507, Fed. Cas. No. 12,066. So the government is entitled to priority of payment out of the effects of the bankrupt whether he be principal or surety, or be solely liable, or jointly with others, and it is immaterial where the debt was contracted. Lewis v. U. S., 92 U. S. 618. But this right of priority is not in the nature of a lien. U. S. v. Hooe, 3 Cranch, 73; U. S. v. Mechanics' Bank, Gilp. 51, Fed. Cas. No. 15,756; and the right is only to priority of payment out of the *general* estate, so that the government has no right to preference over the holder of a valid lien. The Thomas Scattergood, Gilp. 1, Fed. Cas. No. 11,106. It has been held that if the government holds a claim against a debtor in bankruptcy, and with knowledge of the bankruptcy proceedings fails to prove its claim or have it allowed in some form, it cannot assert any rights against the trustee after the estate is fully administered and the fund distributed under orders of court. U. S. v. Murphy, 11 Biss. 415, 15 Fed. 589. But the better opinion appears to be that the trustee in bankruptcy becomes a trustee for the United States, and when he has notice of the debt due the government, he cannot escape personal liability for the amount of it, to the extent of the value of the assets coming to his hands, if he fails to provide for it before making distribution to other creditors. The judgment of a court of competent jurisdiction, directing such distribution, will afford the trustee no justification in such a case, where it does not appear that the United States was made a party to the proceedings in which such judgment was rendered. The government, by omitting to prove its claim in the bankruptcy proceedings until after such distribution is made, does not lose its right to proceed against the trustee personally. The doctrines of waiver, laches, and estoppel cannot be invoked against the sovereign. U. S. v. Barnes, 31 Fed. 705; Field v. U. S., 9 Pet. 182; Lewis v. U. S., 92 U. S. 618. When a person pays the duty on an imported article, in order to get it out of the bonded warehouse, he will be subrogated to the rights of the United States against the failing sureties. In re Chase, 14 N. B. R. 139, Fed. Cas. No. 7,843.

Debts Due a State.

A judgment recovered by the state of New York against a surety in a bail-bond given for the appearance of a person indicted for a crime, is a debt due the state and entitled to priority. In Re Chamberlain, 9 Ben. 149, Fed. Cas. No. 2,580. So a debt due the state upon a contract for the employment of convict labor is entitled to priority of payment. In Re Southwestern Car Co., 9 Biss. 76, Fed. Cas. No. 13,192. But where the warden of a state penitentiary deposits funds in his own name, as warden, in a bank which afterwards becomes insolvent, the warden being liable to the state on his bond for the amount, the state has no claim to priority of payment. In re Corn Exchange Bank, 7 Biss. 400, Fed. Cas. No. 3,242.

Wages and Other Claims.

Orders for goods, drawn by a manufacturing company in favor of their employés, are not preferred claims in the hands of the drawee, against the estate of the bankrupt company. In re Erie Rolling Mill Co., 1 Fed. 585. Where the bankrupt is indebted to several laborers, and one person loans each of them a certain sum, agreeing to collect their dues and pay himself out of the same, and takes an absolute assignment of their claims, his demand against the employer's estate in bankruptcy, for the amounts so advanced, will be entitled to priority. In re Brown, 4 Ben. 142, Fed. Cas. No. 1,974. But an attorney's claim for legal services in preparing the petition and schedules, and for advice in relation thereto, and for disbursements, is not a privileged debt. In re Hirschberg, 2 Ben. 466, Fed. Cas. No. 6,530. Where, by the state statute, mechanics' liens relate back to the commencement of the building, there can be no priority among the mechanics; they all stand upon the same footing and are to be paid in full or pro rata as the funds may suffice. In re Hoyt, 3 Biss. 436, Fed. Cas. No. 6,805.

DECLARATION AND PAYMENT OF DIVIDENDS.

§ 65. *a* Dividends of an equal per centum shall be declared and paid on all allowed claims, except such as have priority or are secured.

b The first dividend shall be declared within thirty days after the adjudication, if the money of the estate in excess of the amount necessary to pay the debts which have priority and such claims as have not been, but probably will be, allowed equals five per centum or more of such allowed claims. Dividends subsequent to the first shall be declared upon like terms as the first and as often as the amount shall equal ten per centum or more and upon closing the estate. Dividends may be declared oftener and in smaller proportions if the judge shall so order.

c The rights of creditors who have received dividends, or in whose favor final dividends have been declared, shall not be affected by the proof and allowance of claims subsequent to the date of such payment or declarations of dividends; but the creditors proving and securing the allowance of such claims shall be paid dividends equal in amount to those already received by the other creditors if the estate equals so much before such other creditors are paid any further dividends.

d Whenever a person shall have been adjudged a bankrupt by a court without the United States and also by a court of bankruptcy, creditors residing within the United States shall first be paid a dividend equal to that received in the court without the United States by other creditors before

creditors who have received a dividend in such court shall be paid any amounts.

e **A claimant shall not be entitled to collect from a bankrupt estate any greater amount than shall accrue pursuant to the provisions of this act.**

UNCLAIMED DIVIDENDS.

§ 66. *a* **Dividends which remain unclaimed for six months after the final dividend has been declared shall be paid by the trustee into court.**

b **Dividends remaining unclaimed for one year shall, under the direction of the court, be distributed to the creditors whose claims have been allowed but not paid in full, and after such claims have been paid in full the balance shall be paid to the bankrupt:** *provided,* **that in case unclaimed dividends belong to minors such minors may have one year after arriving at majority to claim such dividends.**

Practice in Regard to Dividends.

The making or payment of dividends will be restrained in proper cases until further order of court, that an opportunity may be given to any person interested to apply to the court, on proper papers and proper notice, to vacate the order for the dividend. In re New York Mail S. S. Co., 3 N. B. R. 73, Fed. Cas. No. 10,212. But the distribution of the assets of a bankrupt cannot be stayed or prevented by the process of a state court. In re Bridgman, 2 N. B. R. 252, Fed. Cas. No. 1,867. A dividend which has been ordered but remains in the hands of the trustee is not attachable on process from a state court; it remains a part of the estate of the bankrupt in the custody of the court; it is not property of the creditor, but only property that will become his when he shall receive it; he could not maintain a suit against the trustee for it, nor obtain it by any legal process other than by application to the bankruptcy court. Gilbert v. Lynch, 17 Blatchf. 402, 1 Fed. 111. The trustees of an estate in bankruptcy are not bound to pay interest upon dividends which may be declared upon debts which have been fairly and reasonably disputed, from the time that like dividends were declared upon undisputed debts, although it seems that they may be ordered to pay such interest as has been earned upon funds set apart to meet the disputed claim. Hersey v. Fosdick, 20 Fed. 44. Upon the final settlement of a bankrupt's estate, it appeared that two dividends, amounting to 27 per cent. had been declared, and that at the time each was made a sum was retained under section 5092, Rev. St., "sufficient for all undetermined claims which, by reason of the distant residence of creditors, etc., had not been proved," etc.; that afterwards a third dividend of ten per cent. was declared upon claims that had not participated in the first and second dividends; that some claims which had been proven before the first and second dividends did not share therein, although there were then sufficient funds to have paid upon them also a 27 per cent. dividend; and that no fund was specially reserved for their payment; and that the funds remaining were not sufficient to pay upon such claims, and claims since proved, a dividend equal to 27 per cent. Upon this state of facts it was held that the funds remaining should be distributed as follows: first, costs and expenses; second, ten per cent. to creditors that have received no dividend; third, 17 per cent. to those who have received, and shall, under this order, receive, 10 per cent.; and if the fund is insufficient to pay 17 per cent., then it is to be distributed to them pro rata. In re Hovey, 5 Fed. 356; affirmed, First Nat. Bank v. Hovey, 8 Fed. 314. It will be observed that section 58 of the present act provides for notices to creditors of all payments of dividends.

LIENS.

§ 67. *a* Claims which for want of record or for other reasons would not have been valid liens as against the claims of the creditors of the bankrupt shall not be liens against his estate.

b Whenever a creditor is prevented from enforcing his rights as against a lien created, or attempted to be created, by his debtor, who afterwards becomes a bankrupt, the trustee of the estate of such bankrupt shall be subrogated to and may enforce such rights of such creditor for the benefit of the estate.

c A lien created by or obtained in or pursuant to any suit or proceeding at law or in equity, including an attachment upon mesne process or a judgment by confession, which was begun against a person within four months before the filing of a petition in bankruptcy by or against such person shall be dissolved by the adjudication of such person to be a bankrupt if (1) it appears that said lien was obtained and permitted while the defendant was insolvent and that its existence and enforcement will work a preference, or (2) the party or parties to be benefited thereby had reasonable cause to believe the defendant was insolvent and in contemplation of bankruptcy, or (3) that such lien was sought and permitted in fraud of the provisions of this act; or if the dissolution of such lien would militate against the best interests of the estate of such person the same shall not be dissolved, but the trustee of the estate of such person, for the benefit of the estate, shall be subrogated to the rights of the holder of such lien and empowered to perfect and enforce the same in his name as trustee with like force and effect as such holder might have done had not bankruptcy proceedings intervened.

d Liens given or accepted in good faith and not in contemplation of or in fraud upon this act, and for a present consideration, which have been recorded according to law, if record thereof was necessary in order to impart notice, shall not be affected by this act.

e That all conveyances, transfers, assignments, or incumbrances of his property, or any part thereof, made or given by a person adjudged a bankrupt under the provisions of this act subsequent to the passage of this act and within four months prior to the filing of the petition, with the intent and purpose on his part to hinder, delay, or defraud his creditors, or any of them, shall be null and void as against the creditors of such debtor, except as to purchasers in good faith and for a present fair consideration; and all property of the debtor conveyed, transferred, assigned, or encumbered as aforesaid shall, if he be adjudged a bankrupt, and the same is not exempt from execution and liability for debts by the law of his domicile, be and remain a part of the assets and estate of the bankrupt and shall pass to his said trustee, whose duty it shall be to recover and reclaim the same by legal proceedings or otherwise for the benefit of the creditors. And all conveyances, transfers, or incumbrances of his property made by a debtor at any time within four months prior to the filing of the petition against him, and while insolvent, which are held null and void as against the creditors of such debtor by the laws of the state, territory, or district in which such property is situate, shall be deemed null and void under this act against the creditors of such debtor if he be adjudged a bankrupt, and such property shall pass to the assignee and be by him reclaimed and recovered for the benefit of the creditors of the bankrupt.

f That all levies, judgments, attachments, or other liens, obtained through legal proceedings against a person who is insolvent, at any time within four months prior to the filing of a petition in bankruptcy against him, shall be deemed null and void in case he is adjudged a bankrupt, and the property affected by the levy, judgment, attachment, or other lien shall be deemed wholly discharged and released from the same, and shall pass to the trustee as a part of the estate of the bankrupt, unless the court shall, on due notice, order that the right under such levy, judgment, attachment, or other lien shall be preserved for the benefit of the estate; and thereupon the same may pass to and shall be preserved by the trustee for the benefit of the estate as aforesaid. And the court may order such conveyance as shall be necessary to carry the purposes of this section into effect: *provided*, that nothing herein contained shall have the effect to destroy or impair the title obtained by such levy, judgment, attachment, or other lien, of a bona fide purchaser for value who shall have acquired the same without notice or reasonable cause for inquiry.

Liens Voidable by Trustee.

A trustee in bankruptcy has all the rights of creditors to attack conveyances made by the bankrupt in fraud of his creditors. Crooks v. Stewart, 7 Fed. 800. A mortgage which, though valid as between mortgagor and mortgagee, is void as against creditors, for want of record, is voidable by the trustee, who represents the creditors. Moore v. Young, 4 Biss. 128, Fed. Cas. No. 9,782. And so, mortgages and bills of sale of personal property which are void as to creditors under the statute of frauds of the state where the transactions occur, are void as to the trustee in bankruptcy. Edmondson v. Hyde, 2 Sawy. 205, Fed. Cas. No. 4,285; In re Morrill, 2 Sawy. 357, Fed. Cas. No. 9,821. Where a creditor obtains judgment on a debt not yet due, and thereby obtains a lien by levy on the debtor's goods, although this may not amount to a statutory preference, yet the lien will not hold against the trustee in bankruptcy of the debtor; for he takes the property subject to lawful incumbrances only, and he may inquire into the lawfulness of all judgments, because he represents creditors, and therefore is not in privity with the debtor so far as to be prohibited from collaterally attacking judgments against him. Partridge v. Dearborn, 2 Low. 286, Fed. Cas. No. 10,785. Where a chattel mortgage given by the bankrupt is not filed as required by the statute, but is otherwise unexceptionable, it is valid as between mortgagor and mortgagee, but voidable by execution creditors; hence, in a controversy concerning the fund in court arising from the sale of the property covered by such mortgage, between the trustee in bankruptcy of the mortgagor, the mortgagee, and certain execution-creditors, the creditors are to be paid first, and the balance, if any, belongs to the mortgagee, because the trustee takes subject to all valid liens and incumbrances, and this, as between mortgagor and mortgagee, was such. Stewart v. Platt, 101 U. S. 731.

Trustee Takes Subject to Liens and Incumbrances.

Except in the instances specified in the act,—liens void for want of record or otherwise, liens ipso facto dissolved by the adjudication, and fraudulent and voidable transfers, —the trustee in bankruptcy takes the property of the estate subject to all equities, liens, and incumbrances existing against it in the hands of the bankrupt, and takes no greater interest than the bankrupt himself had. Mattocks v. Baker, 2 Fed. 455; Yeatman v. Savings Inst., 95 U. S. 764; Ex parte Dalby, 1 Low. 431, Fed. Cas. No. 3,540; Stewart v. Platt, 101 U. S. 731. Where a bill is filed by a junior mortgagee for the foreclosure or sale of the equity of redemption, neither the mortgagor nor his trustee in bankruptcy has any standing to object to the order in which the priority of valid and subsisting liens on the mortgaged property is fixed by the decree of foreclosure; for the trustee can get nothing in any event until all valid liens have been removed. Jerome v. McCarter, 94 U. S. 734. The trustee cannot avail himself of a claim that an execution was dormant at the time of the vesting of the property in him, if the bankrupt could not. Crane v. Penny, 2 Fed. 187. If a creditor of a bankrupt, having a valid lien upon certain of his property, does not prove his claim in the bankruptcy, and the property upon which he has the lien is not included by the bankrupt in his schedules, the lien survives the bankruptcy proceedings. Clanton v. Estes, 77 Ga. 352, 1 S. E. 163. The acquisition of title by the trustee relates back to the commencement of the bankruptcy proceedings, and, by operation of law, dissolves any attachment sued out within the four months next preceding their commencement, without any action on the part of the court in which the attachment suit is pending. Sullivan v. Rabb, 86 Ala. 433, 5 South. 746. Where a trustee in bankruptcy avoids, as a preference, an execution larger in amount than the value of the goods levied on, he is entitled to the goods or their proceeds as against an execution levied after the preferential execution but before the filing of the petition in bankruptcy. Claridge v. Kulmer, 1 Fed. 399.

Lien of Judgments.

The lien of a valid judgment obtained against the debtor a sufficient period before the commencement of proceedings in bankruptcy is protected under the bankrupt act and is good against the trustee. Webster v. Woolbridge, 3 Dill. 74, Fed. Cas. No. 17,340. In a case where an insolvent person made a fraudulent conveyance of his property to trustees with intent to hinder and delay his creditors; and certain of the creditors, not assenting to this transaction, sued the debtor and recovered judgments,—which, by the law of the state, they could do without first having the fraudulent conveyance set aside,—and these judgments, being duly docketed, became liens on the debtor's property; and afterwards he was adjudged a bankrupt, the bankruptcy court declared the conveyance to trustees to be void, and the trustees conveyed the property to the assignee in bankruptcy; it was held that the assignee took the property subject to the lien of those judgments. In re Beadle, 5 Sawy. 351, Fed. Cas. No. 1,155. And it seems that the same would be true of the lien of an execution in the hands of the sheriff, by the local law, when created more than four months before the bankruptcy. See In re Weeks, 2 Biss. 259, Fed. Cas. No. 17,350. It is competent for a state to provide that the lien of a judgment, in a certain class of cases shall relate back to the institution of the suit, and the bankrupt law preserves such lien. Voyles v. Parker, 9 Biss. 326, 4 Fed. 210. But where the creditor has reasonable cause to believe his debtor insolvent, he acquires no valid lien by taking a confession of judgment. In re Terry, 2 Biss. 356, Fed. Cas. No. 13,835. And a judgment recovered against a person after he is adjudged a bankrupt becomes no lien on his lands. Burgett v. Paxton, 99 Ill. 288.

Mortgages.

So also a mortgage, whether of realty or chattels, executed by the debtor in good faith and without circumstances of fraud, and complying with all the statutory requisites, creates an incumbrance on the property which must be recognized by the bankruptcy court in disposing of the proceeds. In re Collins, 8 Ben. 59, Fed. Cas. No. 3,004. And a mortgage to secure future advances is good as against the trustee in bankruptcy for the amount of advances actually made thereon. Schulze v. Bolting, 8 Biss. 174, Fed. Cas. No. 12,489. A covenant for insurance, in the mortgage, creates a specific equitable lien upon the insurance money which is valid as against a trustee. In re Sands Ale Brewing Co., 3 Biss. 175, Fed. Cas. No. 12,307.

Statutory Liens.

It is entirely within the power of a state legislature to create classes of liens by statutory enactments, in respect of property within the state, and such liens, being otherwise valid, will be protected in the bankruptcy courts. In re Burt, 12 Blatchf. 252, Fed. Cas. No. 2,209. But a lien which derives its existence wholly from a state statute, and the continuance of which is made to depend, by the terms of the statute, upon the institution of a suit in the state court in respect to the subject-matter within a prescribed period, is not preserved as a living incumbrance upon the bankrupt's estate, when no such action has been commenced, and no step has been taken in the bankruptcy court equivalent to such suit, within the time limited; for the mere commencement of bankruptcy proceedings is not a sufficient compliance with the terms of the statute. In re Brunquest, 7 Biss. 208, Fed. Cas. No. 2,055. A national bank has power to enact a by-law creating a lien on the stock of every stockholder for his liabilities to the bank, and such lien is not divested by the subsequent bankruptcy of the stockholder. In re Dunkerson, 4 Biss. 227, Fed. Cas. No. 4,156.

Other Liens.

The lien of a factor for advancements, charges, and commissions, is within the protection of the bankrupt law. In re Roseberry, 8 Biss. 112, Fed. Cas. No. 12,052. The landlord's right to distrain for rent does not, strictly speaking, give him a lien on the goods subject to distress, but yet it may fairly be classed as a lien so far as to be protected in bankruptcy proceedings. Austin v. O'Reilly, 2 Woods, 670, Fed. Cas. No. 665.

Mechanics' Liens.

Where a mechanic's lien, by the local law, arises from the doing of the work and attaches to the building from that time, upon the condition subsequent that the lien-creditor file a certain notice within a given time from the completion of the building, such lien is not affected or impaired by the commencement of bankruptcy proceedings between the doing of the work and the filing of such notice. In re Coulter, 2 Sawy. 42, Fed. Cas. No. 3,276. But where, by the local law, the lien is *created* by the filing of such notice, and not by the mere performance of the labor, and bankruptcy proceedings intervene between the doing of the work and the filing of notice, the property passes to the trustee free of any such lien. In re Dey, 3 N. B. R. 305, Fed. Cas. No. 3,870.

Rights of Secured Creditors.

Where a creditor of a bankrupt holds two classes of security for his debt, to one of which the other creditors have no recourse, the court, in its power to marshal assets, will require him to first exhaust that class of securities from which the other creditors are excluded. In re Sauthoff, 14 N. B. R. 364, Fed. Cas. No. 12,379. The general rule is thus stated by Woods, J., in Wicks v. Perkins, 1 Woods, 383, Fed. Cas. No. 17,615: "A secured creditor can resort to one of these remedies: (1) He may rely upon his security. (2) He may abandon it and prove the whole debt as unsecured, or, (3) he may be admitted only as a creditor for the balance remaining after the deduction of the value of the security. If he takes either of the two courses last named, he must of course prove his debt. But suppose he chooses to rely upon his security; there is no positive provision, nor is there anything in the policy of the bankrupt law, requiring proof of the debt, unless he seeks the aid of the bankrupt court to enforce his lien." So where a creditor has obtained judgment in a state court prior to the institution of bankruptcy proceedings against the debtor, which judgment is a lien on realty, the lien is not lost by a failure, on the part of the creditor, to prove his judgment in the bankruptcy. Cottrell v. Pierson, 2 McCrary, 390, 12 Fed. 805. A mortgage is a security within the meaning of the act; and mortgagees who prove their debt in the bankruptcy proceedings become creditors of the mortgagor's general estate only for the balance of the debt after deducting the value of the mortgaged property, to be ascertained by agreement, sale, or in such other manner as the bankruptcy court may direct. McHenry v. Societe Francaise, 95 U. S. 58. If a person has a judgment for his debt, and proves the debt in bankruptcy without naming the judgment, he will be held to intend to waive, discharge, and surrender the judgment and any lien acquired under it; otherwise, if he proves the judgment itself. Sedgwick v. Stewart, 9 Ben. 433, Fed. Cas. No. 12,625. A secured creditor has not an absolute control of his securities; the court, on the application of the trustee, will interfere and stop a sale, if there is danger that the securities may be sacrificed. The Skylark, 4 Biss. 388, Fed. Cas. No. 12,929. Where a mortgage creditor of a bankrupt, after notice to the trustee, asks for and obtains an order of the court allowing him to foreclose his mortgage by a proceeding in the state court, the trustee being made a party, and the complaint praying that the deficiency arising upon a sale of the mortgaged premises be ascertained and the plaintiff permitted to prove the same in the bankruptcy, and no objection is made until the creditor files proof of the amount of deficiency in the bankrupt court, his action will be considered as sufficiently complying with the provisions of the law regulating the course to be pursued by secured creditors. In re Letchworth, 18 Fed. 822. Although secured creditors may collect from the trustee interest on their claims accruing after adjudication, such interest will not be estimated in determining the relative amount of debts and value of assets on the question of discharge, but the claims will be reckoned with interest only to the date of adjudication. In re Hyndman, 5 Fed. 705.

Who are not Secured Creditors.

The act provides (section 1) that "'secured creditor' shall include a creditor who has security for his debt upon the property of the bankrupt, of a nature to be assignable under this act, or who owns such a debt for which some indorser, surety, or other person secondarily liable for the bankrupt has such security upon the bankrupt's assets." Also under the bankrupt law of 1867, the security was required to be upon the bankrupt's property. Rev. St. § 5075. In view of this limitation it was held that a guaranty given by a third person is not such a security that the creditor must surrender it to the trustee if he desires to prove his debt in full. In re Anderson, 7 Biss. 233, Fed. Cas. No. 350. Neither is an indorsement of a promissory note, of which the bankrupt is maker. In re Broich, 7 Biss. 303, Fed. Cas. No. 1,921. On the same principle it was said: "The court is of opinion that a judgment-creditor of the bankrupt, whose judgment is a lien upon any estate so sold and conveyed by the bankrupt [i. e., to a bona fide purchaser for a valuable consideration fully paid prior to the act of bankruptcy], may claim and secure in the proceeding in bankruptcy his portion of the estate of the bankrupt, in virtue of his said judgment, without accounting or giving credit for anything on account of the lien of his judgment upon the estate so sold and conveyed as aforesaid." McAden v. Keen, 30 Grat. 402. And a creditor of a bankrupt firm who holds security upon the separate estate of one of the partners, may prove his entire claim against the joint estate without releasing his security, even though the partner whose individual property affords the security owes no separate debts. In re Thomas, 8 Biss. 139, Fed. Cas. No. 13,886. Creditors who hold security for their claims on property not the bankrupt's may prove the entire debt as unsecured. In re Dunkerson, 12 N. B. R. 413, Fed. Cas. No. 4,157.

SET-OFFS AND COUNTERCLAIMS.

§ 68. *a* **In all cases of mutual debts or mutual credits between the estate of a bankrupt and a creditor the account shall be stated and one debt shall be set off against the other, and the balance only shall be allowed or paid.**

b **A set-off or counterclaim shall not be allowed in favor of any debtor of the bankrupt which (1) is not provable against the estate; or (2) was purchased by or transferred to him after the filing of the petition, or within four months before such filing, with a view to such use and with knowledge or notice that such bankrupt was insolvent, or had committed an act of bankruptcy.**

Set-Off of Mutual Debts.

"This section was not intended to enlarge the doctrine of set-off, or to enable a party to make a set-off in cases where the principles of legal or equitable set-off did not previously authorize it. The debts must be mutual,—must be in the same right." Miller, J., in Sawyer v. Hoag, 17 Wall. 622. But the term "mutual credits" in the bankrupt act is more comprehensive than the term "mutual debts" in the statutes relating to set-off. The term "credit" is synonymous with "trust," and the trust or credit need not be of money on both sides. Where a creditor has goods or choses in action of the bankrupt put in his hands before the bankruptcy, by a valid contract, by the terms of which the deposit will result in a debt, as if they are deposited for sale or collection, the case of mutual credits has arisen within the meaning of the act. Murray v. Riggs, 15 Johns. 571; Ex parte Caylus, 1 Low. 550, Fed. Cas. No. 2,534; Marks v. Barker, 1 Wash. C. C. 178, Fed. Cas. No. 9,096; Tucker v. Oxley, 5 Cranch, 34. Thus a creditor who holds goods or chattels at the time of bankruptcy, belonging to the bankrupt, with power of sale, or choses in action with power of collection, may sell the goods or collect the claims, and set them off against the debt the bankrupt owes him. In re Dow (Ex parte Whiting) 14 N. B. R. 307, Fed. Cas. No. 17,573. A banker who has for collection drafts of the bankrupt, the proceeds of which come into his hands after bankruptcy, may retain them by virtue of his lien. In re Farnsworth, 14 N. B. R. 148, Fed. Cas. No. 4,673. And the words "mutual credits" are broad enough to include an indorser on a bill which was protested before the commencement of the proceedings in bankruptcy, although he did not pay it until afterwards. Marks v. Barker, 1 Wash. C. C. 178, Fed. Cas. No. 9,096. When there is a debt due on one side, and on the other a delivery of property with directions to turn it into money, the property thus delivered constitutes a credit, and the case becomes one of mutual credits under the bankrupt laws. Goodrich v. Dobson, 43 Conn. 576. So also the discharge in bankruptcy of one of two joint judgment-debtors transforms the debt in equity into a several one against the other, so that the trustee may make it a set-off against a judgment held by the other against him, and thus obtain satisfaction of the latter judgment. Cosgrove v. Cosby, 86 Ind. 511. So where a bailee of an insolvent debtor's goods, prior to the filing of a petition in bankruptcy against such debtor, employed him to assist in the sale and management of the goods, it was held that such employment was not illegal, and that the bailee, as against the trustee in bankruptcy, was entitled to a credit for the amount paid therefor. Catlin v. Foster, 1 Sawy. 37, Fed. Cas. No. 2,519. Again, a claim for loss under an insurance policy may be set off by the insured against his indebtedness to the company. Drake v. Rollo, 3 Biss. 273, Fed. Cas. No. 4,066. But where a claim against a bankrupt insurance company, for loss under its policies, has been assigned, after notice of insolvency, the assignee cannot set it off against his previous indebtedness to the company; the debts and credits are not "mutual" in such case. Hitchcock v. Rollo, 3 Biss. 276, Fed. Cas. No. 6,535. Further, trust-debts cannot be made the subject of set-off under this section. Thus, where the trustee of a bankrupt insurance company sues a stockholder for the unpaid balance of his subscription to its capital, the latter cannot set off a claim against the company for a loss under its policy, for the unpaid stock subscriptions are in reality a trust-fund for the creditors of the company, and therefore the debts are not mutual, and to allow such a set-off would enable the stockholder to turn his fiduciary relation to his own benefit and the detriment of the creditors. Scammon v. Kimball, 5 Biss. 431, Fed. Cas. No. 12,435. So also, money transmitted by the bankrupt to a creditor with directions as to the manner in which it is to be applied, is received under a trust to apply it according to instructions; and if the creditor refuses to so use it, and the trustee sues him for the amount, he cannot offer in set-off his claim against the bankrupt's estate. Libby v. Hopkins, 104 U. S. 303. One who holds the bare legal title to a note given by a debtor cannot set off against it, in bankruptcy, a debt which he owes the bankrupt for goods bought. In re Lane, 2 Low. 305, Fed. Cas. No. 8,043. A joint indebtedness may be proved and set off against the estate of either of the joint debtors who may become bankrupt, and it is immaterial that it may be subject to be marshalled, for the joint debtors are severally liable in solido for the whole debt. Gray v. Rollo, 18 Wall. 629. See, also, In re Carrier, 39 Fed. 193. In one of the cases it appeared that V. and B. were partners in the live-stock business, and V. was adjudged a bankrupt. At the time of his adjudication he was indebted to B. upon transactions not connected with the partnership. Upon the settlement of the partnership accounts there was a balance thereon due from B. to V. It was held that B. had a right to set off against the amount due from him to the bankrupt on the partnership transactions the independent debts due from the bankrupt to himself. In re Voetter, 4 Fed. 632. But a judgment obtained by a trustee in bankruptcy, for a penalty incurred by the violation of a state statute against usury, cannot be set off against a claim of the judgment-debtor against the bankrupt estate. Wilson v. National Bank, 1 McCrary, 538, 3 Fed. 391. A creditor of a bankrupt cannot obtain a preference of his debt by purchasing the property of the bankrupt through the intervention of an agent, and tendering the notes of the bankrupt in payment for the same. And in an action by the assignee to recover the value of such property, the creditor cannot set off the notes of the bankrupt. Fleming v. Andrews, 3 Fed. 632.

Claims Purchased with a View to Set-Off.

A claim against the bankrupt purchased before the filing of the petition, but with full knowledge of the insolvency, and with intent to use the claim as a set-off, was held available for that purpose in a case of *voluntary* bankruptcy under the act of 1867. Lloyd v. Turner, 5 Sawy. 463, Fed. Cas. No. 8,436. But it is to be observed that the present act makes no distinction, in this respect, between voluntary and compulsory cases. "The debtor of a bankrupt cannot set off against the assignee of the bankrupt a claim obtained while proceedings in bankruptcy are pending; such a case being similar in principle to that of the debtor of an intestate seeking to set off a debt due from the intestate purchased by the defendant after the death of the intestate." Wat. Set-Off, § 200; Smith v. Brinckerhoff, 8 Barb. 519. A consent to an assignment of an open account given after the commission of the act of bankruptcy, but before the filing of a petition against the debtor, does not confer any higher or better rights upon the assignee. Rollins v. Twitchell, 14 N. B. R. 201, Fed. Cas. No. 12,027. But it is not unlawful for the creditor of an insolvent to sell his debt to the debtor of such insolvent, although it be purchased for the purpose of being used in set-off. "The defendants were free to sell their notes to any one who would buy them, whether that purchaser could or could not use them in set-off. If he could so use them, there was no wrong done; if he could not, there was no injury." Mattocks v. Lovering, 3 Fed. 212.

Claim already proved cannot be used as Set-Off.

Proving his claim in the bankruptcy proceedings is a waiver by the creditor of all right of action or suit against the bankrupt in respect of such claim. Hence, where the creditor proved his claim, but omitted to credit the bankrupt with a debt due to him from the creditor, and the trustee sued for such debt, it was held that the creditor could not offer the claim already proved, by way of set-off to that suit. His doing so would be equivalent to the prosecution of an original suit for its amount, the right to which he had waived. Brown v. Farmers' Bank, 6 Bush, 198; Russell v. Owen, 61 Mo. 185.

POSSESSION OF PROPERTY.

§ 69. *a* **A judge may, upon satisfactory proof, by affidavit, that a bankrupt against whom an involuntary petition has been filed and is pending has committed an act of bankruptcy, or has neglected or is neglecting, or is about to so neglect his property that it has thereby deteriorated or is thereby deteriorating or is about thereby to deteriorate in value, issue a warrant to the marshal to seize and hold it subject to further orders. Before such warrant is issued the petitioners applying therefor shall enter into a bond in such an amount as the judge shall fix, with such sureties as he shall approve, conditioned to indemnify such bankrupt for such damages as he shall sustain in the event such seizure shall prove to have been wrongfully obtained. Such property shall be released, if such bankrupt shall give bond in a sum which shall be fixed by the judge, with such sureties as he shall approve, conditioned to turn over such property, or pay the value thereof in money to the trustee, in the event he is adjudged a bankrupt pursuant to such petition.**

Seizure of Property.

When the marshal receives the warrant provided for in this section, it is his duty to take possession of all the bankrupt's property in whosesoever hands he may find it. Yet if he takes property from a third person, his warrant will protect him only so far as the goods belong to the bankrupt. If he wrongfully seizes the effects of a stranger, the act is as much a trespass as if committed by a private individual. Marsh v. Armstrong, 20 Minn. 81. But if he seizes property which has been transferred in violation of the bankruptcy law, he is not liable to the transferee. Stevenson v. McLaren, 3 Cent. Law J. 478.

TITLE TO PROPERTY.

§ 70. *a* **The trustee of the estate of a bankrupt, upon his appointment and qualification, and his successor or successors, if he shall have one or more, upon his or their appointment and qualification, shall in turn be vested by operation of law with the title of the bankrupt, as of the date he was adjudged a bankrupt, except in so far as it is to property which is exempt, to all (1) documents relating to his property; (2) interests in patents, patent rights, copyrights, and trade-marks; (3) powers which he might have exercised for his own benefit, but not those which he might have exercised for some other person; (4) property transferred by him in fraud of his creditors; (5) property which prior to the filing of the petition he could by any means have transferred or which might have been levied upon and sold under judicial process against him:** *provided*, **that when any bankrupt shall have any insurance policy which has a cash surrender value payable to himself, his estate or personal representatives, he may, within thirty days after the cash surrender value has been ascertained and stated to the trustee by the company issuing the same, pay or secure to the trustee the sum so ascertained and stated, and continue to hold, own, and carry such policy free from the claims of the creditors participating in the distribu-**

tion of his estate under the bankruptcy proceedings, otherwise the policy shall pass to the trustee as assets; and (6) rights of action arising upon contracts or from the unlawful taking or detention of, or injury to, his property.

b All real and personal property belonging to bankrupt estates shall be appraised by three disinterested appraisers; they shall be appointed by, and report to, the court. Real and personal property shall, when practicable, be sold subject to the approval of the court; it shall not be sold otherwise than subject to the approval of the court for less than seventy-five per centum of its appraised value.

c The title to property of a bankrupt estate which has been sold, as herein provided, shall be conveyed to the purchaser by the trustee.

d Whenever a composition shall be set aside, or discharge revoked, the trustee shall, upon his appointment and qualification, be vested as herein provided with the title to all of the property of the bankrupt as of the date of the final decree setting aside the composition or revoking the discharge.

e The trustee may avoid any transfer by the bankrupt of his property which any creditor of such bankrupt might have avoided, and may recover the property so transferred, or its value, from the person to whom it was transferred, unless he was a bona fide holder for value prior to the date of the adjudication. Such property may be recovered or its value collected from whoever may have received it, except a bona fide holder for value.

f **Upon the confirmation of a composition offered by a bankrupt, the title to his property shall thereupon revest in him.**

Nature and Origin of Trustee's Title.

The trustee's title relates back to the date of the adjudication and accrues as of that date. Conner v. Long, 104 U. S. 228; Zeiber v. Hill, 1 Sawy. 268, Fed. Cas. No. 18,206. Hence it seems that a debtor of the bankrupt who makes payment to the latter, after the institution of the bankruptcy proceedings but before adjudication, and without actual notice or knowledge of the pendency of such proceedings, and in the usual course of business, will be protected against a subsequent action by the trustee in respect of the same debt. See Howard v. Crompton, 14 Blatchf. 328, Fed. Cas. No. 6,758.

Whom the Trustee Represents.

A trustee in bankruptcy, besides being an officer of the court which appoints him, is the representative of the *creditors* of the estate, and is therefore invested with certain powers and privileges which could not have been exercised by the bankrupt himself. Thus, under the bankrupt act, mortgages of realty and chattel mortgages and bills of sale of personalty which, though valid and binding as between mortgagor and mortgagee, are void as to creditors under the local law, for want of record or otherwise, are void as to the trustee. Edmondson v. Hyde, 2 Sawy. 205, Fed. Cas. No. 4,285; In re Morrill, 2 Sawy. 357, Fed. Cas. No. 9,821; Moore v. Young, 4 Biss. 128, Fed. Cas. No. 9,782. He has all the rights in this respect that would belong to an attaching or execution creditor if bankruptcy had not supervened. In re Werner, 5 Dill. 119, Fed. Cas. No. 17,416. He may also enquire into the lawfulness of all judgments standing against the bankrupt, because he represents creditors, and therefore is not in privity with the debtor so far as to be prohibited from collateral attacks on judgments against him. Partridge v. Dearborn, 2 Low. 286, Fed. Cas. No. 10,785. At the same time it must be remembered that the trustee also represents the *bankrupt*, at least in so far as may be necessary to sustain the rule that he takes no greater interest or estate than the bankrupt himself possessed, and that he takes subject to all lawful incumbrances. Thus, where the trustee brings his bill to set aside a sale of the bankrupt's realty, made under a deed of trust, and for leave to redeem, he has no greater rights than the bankrupt would have under the circumstances, and any defense that would be available against the bankrupt may be urged against the trustee. Jenkins v. Pierce, 98 Ill. 646. The trustee represents the bankrupt and his estate in every district and every state and collects the assets wherever found. Cannon v. Wellford, 22 Grat. 195. The bankrupt is, in a certain sense of the term, civiliter mortuus during the proceedings. Yet the individual bankruptcy of a person, who is a stockholder in, and a director and officer of, a corporation which is not in bankruptcy, does not incapacitate him from exercising his functions as such officer of the corporation, nor render inoperative and void as to third parties the acts and conveyances of the corporation done and executed through him as its representative. Atlas Nat. Bank v. F. B. Gardner Co., 8 Biss. 537, Fed. Cas. No. 635. If the trustee himself is adjudged bankrupt, neither his trustees nor his personal representatives are entitled to debts due to the original bankrupt; they must go to a new trustee of the original bankrupt. Merrick's Estate, 5 Watts & S. 9. But it seems that upon the death of an assignee in bankruptcy the right of action for a debt due the bankrupt vests in the executor of the assignee. Richards v. Insurance Co., 8 Cranch, 84. Trustees in bankruptcy do not succeed to the rights of assignees in insolvency whose assignment they have had set aside. Alexander v. Galt, 9 Fed. 149.

Bankrupt's Rights before Appointment of Trustee.

The bankrupt has charge of his own property, during the time between the petition and the appointment of the assignee, as a sort of trustee. Hence where the court orders the marshal to sell a part of the goods, as perishable, the bankrupt cannot become the purchaser. March v. Heaton, 1 Low. 278, Fed. Cas. No. 9,061. And during this interval, the bankrupt has the right to pursue all proper legal measures for the protection of his interests. Myers v. Callaghan, 10 Biss. 139, 5 Fed. 726. In other words, prior to the vesting of title in a trustee, the title to the debtor's real and personal property remains unchanged, except that the court, in certain cases, may in the meantime issue its injunction to restrain the bankrupt or any other person from transferring or disposing of any part of the same, not excepted from the operation of the act. Hampton v. Rouse, 22 Wall. 263.

What Vests in Trustee; Assets Defined.

Assets in bankruptcy are the proceeds of the bankrupt's property which come into the hands of the assignee and are applicable to the payment of his debts. In re Wilson, 2 Hughes, 228, Fed. Cas. No. 17,782.

Property in Bankrupt's Possession.

All property of a bankrupt in his actual possession at the time of the filing of the petition passes into the hands of the trustee the instant he is appointed. In re Vogel, 7 Blatchf. 18, Fed. Cas. No. 16,982. And where a deficit is shown in the assets of the bankrupt's estate, he must account for it by a satisfactory explanation, or pay the amount of the deficit to the trustee. In re Peltasohn, 4 Dill. 107, Fed. Cas. No. 10,912.

But the circumstance that property which belonged to a third party had become subject to the control of the bankruptcy court by reason of the fact that it was in the possession of the bankrupt, and therefore passed into the possession of the trustee, presents no obstacle to the actual owner's regaining possession of his property. He may have it on petition and proof to the court. In re Havens, 8 Ben. 309, Fed. Cas. No. 6,230. "Whatever money or property is in the possession of the bankrupt at the time of filing his petition, which he is actually using and holding as his own, passes to his assignee in bankruptcy, and he cannot set up in defense to the claim of the assignee a title in a third person, merely for the purpose of holding on to it himself. If third persons have the possession, this court cannot, on summary petition, order it to be delivered to the assignee. But if the bankrupt has it, it passes to the assignee, subject to the liens or rights of third persons, whatever they may be. After the assignee gets the property, any third person may, by petition or suit, assert his rights in it." In re Moses, 1 Fed. 845.

Interests in Real Estate.

The equity of redemption in property mortgaged by the bankrupt passes to the trustee and vests in him; and neither the bankrupt nor any court other than the bankruptcy court can affect the title of the trustee by proceedings to which he is not a party. Barron v. Newberry, 1 Biss. 149, Fed. Cas. No. 1,056; Robinson v. Denny, 57 Ala. 492; 1 Daniell, Ch. Prac. *58. Hence a decree of foreclosure against the bankrupt, the trustee not having been joined, is insufficient to extinguish the equity of redemption. Barron v. Newberry, supra. So a vested interest in a contingent remainder passes to the trustee in bankruptcy. Putnam v. Story, 132 Mass. 205; Belcher v. Burnett, 126 Mass. 230; Comegys v. Vasse, 1 Pet. 218. And where the bankrupt is the owner in fee of a public street in a city, subject only to the public easement, the right of the owner therein will pass to his trustee in bankruptcy. Kinzie v. Winston, 56 Ill. 56. But the trustee cannot hold real estate against a third person who bases his claim on an earlier and unrecorded conveyance made to him by the bankrupt. Goss v. Coffin, 66 Me. 432. The title to real estate situated in a foreign country does not vest in the trustee, for a statutory conveyance, such as that directed to be made by the judge to the trustee under Rev. St. § 5044, can have no extra-territorial effect upon real estate. Oakey v. Bennett, 11 How. 33; Barnett v. Pool, 23 Tex. 517. But now, by section 7 of the present act, it is made the duty of the bankrupt to "execute to his trustee transfers of all his property in foreign countries." An estate by the curtesy initiate is such property as will pass. In the case In re McKenna, 9 Fed. 27, it appeared that the state statute provided that the interest of a husband in the real estate of his wife should not, during her life, be sold or disposed of by virtue of any judgment, decree, or execution against him, nor should the husband and wife be ejected or dispossessed of the real estate of the wife by virtue of any such judgment, sentence, or decree, nor should the husband sell his wife's real estate during her life without her joining in the conveyance in the manner prescribed by law in which married women shall convey lands. The wife was seised of lands when the husband became bankrupt, there being issue of the marriage. It was held that the tenancy by the curtesy initiate passed to the trustee in bankruptcy, subject to the statutory right of the husband and wife to continue to hold the land during her life. And it was also held that this state statute and the bankruptcy act did not exempt from the operation of the bankruptcy the whole tenancy by the curtesy for the life of the husband, but only so much as was measured by the life of the wife, and that on her death, pending the bankruptcy proceedings, the assignee was entitled to take the land for the remainder of the husband's life.

Franchises and Licenses.

A franchise in the bankrupt consisting of the right to take tolls for crossing at a bridge or causeway is a species of property which will pass to the trustee. Stewart v. Hargrove, 23 Ala. 429. But it is held that a franchise to construct a turnpike road and take tolls, is a personal trust, not assignable without the consent of the granting power, and therefore will not pass to the trustee of the holder. People v. Duncan, 41 Cal. 507. But in another case it was held that a license to occupy a particular stall in a city market, for which a weekly rental was paid, which license was revocable at the pleasure of the city authorities and could not be assigned to another person without written permission, but which had an ascertainable market value as an article of sale, and could, in point of fact, be transferred without any practical difficulty, was assets in the hands of the trustee, and that the court should order the bankrupt to execute a transfer of the license to the trustee and a request to the city officer to assent to the transfer, so that the trustee might realize the sale value of the license for the benefit of the estate. In re Gallagher, 16 Blatchf. 410, Fed. Cas. No. 5,192.

Membership in Exchange.

It was held in one case that a certificate of membership in a board of trade, although it may have a market value, is not assets in the hands of the trustee in bankruptcy. In re Sutherland, 6 Biss. 526, Fed. Cas. No. 13,637. But on the other hand, a later authority rules that a membership in the New York Produce Exchange is property which passes to the trustee. As remarked by Nixon, D. J., "The bankrupt, before his bankruptcy, had the power of selling and assigning his certificate of membership to any one who was willing to purchase the same and take the risk of an election by the board of managers. It had and has a market value, the statement being made on the argument, without contradiction, that it would bring several thousand dollars. Under the circumstances I have no difficulty, on principle, in holding that membership in such an exchange is property which the creditors of a bankrupt are entitled to have applied to the payment of their debts." In re Warder, 10 Fed. 275. See also Hyde v. Woods, 94 U. S. 523; In re Gallagher, 16 Blatchf. 410, Fed. Cas. No. 5,192.

Trade-Marks.

Under the former bankrupt law, it was held that a trade-mark, consisting of a man's individual name prefixed to the title of the article he manufactures, was not property which would vest in the trustee in bankruptcy. Helmbold v. Helmbold Mfg. Co., 53 How. Prac. 453. But the present act expressly classes such interests with the estate which the trustee takes. But where one sells his distillery, and agrees that during a short period, in which he does not propose to engage in business, the purchasers may use his name in branding whisky, there is no such suspension of the use on his part as will cause him to lose his right to use it thereafter; nor does such right to so use his name pass to his trustee in bankruptcy. Mattingly v. Stone (Ky.) 14 S. W. 47.

Choses in Action.

Where the bankrupt and certain other parties made a contract by which a speculation in real estate was arranged, the bankrupt to have a designated interest and a share of the profits, it was held that he had such an interest in the assets which grew out of the real estate operations as would pass to his trustee. Sherman v. International Bank, 8 Biss. 371, Fed. Cas. No. 12,765. Where the bankrupt is the beneficiary in a policy of life insurance, the premiums on which are all paid by the assured without his aid or interference, he has no such interest in the policy or its possible fruits, during the life of the assured, as will vest in his trustee in bankruptcy.

In re Murrin, 2 Dill. 120, Fed. Cas. No. 9,968, though see Brigham v. Home Ins. Co., 131 Mass. 319. A motion against a sheriff for failing to make money on an execution which had issued in favor of a plaintiff who, after the rendition of the judgment, had been declared a bankrupt, must be made in the name of the trustee in bankruptcy. Gary v. Bates, 12 Ala. 544. The trustee in bankruptcy will not take his wife's choses in action (e. g., a legacy then vested in her but not then payable), for the husband has but a power to reduce them to possession. Shay v. Sessaman, 10 Pa. St. 432. Judgments owned by the bankrupt pass to and vest in the assignee. Hale v. Christy, 24 Neb. 746, 40 N. W. 295. And a claim against the United States for goods seized and destroyed during the war constitutes property and will pass to the trustee in bankruptcy, although from lapse of time, it cannot be judicially enforced. Erwin v. U. S., 97 U. S. 392; Phelps v. McDonald, 99 U. S. 298. But it is otherwise as to claims against the government which are inchoate and imperfect at the time, and are afterwards made available only by an act of grace on the part of the government. Thus, in 1863, the plaintiff paid war premiums on certain vessels insured against capture by Confederate cruisers. In 1868 he was adjudicated a bankrupt, and defendant was appointed his assignee. Under the act of congress of 1882, by which the court of commissioners of Alabama claims was re-established, he applied for re-imbursement for the premiums so paid. Subsequently, under a rule of that court, defendant became a party to that proceeding, prosecuted it to final judgment, and received the proceeds thereof. It was held that, at the time of plaintiff's bankruptcy, this claim, not being an existing right to any property, did not pass to the assignee in bankruptcy. As the payment of enhanced war premiums by the government was a voluntary act, and the act allowing such payment was passed after plaintiff's bankruptcy, his rights under such act do not relate back and carry the claim to the assignee. Kingsbury v. Mattocks, 81 Me. 310, 17 Atl. 126. See, also, Heard v. Sturgis, 146 Mass. 545, 16 N. E. 437; Brooks v. Ahrens, 68 Md. 212, 12 Atl. 19.

Actions for Torts and Penalties.

The general rule is, that the right of action for injuries to the bankrupt's person, reputation, or estate (except in the cases mentioned in the act) will not pass to his trustee. See Dicey, Parties, 399 et seq. Thus, a right of action for slander of the bankrupt will not pass, and hence a plea, in such suit, that the plaintiff, since its commencement, has been adjudged a bankrupt, is not good. Dillard v. Collins, 25 Grat. 343. But in a case where the bankrupt had been induced by the fraudulent misrepresentations of another person to enter into partnership with him, contributing a large sum to the capital of the concern, which money was wholly lost to him in consequence of the deceit and fraud which had been practiced upon him, it was held that the right of action for this deceit passed to the trustee. Hyde v. Tuffts, 45 N. Y. Super. Ct. 56. The right of action against a national bank, to recover twice the amount of usurious interest paid, under Rev. St. § 5198, will pass to and vest in the trustee in bankruptcy of the borrower. Monongahela Bank v. Overholt, 96 Pa. St. 327; Crocker v. Bank, 3 Cent. Law J. 527; Id., 4 Dill. 358, Fed. Cas. No. 3,397; Wright v. Bank, 18 N. B. R. 87, Fed. Cas. No. 18,078; Moore v. Jones, 23 Vt. 739; per contra, Bromley v. Smith, 5 N. B. R. 152, Fed. Cas. No. 1,922. The right to sue for money lost in gaming, given by statute to the loser, is a vested interest and will pass to his trustee in bankruptcy. Brandon v. Sands, 2 Ves. Jr. 514.

Property in the Hands of Receivers and Assignees.

Where an action is commenced in a state court for the dissolution of a partnership and the settlement of its affairs, and a receiver is appointed by the court, who takes possession of the property and effects of the firm, and subsequently bankruptcy proceedings are begun against the firm, and an adjudication is made and a trustee appointed, there is nothing in the bankrupt law which gives the trustee power to take any property out of the receiver's possession, nor is there any provision which, in terms or by implication, confers upon the bankruptcy court a power to interfere in the trustee's behalf in respect of such property; the property must be fully administered by the state court, but the trustee may conduct the action and make all necessary applications to the court. Clark v. Binninger, 39 How. Prac. 363; In re Clark, 4 Ben. 88, Fed. Cas. No. 2,798, though see In re Whipple, 6 Biss. 516, Fed. Cas. No. 17,512. But a valid adjudication of bankruptcy against a debtor has the effect to subject him and his property to the operation of the bankrupt act notwithstanding a previous voluntary general assignment for the benefit of creditors; and the trustee in bankruptcy, as against the assignee under the state law, is entitled to the possession and control of the estate. Hobson v. Markson, 1 Dill. 421, Fed. Cas. No. 6,555; Ostrander v. Meunch, 2 McCrary, 267, 12 Fed. 562. Under the act of 1867 (Rev. St. § 5044), only attachments levied within a certain time were dissolved by the bankruptcy proceedings; and hence it was held that property in the hands of a sheriff under execution from a state court levied before the proceedings in bankruptcy were commenced could not be taken out of his possession by the federal court. Townsend v. Leonard, 3 Dill. 370, Fed. Cas. No. 14,117; Johnson v. Bishop, 1 Woolw. 324, Fed. Cas. No. 7,373; Marshall v. Knox, 16 Wall. 551; though this was doubted in Re Schnepf, 2 Ben. 72, Fed. Cas. No. 12,471. But it will be noticed that the words of the present statute, in relation to the dissolution of liens by an adjudication in bankruptcy, would fully cover the case here supposed.

Property Held by Bankrupt in Trust.

Upon an adjudication in bankruptcy, the debts due a trustee so adjudged, if any, on account of his trust, and his property rights in lands held by him in trust, pass to his assignee, but his duties as trustee remain unaffected by the proceeding. If any claims in favor of the trustee vest in his assignee which are prior liens upon the trust-lands, it is the duty of the trustee to pay them off. Rankin v. Barcroft, 114 Ill. 441, 3 N. E. 97. The general rule upon this subject has been well stated in the following language: "Money delivered to the bankrupt in trust, if ear-marked or separately kept and retained as trust property to be delivered or paid over in the same bills or coin in which it was received by the bankrupt, would not pass under such assignment, but would be considered as trust property; but an amount of money due from the bankrupt as trustee, and which could not be distinguished from any moneys in his possession or under his control, or which was only due from him because he had used trust funds for his own purposes, or otherwise misapplied them, could not be considered as property held by the bankrupt in trust." Hosmer v. Jewett, 6 Ben. 208, Fed. Cas. No. 6,713. The relation between a bank and its customers is that of simple debtor and creditor, not principal and agent, and does not partake of a fiduciary character, and moneys on deposit go to the trustee of the bank. In re Bank of Madison, 5 Biss. 515, Fed. Cas. No. 890; Phelan v. Iron Mountain Bank, 4 Dill. 88, Fed. Cas. No. 11,069. Similarly, a consignor whose property was sold prior to the bankruptcy, and the proceeds mingled with the general assets, has no lien or specific claim against the estate, because the proceeds of such sale, being no longer held *in specie* nor distinguishable from the general fund, cannot be regarded as held by the bankrupt in trust. In re Coan & Ten Broeke Mfg. Co., 6 Biss. 315, Fed. Cas. No. 2,915. But the assets of a firm in the possession of one of the partners are held in trust for the creditors of the firm, and if the partner in possession of them is afterwards adjudged a bankrupt, they do not go to his trustee. Jones v. Newsom, 7 Biss. 321, Fed. Cas. No. 7,484. Where a merchant is induced by the fraudulent representations of a member of a firm to sell goods on credit to the firm, and the goods do not lose their identity nor cease to be distinguishable, he may rescind the contract of sale and follow the goods wherever he can find them; and if, under these circumstances, the firm consents to return the unsold portion of the goods and account for the rest, this arrangement is binding on it, notwithstanding its supervening bankruptcy, and the trustee cannot recover the goods from the merchant again, nor their proceeds. Montgomery v. Bucyrus Machine Works, 92 U. S. 257; Donaldson v. Farwell, 93 U. S. 631.

Beneficial Interest in Trust Estate.

Where land is devised to trustees to be held, with its accumulations, until the beneficiary reaches a certain age, and before that time he is adjudged bankrupt, his interest in the estate will go to the trustee in bankruptcy. Sanford v. Lackland, 2 Dill. 6, Fed. Cas. No. 12,312. See, also, Smith v. Profitt, 82 Va. 832, 1 S. E. 67. But where a will devised certain property to trustees, in trust to pay the net rents and profits to the beneficiary in person, and it was further provided that the beneficiary should have no power to incumber the estate or anticipate the rents, and that the property should descend to the heirs of the beneficiary, it was held that no interest or estate in such property, or the rents and profits thereof, passed to the trustee in bankruptcy of the beneficiary, but the trustee under the will should continue to make payments to such beneficiary in person. Spindle v. Shreve, 9 Biss. 199, 4 Fed. 136. "No case is cited, none is known to us, which goes so far as to hold that an absolute discretion in the trustee [under a will]—a discretion which, by the express language of the will, he is under no obligation to exercise in favor of the bankrupt—confers such an interest on the latter, that he or his assignee in bankruptcy can successfully assert it in a court of equity or any other court." Nichols v. Eaton, 91 U. S. 716.

After Acquired Property.

The earnings and acquisitions of the bankrupt, after the commencement of the proceedings against him, are his own, subject to the condition that they shall remain liable for his debts if he does not succeed in obtaining a discharge. Mays v. Bank, 64 Pa. St. 74; Day v. Superior Court, 61 Cal. 489. Thus where an estate was conveyed to a husband and wife to be held in entirety, and the husband went into bankruptcy, and between the adjudication and his discharge he obtained a divorce, it was held that when the adjudication was made he had no interest in the real estate which could pass to the trustee, and if he gained an alienable interest by the divorce, it was a new acquisition which could not be claimed by the trustee in bankruptcy. In re Benson, 8 Biss. 116, Fed. Cas. No. 1,328.

Executory Contracts.

By the terms of the act the trustee succeeds to the bankrupt's interest in "rights of action arising upon contracts." Whatever those rights are, the trustee can claim and enforce them. It is not the purpose of the bankrupt law to interfere with or avoid contracts made by the bankrupt with other parties or prevent their execution. Foster v. Hackley, 2 N. B. R. 406, Fed. Cas. No. 4,971. But executory contracts in which the personal skill or conduct of the bankrupt forms a material part do not in general pass to the trustee. Dicey, Parties, 195; 3 Pars. Cont. 479; Leake, Cont. 1273; Gibson v. Carruthers, 8 Mees. & W. 333. Contracts of the bankrupt which are to continue for a fixed period, which will probably outlive the bankruptcy proceedings, and which depend upon the future personal services of the bankrupt, are not such property as will pass to the trustee. Streeter v. Sumner, 31 N. H. 542. Where it appeared, from the facts of the case, that the consideration for an agreement to pay money to the bankrupt was not for any interest in property, real or personal, existing at the time of his adjudication, but simply "to buy peace" with reference to certain pretended claims asserted by the bankrupt, it was held that the trustee had no right or title to such agreement. Cullen v. Dawson, 24 Minn. 66.

Burdensome Interests.

A trustee in bankruptcy is not bound to take into his possession property which may be onerous to the estate, or a burden instead of a benefit to it; and if he does not take it, it remains in the bankrupt. Amory v. Lawrence, 3 Cliff. 523, Fed. Cas. No. 336; Copeland v. Stephens, 1 Barn. & Ald. 603; Kimberling v. Hartly, 1 Fed. 571; Glenn v. Howard, 65 Md. 40, 3 Atl. 895; Nash v. Simpson, 78 Me. 142, 3 Atl. 53. So if the trustee and the general creditors are satisfied that a given debt against the bankrupt is valid, and that the property upon which it is secured is of no more value than is sufficient to pay it, he may abandon it to the creditor holding the lien. Second Nat. Bank of Louisville v. National State Bank of New Jersey, 10 Bush, 367.

Property Revesting in Bankrupt.

A bankrupt's interest in his estate is not extinguished by the assignment in the bankruptcy proceedings to the trustee in bankruptcy. In respect to real estate, the interest remaining in the bankrupt after such assignment is, under the statutes of Minnesota, in the nature of a reversion, subject to be defeated by a sale of the trustee. King v. Remington, 36 Minn. 15, 29 N. W. 352. After the bankruptcy proceedings are closed, property of the bankrupt not disposed of by the trustee reverts to the bankrupt. The title which vested in the trustee in bankruptcy cannot be used as an outstanding title to defeat the recovery of land so undisposed of when claimed by the heirs of the bankrupt. Herndon v. Davenport, 75 Tex. 462, 12 S. W. 1111. Compare Oliver v. Sanborn, 60 Mich. 346, 27 N. W. 527.

Recovery by Trustee of Property conveyed in Fraud of Creditors.

While property conveyed to the wife in fraud of the husband's creditors may be pursued by his trustee in bankruptcy, and subjected to the payment of debts, after it has been identified in her hands or in the hands of voluntary grantees or purchasers with notice, yet he cannot abandon the pursuit of the property and have a judgment in personam for its value against the wife or her executors. Phipps v. Sedgwick, 95 U. S. 3; Trust Co. v. Sedgwick, 97 U. S. 304. The bona fide purchaser of negotiable paper, secured by mortgage, before maturity and without notice, takes the mortgage, as he does the notes, freed from any latent equity existing in a trustee in bankruptcy at the time of the assignment of the notes, of which latent equity there is no notice actual or constructive; Myers v. Hazzard, 4 McCrary, 94, 50 Fed. 155; Carpenter v. Longan, 16 Wall. 271; and therefore he is entitled to protection, and to the benefit of his security, as against the trustee, although his immediate vendor held under such circumstances as would have made him liable to an action by the trustee to set aside the security. Myers v. Hazzard, supra. The trustee can also sue to recover land conveyed by the bankrupt, although the conveyance was not made within the time limited before the commencement of bankruptcy proceedings, if the conveyance was fraudulent as to creditors at common law. Knowlton v. Moseley, 105 Mass. 136; Pratt v. Curtis, 2 Low. 87, Fed. Cas. No. 11,375. But if he sues specifically to recover the value of property conveyed by the bankrupt to the defendant by way of illegal preference under the act, he must recover on the case stated in his declaration, and cannot recover on the ground that the transfer was void at common law or under the statutes of the state. Cragin v. Carmichael, 2 Dill. 519, Fed. Cas. No. 3,319.

Trustee's Right of Action Exclusive.

The right of action in the trustee to recover assets, or property which the bankrupt has fraudulently conveyed prior to the adjudication, or which he conceals or fails to surrender, is exclusive; the creditors cannot maintain such a suit, for it is only through his instrumentality that they can proceed. Glenny v. Langdon, 98 U. S. 20; Trimble v. Woodhead, 102 U. S. 647. Thus a petitioning creditor cannot move to set aside an attachment in a state court; that right belongs to the trustee alone. Prichett v. Kelly, 2 Wkly. Notes Cas. 335. And the negligence of the trustee, whereby the action has not been brought within the time limited by the act, will not give the creditors a right to maintain the suit in their own names. Moyer v. Dewey, 103 U. S. 301; Lane v. Nickerson, 99 Ill. 284; King v. Deitz, 12 Pa. St. 156. But see per contra, Bates v. Bradley, 24 Hun, 84. Where the debtor made a general assignment for the benefit of creditors, and afterwards a receiver was appointed by a state court in an independent proceeding against him, and subsequently a trustee in bankruptcy of his estate was appointed, it was held that the trustee was the only party who could attack the assignment and recover the property conveyed under it, and the receiver could not do so. Olney v. Tanner, 21 Blatchf. 540, 18 Fed. 636. But a bankrupt who purchases a claim from his trustee, which was originally due to him, may sue thereon in his own name. Udall v. School Dist., 48 Vt. 588.

THE TIME WHEN THIS ACT SHALL GO INTO EFFECT.

a **This act shall go into full force and effect upon its passage:** *provided, however,* **that no petition for voluntary bankruptcy shall be filed within one month of the passage thereof, and no petition for involuntary bankruptcy shall be filed within four months of the passage thereof.**

b **Proceedings commenced under state insolvency laws before the passage of this act shall not be affected by it.**

Approved July 1, 1898.

Constitutionality of National Bankruptcy Law.

By article 1, § 8, of the constitution of the United States, congress is invested with power to "establish uniform laws on the subject of bankruptcies throughout the United States;" and the constitutional validity of the previous federal statutes on this subject has been fully sustained by the courts. The states, indeed, are prohibited by the constitution from passing laws impairing the obligation of contracts. But since there is nothing in the organic law which forbids congress to enact statutes which may produce that effect, it is universally conceded that a national bankruptcy law, though it includes such features, with provisions compulsory upon creditors, is valid and constitutional. Black, Const. Law (2d Ed.) 211; Evans v. Eaton, Pet. C. C. 322, Fed. Cas. No. 4,559; In re Owens, 12 N. B. R. 518, Fed. Cas. No. 10,632; Keene v. Mould, 16 Ohio, 12; Morse v. Hovey, 1 Barb. Ch. (N. Y.) 404; In re Beckerford, 1 Dill. 45, Fed. Cas. No. 1,209. In fact, the power of congress over the subject of bankruptcy is subject to no other restriction than the requirement that its laws shall be uniform. It is not to be gauged or limited by the British statutes of bankruptcy which were in force at the time of the adoption of the constitution. Although by those statutes, as then in force, the bankruptcy laws applied only to persons engaged in trade, congress is not obliged to limit its laws on the subject of bankruptcy to merchants or traders. In re California Pac. R. Co., 3 Sawy. 240, Fed. Cas. No. 2,315; Kunzler v. Kohaus, 5 Hill (N. Y.) 317. "The power under this clause is sufficiently comprehensive to enable congress to adopt a uniform system of bankruptcy, commit its administration to such of the courts of the United States as it might choose, and to provide the modes of procedure, special or otherwise, as *they* might, in *their* discretion, deem best adapted to secure and accomplish the objects of the act; and if such proceedings should differ from those in ordinary cases and suits, they would, notwithstanding, be obligatory upon the courts, as congress has, by the constitution, plenary authority over that subject." Goodall v. Tuttle, 3 Biss. 219, Fed. Cas. No. 5,533. The power to create and administer a system of bankruptcy is exclusively vested in the federal government; congress has not given jurisdiction to the state tribunals to carry into effect the bankruptcy law, nor would it have power to vest such a jurisdiction in those courts. McLean v. Lafayette Bank, 3 McLean, 185, Fed. Cas. No. 8,885. As to the constitutionality of the penal and criminal provisions of the bankruptcy act, see the case of U. S. v. Fox, 95 U. S. 670, wherein it is said that it is competent for congress to enforce, by suitable penalties, all legislation necessary or proper to the execution of the powers with which it is intrusted, and that any act committed with a view of evading such legislation, or fraudulently securing its benefits, may be made an offense against the United States.

Constitutionality of Exemption Clause.

The provisions of the bankruptcy law allowing an exemption to the extent allowed by the laws of the state in which the adjudication is made are not obnoxious to that clause of the constitution which gives congress power to establish "uniform" laws on the subject of bankruptcy. Dozier v. Wilson, 84 Ga. 301, 10 S. E. 743. A bankruptcy law which, by its terms, is made applicable to all the states alike, without distinction or discrimination, is not unconstitutional merely because its operations may be wholly different in one state from another. Darling v. Berry, 4 McCrary, 470, 13 Fed. 659. In this case it was said: "The circumstances and conditions existing in the states of this Union are infinitely various. No law which human ingenuity could possibly frame would be uniform, in the sense of operating equally or alike in the various states, with their different conditions and diversified interests. * * * Suppose congress should, in a bankruptcy law, as it did in 1867, adopt the homestead exemptions provided by state laws in force at a specified time; and suppose there should in some states be no law giving homestead exemptions, while in others such exemptions should by law exist,—then the operation of the bankruptcy law would not be uniform with respect to the homesteads; but would it be for that reason unconstitutional? All that the constitution intends is that congress shall not pass partial revenue and bankrupt laws. It shall not prescribe one law for this state or section, and a different law for that state or section. The law must be general and uniform in its provisions, but its working and operation may be very different in different states, owing to their diverse conditions and circumstances." The system of bankruptcy is, in a relative sense, uniform throughout the United States, since the trustee takes in each state whatever would have been available to the recourse of execution creditors if the bankruptcy law had never been passed. Though the states vary in the extent of their exemptions, yet what remains the bankruptcy law distributes equally among the creditors. The law does not in any way vary or change the rights of the parties. In re Beckerford, 1 Dill. 45, Fed. Cas. No. 1,209; In re Jordan, 8 N. B. R. 180, Fed.

Cas. No. 7,514; In re Appold, 1 N. B. R. 621, Fed. Cas. No. 499.

Bankruptcy and Insolvency Laws Distinguished.

In connection with the question of the validity of national bankruptcy laws and of the insolvency laws of the several states, and the effect of the one upon the other, numerous attempts have been made (but without any marked success) to draw a sharp line of distinction between a bankruptcy law, properly so called, and an insolvency law. In the case of Adams v. Storey, 1 Paine, 79, Fed. Cas. No. 66, will be found a detailed discussion of the nature of bankruptcy and insolvency laws and the differences between them, and the constitutional power of the states with reference to the enactment of such laws. But in point of fact, as pointed out in Martin v. Berry, 37 Cal. 208, the only substantial difference between a bankruptcy law and an insolvency law lies in the circumstance that the former affords relief upon the application of the creditor, and the latter upon the application of the debtor. In the general character of the remedy there is no difference, however much the modes in which the remedy may be administered may vary. An act which (like the present one) embodies provisions for both voluntary and involuntary proceedings is in effect both a bankruptcy law and an insolvency law. In matters of detail, however, and even in the general theory of the proceeding, there may be wide differences between the national bankruptcy law and any particular insolvency law in force in a given state. Thus, for example, an assignment in bankruptcy, under the federal law, differs from a cession under the insolvency laws of Louisiana in that it divests the bankrupt of the title to all his property, and transfers the same to the assignee or trustee. May v. New Orleans & C. R. Co., 44 La. Ann. 444, 10 South. 769. And it should be observed that there is a substantial and important difference between the terms "bankrupt" and "insolvent," as applied to persons. A person is said to be "bankrupt" when he has done or suffered some act which the law declares to be an act of bankruptcy, or when proceedings in bankruptcy have been instituted by or against him, or when he has been adjudicated a bankrupt. He is "insolvent" when he cannot pay his debts as they mature in the ordinary course of his business. Thus he may be insolvent without being bankrupt. Barr v. Bartram & F. Mfg. Co., 41 Conn. 502.

Effect of Bankruptcy Law on State Insolvency Laws.

Insolvency laws may be passed by the states, authorizing the discharge of debtors from their obligations and liabilities on just and reasonable terms. But these laws are subject to three important limitations. First, there must be no national bankruptcy law in existence at the time, for such a law suspends all state laws on the same subject while it continues in force. Second, state laws of this kind cannot apply to citizens of other states having claims against the debtor, for the state has no jurisdiction over them, unless they voluntarily submit their claims to the jurisdiction and agree to participate in the distribution of the estate. Third, such laws cannot apply to contracts entered into before their enactment, for that would impair the obligation of such contracts. Ogden v. Saunders, 12 Wheat. 213; Baldwin v. Hale, 1 Wall. 223; Gilman v. Lockwood, 4 Wall. 409; Brown v. Smart, 145 U. S. 454, 12 Sup. Ct. 958; Hempsted v. Bank, 78 Wis. 375, 47 N. W. 627; Roberts v. Atherton, 60 Vt. 563, 15 Atl. 159.

The passage of a national bankruptcy law by congress renders it supreme. The state laws in force must yield to it, and can no longer operate upon persons or cases within the purview of the federal statute. The latter does not, indeed, repeal or destroy the state laws on the same subject, but it suspends their operation. If the state law and the federal act operate upon the same subject-matter, upon the same property, upon the same rights, and upon the same persons, creditors as well as debtors, or may so operate, they cannot go together without direct and positive collision, and in such case the federal enactment suspends or supersedes the state law. Sturges v. Crowninshield, 4 Wheat. 122; Ogden v. Saunders, 12 Wheat. 213; Baldwin v. Hale, 1 Wall. 223; In re Reynolds, 9 N. B. R. 50, Fed. Cas. No. 11,723; Ex parte Eames, 2 Story, 322, Fed. Cas. No. 4,237; West v. Longis, 20 La. Ann. 15; Van Nostrand v. Carr, 30 Md. 128; Lavender v. Gosnell, 43 Md. 153; In re Reynolds, 8 R. I. 485; Judd v. Ives, 4 Metc. (Mass.) 401; Atkins v. Spear, 8 Metc. (Mass.) 491; Chamberlain v. Perkins, 51 N. H. 336. Nevertheless it is competent for the legislature of a state to enact an insolvency law, although a national bankruptcy law may be then in force. Such a law, passed at a time when an act of congress establishing a uniform system of bankruptcy is in force, is not, indeed, void, but it does not become operative (so far as it may be in conflict with the federal act or concurrent with it) while the latter continues in force; but on the repeal of the federal law, the state statute becomes operative without re-enactment. Tua v. Carriere, 117 U. S. 201, 6 Sup. Ct. 565; Seattle Coal Co. v. Thomas, 57 Cal. 197. See, also, Thornhill v. Bank of Louisiana, 1 Woods, 1, Fed. Cas. No. 13,992. On this point we quote the following from an opinion of Chief Justice Appleton in Maine: "We come now to the question whether a state can pass an insolvent or bankrupt law during the existence of an act of congress on the subject, in other words, whether the act under discussion is in force. Its validity is unquestioned, unless absolutely void in its inception. No constitutional provision has been violated, for the passage of such a law is not merely not prohibited, but it is impliedly sanctioned by the clause giving congress power over the subject of bankruptcies. The legislature may pass a law to take effect instantly, or at a future day, or on the happening of a future event. If the statute had said it was to take effect upon and after the repeal of the bankrupt law of congress, there could have been no doubt of its validity. But such is the precise effect of the law without the intervention of any such provision. The act of congress is the paramount law on the subject when called into action. The law of the state is subordinate to it. The efficient action of the state law is suspended for the time being, precisely as in the cases already considered, when a national bankrupt law was passed subsequent to a state law on the same subject. The state may pass a law which is subordinate to the paramount authority of national legislation, and is only subordinate to that, but which, when that ceases to have force, by reason of its repeal, has at once the vigor of law. Whether the law of the state is existent and superseded by the subsequent legislation of congress, or is inoperative by reason of precedent congressional action, can make no difference. In either case, the efficiency of the state law is alike suspended and in abeyance while the act of congress is in force, and when that is repealed, the law of the state at once and instantly becomes operative, and action may be had under its provisions." Damon's Appeal, 70 Me. 153. And see Lewis v. Santa Clara Co., 55 Cal. 604.

Pending Proceedings Under State Laws.

If a state court has acquired jurisdiction under a state law of a case in insolvency, and is engaged in settling the debts and distributing the assets of the insolvent, before or at the date at which the act of congress upon the same subject takes effect, the state court may nevertheless proceed with the case to its final conclusion, and its action in the matter will be as valid as if no federal law upon the subject had been enacted. Martin v. Berry, 37 Cal. 208; Meekins v. Creditors, 19 La. Ann. 497; Judd v. Ives, 4 Metc. (Mass.) 401.

Judicial Notice.

The courts of the various states, being officially çognizant of the law of the land, will take judicial notice of the national bankruptcy law and its provisions. Mims v. Swartz, 37 Tex. 13.

Nature of Proceedings in Bankruptcy.

A proceeding against a debtor to have him adjudged a bankrupt is a civil proceeding, and not a criminal proceeding. In re De Forest, 9 N. B. R. 278, Fed. Cas. No. 3,745.

Construction of Bankruptcy Law.

The national bankruptcy law should not be subjected to a strict or narrow construction, but must be interpreted reasonably and according to the fair import of its terms. In re Muller, Deady, 513, Fed. Cas. No. 9,912. In this case it was said by Deady, J.: "Counsel have insisted that this is a special proceeding, purely statutory, and that the act must be taken most strictly against the creditor and in favor of the bankrupt. In my judgment, this view of the matter is not supported by reason or authority. The act does not attempt to punish the bankrupt, but to distribute his property fairly and impartially between his creditors, to whom in justice it belongs. It is remedial, and seeks to protect the honest creditor from being overreached and defrauded by the unscrupulous. It is intended to relieve the honest but unfortunate debtor from the burden of liabilities which he cannot discharge, and allow him to commence the business of life anew. The power to pass bankrupt laws is one of the express grants of power to the national government; and history teaches that the want of a uniform law on this subject throughout the states was one of the prominent causes which led to the assembling of the constitutional convention and consequent formation and adoption of the federal constitution. Such a statute is not to be construed strictly, as if it were an obscure or special penal enactment, and this was the sixteenth instead of the nineteenth century. The act establishes a system, and regulates, in all their details, the relative rights and duties of debtor and creditor. Such an act must be construed—as indeed should all acts—according to the fair import of its terms, with a view to effect its objects and to promote justice."

TABLE OF CASES CITED.

[THE FIGURES REFER TO PAGES.]

[The figures refer to pages.]

[The figures refer to pages.]

[The figures refer to pages.]

D

[The figures refer to pages.]

I

J

[The figures refer to pages.]

[The figures refer to pages.]

M

[The figures refer to pages.]

N

[The figures refer to pages.]

O

P

[The figures refer to pages.]

[The figures refer to pages.]

[The figures refer to pages.]

T

U

[The figures refer to pages.]

[The figures refer to pages.]

Y

Z

INDEX.

[THE FIGURES REFER TO PAGES.]

A

[The figures refer to pages.]

[The figures refer to pages.]

[The figures refer to pages.]

B

[The figures refer to pages.]

[The figures refer to pages.]

C

[The figures refer to pages.]

[The figures refer to pages.]

[The figures refer to pages.]

[The figures refer to pages.]

D

[The figures refer to pages.]

[The figures refer to pages.]

[The figures refer to pages.]

[The figures refer to pages.]

E

[The figures refer to pages.]

F

[The figures refer to pages.]

[The figures refer to pages.]

G

H

I

[The figures refer to pages.]

[The figures refer to pages.]

[The figures refer to pages.]

[The figures refer to pages.]

[The figures refer to pages.]

N

O

P

[The figures refer to pages.]

[The figures refer to pages.]

[The figures refer to pages.]

[The figures refer to pages.]

[The figures refer to pages.]

[The figures refer to pages.]

[The figures refer to pages.]

S

[The figures refer to pages.]

[The figures refer to pages.]

[The figures refer to pages.]

[The figures refer to pages.]

U

V

[The figures refer to pages.]

W

WEST PUBLISHING CO., PRINTERS AND STEREOTYPERS, ST. PAUL, MINN.